Also by Michael Harrington
The Twilight of Capitalism
Accidental Century
Fragments of the Century
The Other America: Poverty in the United States
Retail Clerks
Socialism
Toward a Democratic Left

The Vast Majority A Journey to the World's Poor *Michael Harrington*

 Simon and Schuster | New York

Designed by Irving Perkins
Manufactured in the United States of America
1 2 3 4 5 6 7 8 9 10

Library of Congress Cataloging in Publication Data

Harrington, Michael.
  The vast majority.

  Bibliography: p.
  Includes index.
  1. Underdeveloped areas.   2. Economic assistance,
American.   3. Poor.   I. Title.
HC59.7.H353   330.9'172'4   77-9525
ISBN 0-671-22529-4

I want to acknowledge help in defraying travel costs from the Kaplan Fund, the Queens College Fund, the United States Educational Foundation in India, and W. H. Ferry. The hospitality of Peter and Odette Jankowitsch greatly facilitated my contact with Third World diplomats at the United Nations.

To Julius K. Nyerere of the South and Willy Brandt of the North, to some whose names I cannot mention, to many more whose names I do not know, to all those who struggle daily with the contradictions described here, this book is dedicated.

Contents

Chapter One **The Cruel Innocence**

In the nineteen hundred seventies, the government and the people of the United States are turning their backs on the wretched of the earth.

They do so with the best will in the world. Indeed, for at least eighty years, America has worked against the poor of the planet in a spirit of sincere compassion. And one point of this book is, precisely, to deprive us of this cruel innocence which prevents us from even seeing the wrongs we perpetrate.

I do not write these things arrogantly, in the spirit of ritual anti-Americanism that sometimes demeans the Left. On the contrary. I speak in this way because I identify with—and have inherited—my country's instinctive sympathy for the downtrodden. That is also why I permit myself to hope. We are a decent people. But intricate economic mechanisms, whose very existence is a mystery to most citizens, subvert that innate generosity and perpetuate misery around the globe. And yet, if this nation would become aware of the unwitting evil it does, and if there were a democratic movement capable of offering serious alternatives to it, then it could, and would, change.

So, I do not propose a theory of American malevolence. Rather, I will show how the United States is normally an unconscious participant in, and beneficiary of, a global system of injustice that warps or destroys the minds and bodies of hundreds of millions of human beings. Seen from its most terrifying aspect, we are accomplices in a process that retards the genetic potential of fetuses and babies. I distrust any analogy between American and Nazi society, not the least because this country, whatever its structural inequities may be, has never produced anything remotely as monstrous as Hitlerism. And yet, if one understands these references carefully and precisely, there is a sense in which most of us are "good Germans." That is, we are inexcusably unaware of the evil that is done in our name.

The basic facts are outrageous, but so well worn and familiar that they bore us with the tedious details of degradation. Let one family or one town suffer some terrible fate and the good heart of this country—I write here utterly without irony—will pour forth in gifts and concern. Let a billion men and women and children rot day after day, and the very enormity of that reality tends to dull the moral sense. I do not speak out of a presumed superiority. In India, I too grew tired of, and even angry at, the continual wheedling of leprous beggars. Moreover, this point is not merely psychological. It bears most importantly on the method and strategy of this book.

If one exaggerates the suffering of the Third World, even if for the most humane reasons, that is to make justice even more difficult to achieve. For example, the Food and Agricultural Organization (FAO) of the United Nations used to sometimes make dire predictions about the number of people who were, or soon would be, menaced by starvation. The decency that inspired those projections is obvious: a desire to shock the affluent public into a crusade to avert an impending calamity. But by overstating the problem of hunger, these advocates convinced some people that no action could possibly affect it. The truth is bitter enough—that there are in the Third World over 400 million people who have an insufficient protein-energy supply, perhaps 70 million of them immediately threatened by starvation. That is intolerable *and* a crisis that the mind can conceive, grapple with, plan to overcome.

So it is not a mere literary flourish when I say that I want to write with a passionate objectivity. I am deeply convinced that it is the truth, put candidly and in all of its complexity, that serves our cause. I think, for instance, that some of the leaders of the world's poor have been bombastic, hypocritical, the purveyors of an empty, purely verbal, radicalism. Pretending that such things are not true is hardly to act in solidarity with the oppressed of the globe, some of whom suffer at the hands of the tribunes who speak in their name. I will refer to such posturing—or worse, the murderous megalomania of an Idi Amin—by its proper name.

In the same spirit, I will document the assertions I make. I will not, however, do this in a traditional, scholarly fashion, with an apparatus of footnotes and citations attached to the text. Those will be found at the end of the book.* I proceed in this way because the issues that I raise do not merely relate to the American intellect; they must touch the American soul as well. I therefore want to speak factually, but directly to the reader, to engage him or her in a dialogue, to admit honestly when I feel that my own case is incomplete or imperfect.

But when all of the complexities are properly sorted out and all of the ambiguities recognized, I return to my opening statement: America is turning its back upon the wretched of the earth. If that is a simplification, it is the valid simplification of an unconscionable fact.

Who are the wretched of the earth?

Some of them are people in countries where one child in two dies before reaching age five. They are the overwhelming bulk of the 70 percent of the world's population without safe water. Four hundred and fifty million of them are afflicted by schistosomiasis and filariasis, the leading causes of blindness. They are the more than two billion human beings—54 percent of mankind—who live in countries where the per capita Gross National Product in 1973 was under $200. The poorest among them, 30 percent of the world's population, have 3 percent of its income. And they are the impoverished citizens in nations which are statistically "well off," like the 50 percent of the Brazilians who have been excluded from—and even injured by—an economic "miracle."

* In each chapter, major sections of the text will be marked with numbers that refer to notes in the back of the book; these will provide the corroboration for *all* the statements in that section.

Another way of describing the wretched of the earth is to define them as the citizens of those countries that have been falling behind the economic levels of the West during the past four centuries. Between 1952 and 1972, the gross product of the advanced capitalist nations increased from $1.25 trillion to $3.07 trillion. That *increment* of $1.82 trillion dollars was three and a half times the *aggregate* product of the underdeveloped world in 1972, which was $520 billion.* Using constant (1973) dollars, the rich lands saw their per capita income move from $2,000 to $4,000, while that of the poor countries went from $125 to $300. The major capitalist powers have two thirds of the globe's income, but only 20 percent of its population; the underdeveloped nations, with more than 50 percent of the people, have less than 13 percent of the income.

All this, however, is not to suggest that the Third World is a homogeneous phenomenon. Argentina had a per capita GNP of $1,290 in 1973; Yemen had $90. In Kuwait in 1970, 69 percent of the teen-agers were in school; in Haiti, 4 percent. But even these obvious statistics can be deceptive. Africa has the lowest per capita income of all the continents. Does that mean that it is the worst off? Not exactly, for it does not have those massive concentrations of urban suffering that are typical in southern Asia. India alone has three times the population of Africa. And yet—and this anomaly is, as we will see, part of the very structure of underdevelopment— India also has the ninth-largest industrial sector in the world, the fourth-largest army, and the sixth-ranking atomic capacity. So I am speaking now in terms of rough indicators, with the complications behind them to be unraveled later on.

Given this caution, it is possible to identify a "Fourth World" of the very poor. Taking those countries with less than $150 per capita GNP in the early seventies, they contained about 1.1 billion people. More than 915 million were found in Asia; around 170 million in Africa; about 8 million in the Middle East and 6 million in the Caribbean. And these figures exclude China with an estimated per

* There has been a good deal of euphemism, much of it politically motivated, with regard to how one speaks about the poor countries. At first they were called "underdeveloped"; then "developing"; and most recently, "less developed." In fact, they were, and are meant to be, *underdeveloped*. I do not use the word contemptuously or chauvinistically, but because I think that even in semantics, realism is in the interest of justice.

capita product just above our cutoff—$170 in 1973—and a population of 800 million.

At the other pole of the Third World are the countries that have been described as part of the world's "new middle class." They include nations with key raw materials, like the oil powers; those with highly competitive manufacturing sectors, like South Korea and Taiwan; those with a large and growing market; and those, like Brazil and Iran, with all three characteristics. The existence of this stratum has given rise to an unjustified euphoria. As one writer put it, "a perceptible shift appears to be taking place in the global balance of economic power from the owners of capital to the owners of natural resources." But the fact of the matter is that even the most favored economies in the Third World are systematically subordinated to an unjust system that shapes, and distorts, their very gains. Brazil, that dictatorial and militaristic model of modernization, whose 10 percent growth prior to the oil crisis was the joy of conservatives around the world, is a victim—a much more affluent victim, to be sure—of the same structure that oppresses Bangladesh.

So there is a common fate that binds the Third World together, even though there are enormous, and sometimes murderous, differences between these countries. And there is a subgroup, a Fourth World, of more than a billion people—one quarter of mankind— which lives a daily agony. These are the wretched of the earth. These are the people upon whom America is turning its back. I write, then, about the vast majority of humankind.

The fact that America has become wearily angry with these driven and hungry millions is easy enough to document. We know from polling data that, between 1956 and 1964, popular support for foreign aid rose slightly and reached 59 percent. That figure is, I think, a fair, if rough, index of sentiment toward the world's poor. But then, between 1964 and 1968, those in favor of such programs declined to 46 percent, and those openly hostile to them increased from 21 percent to 32 percent. In considerable measure, this shift was obviously related to America's catastrophic intervention in Vietnam, an intervention that led, particularly among the poor and the poorly educated, to a "fundamental mistrust of leaders on such issues as aid, and hostility toward all international involvement." As Zbigniew Brzezinski, now National Security Advisor to President Carter, put it, there is a "fundamental shift in the way that Americans perceive themselves in relation to the rest of the world." Americans, Brzezinski went on, "recoil in horror from a world that appears to them headed in the wrong direction," suffering "anxieties regarding the egalitarian values proclaimed by the newly emancipated countries."

It was not just the catastrophe of Vietnam that changed this country's mind about the globe; it was also a hostility toward the demands for a new, international economic order put forward by Third World leaders.

Perhaps the most dramatic, summary case in point is provided by Senator Daniel Patrick Moynihan's brief tenure as the United States Ambassador to the United Nations. Moynihan became immensely popular among the American people by taking the offensive against the new nations. He liked to quote a French saying—*cet animal est méchant; quand on l'attaque, il se défend* (this animal is nasty; when you attack it, it defends itself)—but there was more than pugnacious emotion in his attitude. In a speech before the AFL-CIO Convention in October 1975, Moynihan synthesized his intellectual position.

First of all, there is the traditional, and no doubt sincere, assertion of American blamelessness. "There are those in the country," Moynihan said, "whose pleasure, or profit, it is to believe that our assailants are motivated by what is wrong about us. *They* are wrong. We are assailed because of what is *right* about us. We are assailed because we are a democracy." And, "We repudiate the charge that we have exploited or plundered other countries, or that our own prosperity has ever rested on any such relation. We are prosperous because we are—or were—an energetic and productive people who have lived under a system that has encouraged the development of our productive capacities and energies. We also consider that we have been reasonably helpful and generous in our economic dealings with other countries." That last quotation, I would suggest, accurately reflects the feelings of most Americans, which is what gave Moynihan's words such a national resonance.

In another passage, Moynihan became even more dramatic. "In the United Nations today there are in the range of two dozen democracies left. Totalitarian Communist regimes and assorted ancient and modern despotisms make up all the rest. And nothing so unites these nations as the conviction that their success ultimately depends on our failure. . . . It is sensed in the world that democracy is in trouble. There is blood in the water, and the sharks grow frenzied. They commence, of course, to consume one another, and the chaos mounts."

"The old dream of an international economic order in which one single nation dominated," Moynihan said a little later on, "is being replaced by a not so different vision of the domination of a single idea, the idea of an all-encompassing state, a state which has no provision for the liberties of collections of individuals, such as trade unions."

That speech articulated, in somewhat sophisticated fashion, what tens of millions of Americans were feeling. We, an innocent nation whose only sin is its enormous productivity, are being assailed by ungrateful, incompetent dictatorial regimes that wish to take what is rightfully ours.

I expect this attitude to continue in the new period in American life under President Jimmy Carter. This is not to say that there is no difference between Democrats and Republicans in the area of international economic policy. The Democrats are obviously more liberal than the Republicans, and they increasingly have the support of the college-educated stratum in this country, which is more sympathetic to foreign-aid programs than any other group. Sometimes this Democratic internationalism has tragic consequence, like defending "freedom" in Indochina by giving massive military backing to various dictators in Saigon. But on many other occasions, the Democrats have demonstrated a much greater sensitivity toward the claims of the world's poor than the Republicans have. Where President Eisenhower honored every Latin American tyrant he could find in order to bind them to the "Free" World, President Kennedy launched the Alliance for Progress, an effort designed to create a non-Communist road out of poverty.

But even the Alliance, for all of the decency of its intentions, was basically flawed. It shared a crucial assumption with Eisenhower, that what was needed in Latin America (or in the Third World generally) was a capitalist revolution. To be sure, Kennedy wanted a capitalism much more left-wing, even socialistic, than that of

Eisenhower. Still, the two leaders held to the same underlying conception: that the poor nations must now go through the American experience, for ours is the only effective way to modernity.

That is not simply wrong. It also gives continuity to American policy throughout the entire postwar period. It is the theoretical basis of Moynihan's—and the American people's—belief that we have been "reasonably generous" with the world's poor and they have responded by perversely rejecting our humane and shrewd advice and insisting on crazy schemes for a new international economic order. I do not equate Democrats and Republicans as Tweedledum and Tweedledee; and indeed I have some cautious hopes for modest gains under a Carter Administration. In Mr. Carter's speech to the United Nations in March 1977, for instance, he declared that this country was now willing to consider the establishment of a common fund to stabilize world commodity prices. This was a significant concession to a key Third World demand, and the Administration followed it up. In May 1977, C. Fred Bergsten, the chief Treasury spokesman in this area, said that we would take a "much more positive position" on the issue in North-South negotiations. This was not, to be sure, a burst of sheer idealism. Even sophisticated corporate ideologists, like the editors of *Business Week*, had come to similar conclusions. Still, the Democrats are more internationalist than the Republicans and contain constituencies—the minorities, the reform activists—which are deeply concerned with economic injustice. As I was finishing this book, then, there was some reason to expect movement and modest gains as a result of the Carter victory. Still, if there is to be a breakthrough of the kind that might significantly alleviate the abject misery of the more than a billion people in the Fourth World and change the system of injustice which afflicts even the better-off of the Third World, what is required is a basic critique of the Democratic-Republican assumptions. Just before he made his concession to the Third World in that UN speech, Carter reiterated the classic, and erroneous, American position: that an "open international trading system" is the answer to global poverty. In fact, as we will see, it is one of the main causes of global poverty.[1]

To which a Machiavellian might say, Why bother?

It is, it could be argued, downright silly to talk about a redistribution of the world's wealth that will be accomplished voluntarily, democratically, by the advanced capitalist nations. (The same thesis would hold for Communist totalitarianism, where the bureaucratic ruling class is also unlikely to freely surrender its privileges, not even to its own people, and most certainly not to destitute foreigners.) There is obviously considerable force to this objection. Still, I am convinced that the most strenuous efforts must be made to overcome this obstacle, and that those efforts might even prevail.

This conviction is not motivated, of course, by the self-serving pragmatism that caused the American government to make a tactical shift on these matters in 1975 and 1976. After blustering against the Third World demands for a new economic order and trying to break up the OPEC cartel, Henry Kissinger decided to make a few positive gestures. These will be examined in greater detail in the next chapter. For now, two aspects of the Kissinger move are relevant. First of all, the American Secretary of State wanted a *quid pro quo* for the marginal modicum of decency that he offered. He wanted guaranteed Western access to Third World materials and markets; OPEC had taught a bitter lesson. And secondly, I am quite convinced that Mr. Kissinger believed his proposals to be substantial and generous and in the interest of the wretched of the earth. He did not *intend* to create a more rational, conflict-free order of injustice. That was, however, the predictable outcome of his benevolence. The same ambiguity was present in Mr. Carter's 1977 initiative.

Kissinger's scheme was clearly not a response to the Machiavellian objection—it was an exercise in Machiavellianism. However, there are three arguments, two of them rather practical and one purely moral, that do give an answer. To begin with, if the system of planetary inequity continues essentially as it is, there may be, as Robert Heilbroner has suggested, nuclear "wars of redistribution." There is, after all, already nuclear capacity in the Third World, in India. And competition among the Western powers is exacerbating the danger that Heilbroner fears. In 1974, West Germany agreed to sell reactors to Brazil. As Senator Abraham Ribicoff told his colleagues at the time, "The capacity to produce nuclear explosives is spreading 'like a plague,' in the words of the Inspector General of the International Atomic Energy Agency." No one listened to Ribicoff or the Inspector General; in 1976 France sold a nuclear plant to Pakistan.

Given the political volatility in the poor countries—and given the fact that the maldistribution of the world's wealth offends two of the most powerful emotions of the modern age, national and racial pride—Heilbroner's grim prospect is more of a possibility today than when he first suggested it. Phillip J. Farley, writing in a volume sponsored by the exceedingly sober and establishmentarian Brookings Institution, noted the possibility that "the proliferation of nuclear weapons would increase and disperse the number of people with the practical knowledge to construct nuclear explosives and to handle them or the requisite plutonium. The pool of people from which terrorists, blackmailers, or insurrectionists could be drawn would thus be significantly enlarged, at the same time that political and moral barriers to the use of nuclear weapons—now high—might be lowered."

Consider, then, a fantastic but possible scenario. A small fanatic group of Third World militants comes into possession of a nuclear bomb, manages to plant it in a major Western city and then holds millions of people hostage, demanding an impossible ransom. That such an action would be both indefensible and suicidal is beside the point. It is possible. But if the globe were making steady progress toward redistribution voluntarily, this horror—and many lesser, but dangerous, outbursts—could become less likely.

Robert Tucker thinks that the potential for Third World disruption has been exaggerated by writers like Heilbroner. He reaches that wrong conclusion, I think, because he focuses on conventional military power rather than terrorism. But he concedes an analagous possibility. It could be, he suggests, that the rich will be politically unable to maintain the old order while the poor will lack the capacity to create a new order. Such a situation, he concludes, could lead to "chaos." It is of some moment that a principled (and sophisticated) opponent of egalitarianism sees such potential for upheaval in the present system. So whether one thinks of the issue in terms of redistributive wars and terrorism, or as a chaotic void in the world economy, there are self-interested reasons for compassion from the North.

Secondly, the United States is much more deeply involved in

the world economy than ever before. In 1960, 7 percent of American corporate profits derived from abroad; in 1974, 30 percent. It is true, as this book will document later on in detail, that the bulk of American economic activity overseas is in the affluent capitalist economies. But it is also true that the world is becoming, in the fashionable cliché of the seventies, more and more "interdependent." The poor of the globe suffered more than anyone else from the recession that afflicted the United States, Europe and Japan in 1974 and 1975. But the rich would also lose if Asia, Africa and Latin America were closed to them. The patterns of the nineteen thirties, when each nation tried to "beggar its neighbors," could return.

So there are eminently practical arguments, based on averting the possibility of nuclear terrorism and an intensification of the internal problems of the wealthy countries on an international scale. Ultimately, however, I am convinced that the most compelling reason for action is moral. It is here that my fundamental optimism about the basic decency of the American people comes most prominently into play. I am convinced that if they are persuaded of the immorality of the present order of world injustice, it will make a difference in American politics.

John Rawls has developed an "intuitive" concept of justice which is apropos of this point. I disagree with significant aspects of Rawls's analysis, including his failure to deal with the international dimensions of his subject, but I find this definition most powerful.* A system is fair, Rawls says, if a person can accept it even though she or he does not know her or his place in it. Obviously, most people would not regard a proposed society as just, or even tolerable, if 99 percent of its people were to be slaves of the 1 percent and they did not know to what group they belonged. And almost as obviously, a world in which the poorest 30 percent of humanity has 3 percent of the income, while the top 20 percent has 66 percent, is purely and simply wrong. It is an offense to a minimal sense of fairness. It should be changed.

I wish the issue could be resolved thus, intuitively, emotionally. Unfortunately, it can't be and there is no point in trying to hide from a most significant complexity. There is a brilliant, well-docu-

---

* Lester Thurow's succinct critique of Rawls in *On Generating Inequality* (New York: Basic Books, 1976) is excellent.

mented case against the pursuit of global justice. It has the support of more than one hundred years of academic thought in the West and, more to the point, of the major Western powers, the United States the most enthusiastic among them.

This attitude is an internationalized version of a policy and point of view that utterly dominate American domestic life. (It is somewhat less powerful in Europe, where socialist movements and ideas are much more of a counterweight to it.) The intelligent reformer, it is argued, should avoid all questions of equity. What is important for a national economy is that there be growth that creates more and more resources to be divided up. If this demands tolerating some inequality, the thesis continues, that is actually to the benefit of the least equal in the society, for even though their share of the wealth remains unfair, their absolute consumption is steadily on the increase. Rawls himself holds a version of this concept, and there is even a socialist edition of it, developed by the late Anthony Crosland in *The Future of Socialism*. The best, it is said, is the enemy of the good.

Now this "trickle down" theory has gone global. Efforts to redistribute the world's wealth, American spokespeople hold, can only interfere with that harmonious, interdependent growth of the international economy which is the one sure way of truly promoting the interests of the poor. Perhaps the most powerful statement of this theme was made some time ago by Ortega y Gasset. In *The Revolt of the Masses*, Ortega warned against hungry mobs that would, in their righteous anger, burn down the bakeries. Isn't such a self-destructive passion the real core of the Third World demand for a new international economic order? And mustn't it, then, be rejected in the name of the objective self-interest of those who foolishly propose it?

Herman Kahn and his associates at the Hudson Institute put this idea in more contemporary—technocratic—form in their appalling book, *The Next 200 Years*. They wrote:

As far as we can tell, arithmetic differences (as opposed to ratios) in per capita product [as between the rich and poor countries] will generally increase for the next 100 years with (of course) many exceptions. But this should not be disastrous, either morally or politically, since there are very few peasants, workers or even businessmen in developing nations who care much about gaps (whether arithmetic or geometric), no matter how much intellectuals, academics and some businessmen may profess to.

Kahn and company are the advocates of a shocking complacency that sees an essentially linear progress bringing global economic happiness during the next two hundred years, if only the underdeveloped lands will accept the system that the advanced economies have imposed on them. Unfortunately, in this defense of the function of inequality in the world economy, they are the spokespersons of a widely misunderstood, and widely held, academic theory.[2]

In a sense, the rest of this book will be a documented refutation, not simply of this attitude but of the American international economic policy based, sometimes consciously, on it. For now, I will simply introduce five basic concepts that will be used in this undertaking. These are my *Leitmotifs:*

First, the linear notion of global economic development is wrong. According to that thesis, the Western capitalist experience represents the normal, natural path of modernization and growing productivity. Where societies deviate from it, they become inefficient, wasteful and antidemocratic, as under Communism. W. W. Rostow's *The Stages of Economic Growth* is a clear statement of this theme, one that had a significant impact upon the administrations of both John F. Kennedy and Lyndon B. Johnson. For Rostow, "all societies, in their economic dimensions . . . [lie] within one of five categories: the traditional society, the preconditions for take-off, the take-off, the drive to maturity, and the age of high mass-consumption." These stages, it will be noted, describe a ladder, one that has been scaled only by Western capitalism. For Rostow and Kahn, they also define the necessary way into the future for any society that wishes to become affluent.

Ironically, Rostow's book, subtitled "A Non-Communist Manifesto," repeated one of Karl Marx's own errors. Marx, too, held that the development on the colonial periphery would essentially repeat the experience in the capitalist center, that India would fairly rapidly grow to resemble the Britain whose imperial power had brutally started it on the road to modernization. Marx was wrong. (So was Lenin, who followed him on this point.) But, then, Marx had the excuse of not being able to observe history disprove him. (And he also wrote in a contrary, and correct, vein on other occasions.) Rostow *et al.* have no such escape hatch. For more than a century, reality has not borne out the expectation of mainstream economic theorists—which has not prevented them from packaging, and repackaging, their discredited theories.

There are many reasons for this mistake and many ways in which it manifests itself, but its central flaw is rather simple to grasp. When Western capitalism emerged, there was no preexisting capitalist system dominating a world market that was itself structured so as to frustrate the economic development of new modernizers. Having climbed through stages that bear some resemblance to Rostow's model, these now-affluent nations did all they could to take the ladder with them. So, the present poor countries confront an integrated, global system that is hostile to their development, and this makes much of the American and European past, which did not take place under any such constraint, irrelevant or, worse, illusory.

Secondly, it may be argued with some force (though I am not at all convinced) that "trickle-down" works *within* an affluent nation. But to say that it operates *between* the rich and poor countries is an entirely different, and erroneous, proposition. The economies of the great capitalist powers are more or less coherent, even though many have backward regions. That is, an economic stimulus will, more or less, travel through the entire system. That is indeed what makes it a system. In sharp contrast, an underdeveloped nation is in great measure defined by the very fact that its economy is not internally coherent, that it lacks the transmission belts found in the wealthy economies of the world's North. One of the characteristics of the South, then, is precisely that trickle-down doesn't, and cannot, function there. This point, I should emphasize, is not the private property of radical critics. Important aspects of it are, it will be seen, asserted by contemporary classicists like John Hicks and Hyla Myint and by Keynesians like Roy Harrod, as well as by Marxists like Samir Amin. And perhaps the most brilliant statement of it was made by the Nobel laureate Gunnar Myrdal more than forty years ago.

Thirdly, I do not make the claim that all the actions of the capitalist powers lead to pure and unmitigated evil in the Third World. There are some on the Left who sometimes talk as if this is the case, and they simply provide the defenders of the status quo with a straw man that any intelligent child can pull apart. Of course, multinational investments in poor countries can create employment and production, generate skills, and so on. But it does so under present circumstances at much too high a price and in a distorted way. This kind of development reinforces the structures of under-development; it perpetuates rather than solves the basic problem. It fits neatly into the incoherence that has just been described; it can even intensify it. Thus, the perpetuation of the *relative* inferiority of the poor countries is programmed into their "progress." In André Gunder Frank's phrase they "develop" underdevelopment.

Fourthly, and closely related to the previous two concepts, the abject misery of the Third World is so intense that many countries must first benefit from a greater relative share of the world's wealth before they can even begin to better themselves, either relatively or absolutely. Gunnar Myrdal has given us a brilliant case in point. In the West, the unemployed have more or less the same social characteristics as the employed. Therefore, if a significant increase in investment is stimulated by a Keynesian government, one can confidently expect that there will be people waiting for the new jobs thereby created for them. In the globe's South, however, great masses of people live on the margin of human existence, lacking the caloric intake of energy that would allow them to participate in a process of economic growth, assuming that the opportunity was given. Under these conditions, an increase in personal consumption for the people will probably be more of a "productive" investment than the building of a mill.

More broadly, the level of misery in many formerly colonial countries is so intense that an increase in justice, in their relative share, is a prerequisite for incremental gains. The West did not merely have the enormous advantage of being first; its absolute levels of consumption were higher two hundred years ago, at the time of the "take-off," than all of the Fourth World and a good part of the rest of the Third World today. For instance, measured in 1965 dollars, the United States had a per capita Gross National Product of $474 in 1834–43—a figure that is higher than that of all Third World countries except the most prosperous of the Latin Americans. Moreover, it was precisely the existence of a socialist working-class movement demanding a redistribution of wealth that forced the Western rulers to that reluctant minimum of social decency that turned out to be so profitable for them. In the scenario of Kahn and Rostow, development is an impersonal, technocratic process and one surveys the centuries from lofty statistical heights. In reality, Western modernization was marked by bitter class struggles; and, if one liked to play with analogies it could be argued, only somewhat facetiously, that the campaign of the globe's poor for a new international economic order will benefit the rich as well.

So, there is a practical case for justice to the Third World: that it is the most productive investment the rich countries can make; that it is a precondition of relative, incremental growth; that it is likely to benefit the entire world and not simply the world's most miserable people. And, even in this excessively pragmatic age, I would add the consideration that really moves me as a person. Justice for the Third World is right.

This issue of justice is intimately involved in the last of these basic concepts, the notion of an international *caste* system. Herman Kahn and his associates blithely and without argument assume that their scheme would not "be disastrous either morally or politically . . ." In fact, it is both. When advanced capitalism developed, the exploiters and the exploited within the home country were usually of the same race. (Blacks in America are, of course, a major exception.) Moreover, there was some social mobility within these societies even in their early, brutal period. If the Third World were to follow Kahn's advice to accept a century or so of systemic inferiority in order to achieve equality sometime around the year 2100 (a false projection in any case), a completely different situation would ensue. There would be a world division of labor—there is already—in which the menial positions would all be assigned to nonwhites. The result would be, not the inequities of a class system, but the much more morally unacceptable and politically explosive rigidities of a caste system.

This situation is immoral on the very face of it, since it makes a national or racial accident of birth into a permanent social and economic fate. And calling it politically explosive is not merely a literary device. The example of South Africa is most instructive on this count. That country has the highest black living standard in all of Africa. It exists, not because the whites have any great concern for the people whom they have assigned to *apartheid*, but because the imperatives of capitalist development, above all the need for

labor, mandated it. And yet, as the bloody, violent events of 1975–
1976 have demonstrated, there is a vast, seething rage among the
blacks. It was not a handful of discontented intellectuals who went
into the streets, willing to die for their cause. Given those events,
Robert Heilbroner's seemingly fantastic vision of the possibility of
nuclear "wars of redistribution" is infinitely more realistic than
Kahn's complacency.[3]

These, then, are the five concepts that underlie this book. They
will not, however, be presented simply as the means of an abstract
analysis. Since I propose to speak to the American heart as well as
to its mind, I will recount some of my own experiences in the Third
World, or in contacts with its leaders at the United Nations, in the
hope that they may make some of the statistics come alive.

There is, however, a problem here. My contact with the Third
World is quite minimal and I do not for a moment pose as an
existential expert on its suffering. I have been a tourist of degradation; I have talked to a few from the poor's elite. That is all, and I
do not want to make any great claims for the profundity of my
observations and conversations. Yet, they have a value. When I
spent a year in Paris in the early sixties, I discovered that what you
learn in the first several weeks—simply what the place looks like,
the aroma of its cigarettes and beer, the way the people count their
change at a small shop—is probably more significant than anything
you will find out in the months to come. To know a country from
the inside, one must live there for years; to know it infinitely better
than someone who has never been there, weeks will suffice. An
incident in India focused this insight anew for me and related it
to this book.

It was an insomniac night in New Delhi in January 1976. I had
decided not to fight my sleeplessness and was rereading Hegel's
Phenomenology of Spirit. Suddenly that incredibly rich and complex masterpiece became relevant to my trip and to this volume. I
had been worrying about the arrogance of pretending to uncover
something of importance in a three-week excursion into the second-
most-populous land on the face of the earth, the site of several
ancient and intricate civilizations, a land that was at that time in
the throes of a political upheaval as Mrs. Gandhi took on near-
dictatorial power. It seemed preposterous to think that the meager
gleanings of my daily brushes with this massive, convoluted reality

could have any worth at all. It was then that I realized that a
phenomenological report might be valuable.

For Hegel, one of the meanings of *phenomenology* is an account,
not of the essence of reality, of things as they really are, but of how
that reality appears to us. In his book, he studies the simplest levels
of perception and experience with the same care that he lavishes on
his most profound insights (not least because he sees the profun-
dities evolving out of the simplicities). It occurred to me that I
could do something like that in describing my travels. I would
not communicate the deep truth about India (or Africa or Latin
America), because, if there is such a thing, I would not even begin
to perceive it in a matter of weeks. But I could tell what it is like
for a Western man to come face to face with these bewildering
societies—how that man felt, not what the society really is.

Later on in India, that project struck me as all the more valuable
when I was forced to realize anew how ordinary, how typical, I
am. I am not engaging in false modesty. Of course, I brought a
greater intellectual, theoretical background to India than most
tourists. I had already written seven books of social criticism and
observation. But, I came to understand, I am also a very mundane
member of the Western middle class, with commonplace emotions.
Paradoxically, it is in that ordinariness that I see the special value
of my autobiographical notes. For I claim to be representative of
most of the people who read this book: unheroic, immersed in
Western comforts, no Saint Francis of Assisi. I am a contradictory,
compromised and somewhat baffled person. If I can transmit the
passion for change with which these experiences flooded my
middle-class soul, perhaps others will feel them.

I will not, of course, confine myself to that personal dimension.
The cruel innocence of the mass of Americans derives, in part,
from the sophisticated, willful innocence of academic economists
who have described the world economy as an idyll for well over a
century. I must confront some of the theoretical complexities that
are involved in that eminently political stance that usually mas-
querades as an "objective," "scientific" view. However, because of
the purposes of this book, I will do these things in a very specific
way.

I will avoid all the intellectual complications that are not ger-
mane to my theme. That is not to say that these issues are unim-

portant, but simply that they do not belong in this book. In a similar spirit I will, wherever possible, base my factual statements and even some of my analyses on the most conservative authorities available. If neoclassicists like John Hicks or Hyla Myint agree with me, that, I think, makes my case all the more compelling. However, it will obviously be impossible to build an entire radical critique on conservative foundations. But even when I take up Marxist insights, I will do so in a certain way. There is a tremendous amount of intramural feuding among Marxists. The disputes involve issues of real substance, but I will venture into that thicket only when it is necessary for my present purposes. I want to write, not a book for scholars and specialists, but a book whose documentation is impeccably scholarly.

In broad outline, Chapters Two, Four, Five and Six will be primarily analytic, albeit in the mode I have just described. Chapter Two will focus on the theory and practice of current American economic policy in the world; Chapters Four and Five will deal with the history and structure of imperialism; Chapter Six will treat the problem of global hunger as a terrifying case in point of the mechanisms detailed in the earlier parts of the book. Chapters Three, Seven and Eight will contain personal observations and entries from journals. They will focus on India, Mexico, Guatemala, Kenya,Tanzania, and the United Nations. Finally, Chapter Nine will attempt to outline positive proposals for the alleviation of the miseries recorded here, and Chapter Ten will be a brief epilogue.

Let me be candid about Chapter Nine. My negative critique of how the United States, and the advanced capitalist powers generally, oppress the poor of the planet is, I believe, quite persuasive. But when one shifts from what is wrong to how to make it right there are enormous difficulties. On the one hand, it is almost impossible to imagine a complete plausible alternative to the existing world economic system. The present reality is, after all, an intricate and vast system, a living, global organism. Even if one could omnisciently work out a total substitute for it, making that work of the mind as real as reality is beyond our powers.

But, on the other hand, if one accepts the current system as a given and simply projects incremental changes in it, there is a profound tendency for the system to overwhelm—to co-opt—those changes. So, a radical transition to a new international economic order is all but indescribable—a problem that confronts Third World statesmen as well as the writers of books—but reformist gains often merely rationalize the system of injustice. The reader, then, is put on notice that my positive proposals will be, of necessity, less solid—less "real"—than my negative critique. Which is to say that we will not easily transcend an unfair planetary structure that has been four centuries in the making.

But we must try to transcend that structure. If one has seen the ragged children selling chewing gum on the streets of Mexico City or the Indians in the mountains of Guatemala who are drunk with an alcoholism that is, quite literally, a social disease; if one has suddenly turned, sitting in a cab in Bombay, startled by the soft, insistent voice of a little girl begging; if, driving outside of Nairobi, you have seen women and children carrying firewood on their backs, bent halfway to the ground; then there is no alternative to seeking those difficult, improbable changes. For you are a haunted person. I want to share that with the reader; I want to take his or her innocence away.

The huge and unconscionable fact of the matter is that, difficult as it may be to abolish this suffering, it can be done. In 1976, Wassily Leontiev, the Nobel laureate, published the results of a careful econometric study of the world economy. He concluded: "The principal limits to sustained economic growth and accelerated development are political, social and institutional in character, rather than physical. No insurmountable physical barriers exist within this century to accelerated development of the developing regions." A Club of Rome Task Force under another Nobel laureate, Jan Tinbergen, came to the same conclusion.

Typically, when the Leontiev report came out, *The New York Times* casually ignored the fact that it endorsed all of the Third World demands made at the Seventh Special Session of the UN— that is, that it demanded far-reaching changes in the United States —and concentrated solely on Leontiev's insistence that there also had to be great efforts among the poor for self-development. That allowed the *Times* to maintain a most cherished Western myth: the problem of global poverty is *them*. In fact, a good part of the problem—the part this book is about—is *us*.[4]

We Americans are too innocent for our own, or the earth's, good. In the heyday of imperialism, when Europe scrambled to divide

Africa, we acquired only a few colonies. The world had already been portioned out to other imperial powers, so America's imperial self-interest spoke in the rhetoric of anti-imperialism. Let everyone simply open all the doors, we said; just let there be a free competition. We did not add the truth we knew: a competition we will win. We do not, then, have the legacy of guilt that is the birthright of an Englishman or a Frenchman. We have to learn about our wrongdoing by way of an arduous effort.

Because of my deep commitment to the best—the most generous and egalitarian—in the American spirit, I want to help rob it of its innocence—both the naïve and cruel innocence of the popular consciousness and the sophisticated and cruel innocence of the academic theories. The point is not to make my fellow citizens feel guilty—though that certainly will be a by-product of this book if it succeeds in its aim—but to persuade a decent people to turn toward the wretched of the earth and to cooperate with them in the work of justice.

Chapter Two **The Status Quo as Utopia**

There is a utopia that has the passionate support of the most powerful people on the planet. It is a visionary rationalization of present misery.

It is an extraordinary idyl on the face of it. It does not simply assert that trade between the rich and poor will in the long run lead to more international equality. It holds that an explicitly unfair bargain between those parties, one in which the disadvantaged give more than they get, will lead to that happy result. It has been approximately a century and a half since this remarkable providence was discovered working through the injustices of the world market. For roughly one hundred and fifty years, reality turned out to be exactly opposite to what was predicted: global inequality grew. Then, during the past quarter of a century, inequality merely stagnated. Nothing daunted, academic economists continued to turn out more and more sophisticated versions of a theory that so spectacularly failed all empirical tests. And the statesmen, delighted to learn that the pursuit of national profit was actually a contribution to the welfare of mankind, kept on repeating this thesis.

We already know, as the last chapter documented, that President Carter is committed to this theory—and that he is likely to apply it in a more generous, humane fashion than his predecessor. However, there is not yet an extensive Carter record in this area; it is simply too early for that. Therefore, most of the examples in this chapter will be taken from the words and actions of Henry Kissinger. These will not accurately predict in detail what Carter will do in the future, but they will define the underlying assumptions of his—and, for that matter, all, post-World War II— policy.

This is not to suggest that nothing changes in this area. Kissinger himself, after an initial bout of intransigence, used this utopia to adapt the United States to some momentous developments, including the new power of the oil producers united in OPEC, the growth of multinational corporations, and a shift in the international division of labor in which the global South was allowed to take over some used industrial revolutions from the North. But what was, and is, fascinating is that these flexible applications of the traditional doctrine carefully preserved its central core, that faith in the egalitarian tendencies to be found in unjust deals between unequals.

The truth is roughly the contrary of what the practical men of power have predicted for these one hundred and fifty years. International trade has not put the underdeveloped countries in a position to make long-run, systemic gains. Rather, it has institutionalized their inferiority. Our dominant theory, then, describes a utopian status quo.

I

The classic statement of this theme was made by the great British economist, David Ricardo, in 1817. One can get some sense of the awe in which his theory of "comparative advantage" is held through an anecdote told by the Nobel laureate Paul Samuelson. One day Samuelson was talking with a mathematician, Stanislaw Ulam, who challenged him to " 'name one proposition in all of the social sciences which is both true and not trivial.' This was a test I always failed. But now, some years later, on the staircase so to speak, an appropriate answer occurs to me: the Ricardo theory of comparative advantage; the demonstration that trade is naturally profitable even when one country is absolutely more—or less—productive in terms of every commodity."

Ricardo's theory has more than a few intricacies, but its basic assertions are simple enough to state clearly, and significant enough to linger over for a moment. "It is quite important to the happiness of mankind," Ricardo wrote, "that our enjoyments should be increased by a better division of labor, by each country producing those commodities for which by its situation, its climate and its other material or artificial advantages, it is adapted, and by their exchanging them for the commodities of other countries." And, "Under a system of perfectly free commerce, each country naturally devotes its capital and labor to such employments as are most beneficial to each. This pursuit of individual advantage is admirably connected with the universal good of the whole."

So far, this might seem to be a mere repetition of Adam Smith. Ricardo, however, took a giant step beyond Smith by showing that there would be mutual advantage to all parties, even if some were more developed than others and even though one country was forced to give another a bargain. He did so by means of a two-nation model. Suppose that the production of a quantity of cloth takes the labor of 100 men for one year in England whereas a quantity of wine requires the labor of 120 men. In Portugal, the wine costs 80 men's labor; the cloth, 90. Under these circumstances, it makes sense for England to exchange its cloth for Portuguese wine even though it thereby receives 80 man-years of labor in return for 100. It still has saved the 20 man-years that domestic production of the wine would have cost. And although the Portuguese could produce the cloth at home for less of an outlay than goes into the cloth it imports, they still save ten man-years of labor, paying only 80 man-years for a cloth on which they would have had to expend 90 man-years at home.

The beauty of this thesis from the point of view of an advanced country should be immediately apparent. It shows that it is in the self-interest of a poor nation to exchange more labor in return for less. The inequality of the world, then, actually facilitates efficiency and the mutual interest of all, for it permits each country within this interdependent system to make the best use of its resources. Small wonder that Henry Kissinger came forward as a modern-day

Ricardian at the Seventh Special Session of the UN General Assembly in 1975. He said in classic terms, "Comparative advantage and specialization, the exchange of technology and the movement of capital, the spur to productivity that competition provides—these are central elements of efficiency and progress. For developing nations, trade is perhaps the most important engine of development."

There is a complicating irony in all of this: the Soviet Union agrees with Kissinger. As one Russian expert put it, "If commodities are exchanged at fair world prices based on the international value of commodities, then foreign trade is mutually advantageous for countries that are on different levels of economic and technological development." I will not go into the question of why Communist writers approve of such an eminently bourgeois theory. I will only note that it is one more reason for regarding Moscow's "Marxism" as spurious and Soviet power as a beneficiary of the injustices of the world division of labor. On this point, fat Communists are very much like fat capitalists.

So the advanced powers on both sides of the twentieth century's ideological divide are agreed on the theory of comparative advantage. That raises two obvious questions. What, precisely, was wrong with Ricardo's reasoning? Secondly, if this thesis is so clearly contradicted by one hundred and fifty years of contrary evidence, why does it retain such a hold over the minds of honest, and genuinely brilliant, thinkers?

The most persuasive and comprehensive answer to both counts has been formulated by Gunnar Myrdal in several seminal books.* Myrdal is a social democrat, but not a Marxist; yet his theory is in

---

* Even though Myrdal is a Nobel laureate in economics, I believe that his extraordinary accomplishments as a *theorist* have not been sufficiently appreciated. The intellectual public often thinks of him as the inspired empirical researcher of *American Dilemma* and *Asian Drama*. It ignores the remarkable methodological appendices in both books, as well as *The Political Element in the Development of Economic Theory*. One of the reasons, I think, is that Myrdal speaks in lucid prose, rather than in mathematics, which many people think must mean that he is somehow less profound than the equation writers. And then, as Myrdal himself remarked in another context, "Ignorance is seldom random, but instead highly opportunistic." The opportunistic ignorance in this case derives from the fact that most modern Ricardians are citizens of countries which benefit from not too closely examining the reality that treats them so well.

essential agreement with Christian Palloix's Marxist analyses and can even draw support from some modern classicists like Hyla Myint and John Hicks, or, for that matter, from Albert Tucker, the vigorous critic of the proposals for a new international economic order. The point of view that I present, then, deviates from the current academic consensus—a version of Ricardo developed with great sophistication by Heckscher, Ohlin and Samuelson—but it has some weighty support. Its supreme virtue is that it deals with the facts.

If every country in Ricardo's rather static model specialized in the same kind of technology, then his theory might work out. In point of historical fact, one group of countries concentrated on the most advanced high-productivity pursuits; the others, through no choice of their own, were assigned labor-intensive and low-productivity jobs. Such a division of international roles clearly helped to promote inequality. Secondly, the traditional (small-scale, handicraft) industries in the poor nations were often wiped out by the competition of the new manufactures from the rich. A related point, stressed by Hyla Myint, is that Ricardo assumed fully employed and given resources in the two countries that traded with each other. He did not consider the possibility that one of them would be only marginally in the world market. Finally, John Hicks remarks that the first powers to benefit from free trade carefully saw to it, through a variety of policies, that no other economies would duplicate their good luck. This point will be much more fully developed in Chapters Four and Five.

Ricardo's theory, then, did not explain reality. But why has it persisted to this very day? The intellectual stature of the thinkers who have developed the current update of Ricardo, the Heckscher-Ohlin theorem, precludes a crass theory that they were simply the flunkies of those who stood to gain by rationalizing a sordid economic reality by means of a pretty utopia. One reason that they kept to this thesis in spite of the facts is that it is even more abstract than most economic theories. Economists often have a self-avowed—but never justified—penchant for preferring "elegant" analyses to the inelegant. This aestheticism may be at work in this case. Moreover, the very intricacy of the theory, particularly the enormous number of contrary-to-fact assumptions that it contains, provides more than enough escape hatches when some critic remarks that reality deviates so profoundly from what it is supposed to be.

But why continue to play such games? Myrdal poses the problem well: "The question . . . arises what a general *practical* postulate for *concrete* action really means when it is delimited by *abstract* assumptions and reservations." To account for this, I am afraid that one must look to extra-intellectual and self-interested factors. I say that I am afraid that one must do so without any irony. As a rule, I regard conspiratorial explanations of serious intellectual work—that an idea is merely a rationalization of a greedy economic interest that profits from it—as thin and utterly unsatisfying. That, I pointed out in two books, is a "vulgar Marxism," which caricatures the much more complex epistemology of the authentic Marxism. Only, in this case, I am literally forced in that direction, because reality itself seems to be rather vulgarly Marxist.

Ricardo's theory was developed in Britain and it was sold to the political leadership on the grounds that, while promoting the welfare of the entire world, it would, first and foremost, improve Britain's position more than that of any other nation. It was not a conscious rationalization in the sense of deliberately misrepresenting the facts in order to serve some selfish purpose. It was, however, an analysis that was quite well aware of how Britain would gain from the extraordinary providence that it described. Free trade, Joan Robinson has said, is "just a more subtle form of mercantilism. It is believed only by those who will gain an advantage from it."

Finally, Thomas Ballogh, a highly respected Labour economist in Britain today, sees the function of Ricardo's analysis in terms of conscience and morality. The British, Ballogh argues, were appalled at the wretched mass of humanity over which they presided in the Empire. Being good and decent folk in their own self-definition—"Christians" who were proud of their superior ethics—they needed a justification for what they were doing. The notion of comparative advantage did this admirably well. It gave imperialists a sophisticated reason for picturing themselves as the humble servant of economic laws that would ultimately do more to better the globe than any sentimental attempts at redistribution of wealth.[1]

The United States, Britain's successor in the leadership of world capitalism, still believes in that Ricardian providence. I now turn to its contemporary exercise in pragmatic, self-serving utopianism.

II

In September 1975, America changed its tone of voice.

Earlier that year, Secretary of State Kissinger had been threatening the Third World, observing only a minimum of diplomatic tact. The majority in the United Nations, he said in a Milwaukee speech, was subverting the usefulness of the General Assembly. "Tragically, the principal victims will be the countries which seek to extort what could substantially be theirs if they proceeded cooperatively." A little later, he delivered an understated, but unmistakable, rebuke to those who complain of American imperialism. "Those who do not want investment from abroad," he commented sardonically, "can be confident they will not receive it."

But then in his speech before the Seventh Special Session of the General Assembly (which Daniel Patrick Moynihan actually read), Kissinger began talking of building "a better world, by conscious purpose, out of the equality and moderation of states." More to the point, he made a series of proposals that seemed to promise new resources for the modernization process in Africa, Asia and Latin America. His apparent change of mind and heart was, on the whole, greeted enthusiastically by the ambassadors of the poor. Most of them did not notice that they were getting an edited, updated version of Ricardo's imperial theory.

This is not to say that Kissinger's transition from bully to cooperator was a charade. Far from it. The new tone of voice was one minor refraction of a major shift taking place in the world economy, or rather a sign that the State Department had finally become aware of that shift. In the era of the OPEC cartel, the United States needs access to the raw materials and resources of the periphery without having to worry about expropriations. And the multinationals—two thirds of them American—want to be able to shift a certain amount of manufacture to the Third World. An argument to show why the underdeveloped economies should accede to both these desires was required. Reenter the durable David Ricardo.

Actually, Kissinger had made his central theoretical point in the

Milwaukee speech when he was still talking tough. He said, "We believe that economic development is in the first instance an internal process. Either societies create the conditions for saving and investment, for innovation and ingenuity, for enterprise and industry which ultimately lead to self-sustaining economic growth, or they do not." In other words, all countries are to follow the American (European) path to modernity. Since economic development is thus a problem that is internal to each nation, there need be no "North-South" conflict. On the contrary, sophisticated statesmen will realize that the world is interdependent. At this point the unmistakable accents of Ricardo are heard.

"The reality," Kissinger told the UN, "is that the world economy is a single global system of trade and monetary relations on which hinges the development of all our economies. The advanced nations have an interest in the growth of markets and production in the developing world; with equal conviction we state that the developing countries have a stake in the markets, technological innovation and capital investment of the industrial countries." Only, the poor countries perversely refuse to recognize this proposition. At the Nairobi meeting of the UN Conference on Trade and Development (UNCTAD) in 1976, Kissinger admonished his listeners:

For, paradoxically, resource development is often discouraged by the very countries which are most in need of it. Nationalization and forced change in the terms of concessions in some developing countries have clouded the general climate for resource investment in the developing world. Social and political uncertainties have further complicated investment prospects. As a result, commercially viable projects have been postponed, canceled or relocated; and capital, management, and technology have been diverted to production of higher-cost raw materials in the industrialized world.

In short, if the Third World will only become reasonable, then it can get the benefits of all those comparative advantages that are built into the world market. Nationalization of foreign corporations is bad—and multinationals are good.

Transnational enterprises [Kissinger continued] have been powerful instruments of modernization both in industrial nations and in the developing countries where there is often no substitute for their ability to marshal capital, management skills, technology and initiative. *Thus the controversy over their role and conduct is itself an obstacle to economic development.** [Emphasis mine.]

So Kissinger tells the UN—which had had the temerity to sponsor an investigation into the "role and conduct" of the multinationals—that these institutions are so hallowed and beneficial that one may not even discuss their shortcomings.

All of this theorizing had the very real function of rationalizing America's basic international economic policy: to get guaranteed, secure access to raw materials and to defend multinationals on the grounds that private capital offers the greatest hope for the economic development of the Third World. So, for example, Kissinger proposed at the Seventh Special Session that the World Bank's International Finance Corporation (IFC)—its organization for the support of private enterprise in the underdeveloped countries, a brainchild of Nelson Rockefeller—expand its 1975 capital of $100 million to "at least" $400 million. And at the UNCTAD meeting in Nairobi, he urged creation of an International Resources Bank, which would participate, with private investors and host governments, in development projects. In this scheme, the foreign investor would actually get a share of what was produced rather than an interest payment. This is a somewhat subtle way of rejecting a major Third World demand—that the advanced economies "unpack" their take-it-or-leave-it combination of capital, technology and management.

The point of these proposals, as the London *Economist* noted candidly, was to put a "cushion between multinational corporations and the developing countries." If the multinational has, in effect, an international "front" sanctioned by the UN, then expropriations and other acts of national impertinence can be ruled out. This is a not unimportant consideration given the fact that in 1973–74, in eighteen African countries, there were some 37 major acts of

---

* In UN terminology, multinationals are "transnationals." The UN writers want to make clear that these entities are not genuinely multinational—that is, run by people from various countries. *Transnational* focuses on the fact that these companies produce in more than one country, which is indeed their distinguishing characteristics. I agree with the UN point entirely, and I use the term, multinational, only because it is the generally accepted name in the United States.

nationalization that involved between 40 and 100 percent of the affected foreign assets.

In America's very pragmatic utopia, then, the multinationals, the foreign investors and the United Nations, working to protect and facilitate the movement of private capital and enterprise, are good; nationalizations, tough bargaining and militance on the part of poor countries are bad. If the latter can only be avoided; then the long-promised Ricardian equilibrium will surely assert itself, even if it is a century and a half late. The rest of this book will show, among other things, that every single one of the dogmas undergirding the United States' ideology is either seriously defective or simply wrong. For now, however, it is important to turn to another aspect of the tactical move from truculence to comparative-advantage idyls. It is a certain shift that is taking place in the global economy, one that Kissinger's sweet reasonableness was designed to help.

Writing in the London *Economist* in 1975, Norman Macrae quite accurately summed up the basic, ongoing trends on the world market. "The key strategies for American business corporations," he wrote, "should be to (1) move the boring manufacturing jobs down to the poor south of the world, at maximum profit to the poor south and themselves; (2) to redesign their domestic structures to fit the new knowledge-processing, un-obsequious, post-manufacturing age." Even the *Economist*'s imperial flippancy is to the point. It suggests the essence of the matter: that whatever changes take place will promote the advantages of the major capitalist powers. There is a ritual nod to Ricardo's egalitarianism—these moves will be to the "maximum profit" of both North and South—but then the real purpose is hardly even disguised. The Southerners are to get "the boring manufacturing jobs," the Northerners the sophisticated, high-productivity technology. This "new" trend will thus replicate the basically unfair world division of labor.

This point is an extremely important one, because the unwary reader is more than likely to be reading in the near future about how manufacturing is increasing among the once-poor countries. There will be a certain truth in these reports (though it needs to be carefully qualified, as will be seen), but that will almost certainly obscure what is truly critical. The underdeveloped nations will be given a certain limited license to industrialize at precisely that

moment when it suits the needs of the advanced economies. Paradoxically, the growth of manufacture in the South of the globe in
this fashion will, under multinational corporate auspices, be one
more sign of that region's subjugation, not a portent of its emancipation.

The original international capitalist division of labor (which will
be examined more carefully in Chapters Four and Five) was for-
malized in the nineteenth century. On the one side, the rich were
the industrialists; on the other, the poor were the producers of raw
materials and agriculture. Between World War I and World War II
there was either stagnation or depression on the world market. But
then, after World War II, a new structure began to evolve. This
is the reality that the American Secretary of State was trying to
cope with in those speeches to the UN in 1975 and 1976.

In the post-World War II period, the colonial revolution brought
an end to formal Western hegemony throughout the world. Economically, the former colonies began to develop light industry and
even some heavy industry. The advanced economies now began
more and more to provide the capital goods that permitted the
growth of those industries on the underdeveloped periphery. Between 1960 and 1973, for instance, Third World manufacturing
output climbed from $26.8 billion to $64.5 billion, with about half
of that growth in heavy industry and half in light. Even though
such numbers describe a significant change, they can be deceptive.
The top three manufacturing powers in the Third World accounted
for more than half of its manufacture; the top ten, for 80 percent,
the top twenty for 90 percent. Moreover, the basic trend was one
of export-led industrialization—that is, these countries produced
for the big capitalist nations. In other words, even in a favorable
period for the minority of the best-off poor countries, their growth
was geared to the needs of the old imperial powers.

Most important of all in terms of this analysis, this increase in
manufacturing in the underdeveloped areas primarily reflected the
activity of multinational corporations. Under the old imperial system, the advanced powers exported commodities and finance; now,
production itself was becoming international as technology and
management roamed the world in the search of profits. Indeed,
this is precisely the specific difference that sets the multinational
corporation apart from those businesses that traditionally have

operated in international trade. The multinationals send plants, and not just products or money, around the globe. The main beneficiaries of this process, we shall see, are the advanced powers that have been investing in one another's affluence more than in Third World poverty. But there is a certain ambiguous spin-off to the poor countries, and that is the major source of the growth in their manufacture.

Why was some manufacturing thus shifted to the Third World? I want to take great care with the answer, for simplistic Leftists have sometimes given dramatically inaccurate responses, which have been a godsend to their enemies. I would like to begin by rejecting some easy explanations and then turn to the actual complexities.

This shift did not take place because the United States, or the advanced capitalist powers in general, were becoming more dependent on the Third World in the post-World War II period. It is true that 25 percent of all American corporate investment is taking place abroad in the middle seventies, and that 25 percent of the profits (50 percent in the case of some companies) are made overseas. And liberals join Marxists in arguing that this trend may be the result of a surfeit of capital in the big powers and a lack of high-yield investment opportunities there. All that has a Leninist ring to it. But on the other hand, more than 70 percent of those exported American dollars are placed in wealthy capitalist societies. Of the rest, Latin America accounts for over half, which means that there is no great rush to exploit Africa and Asia.

Secondly, "superprofits" are not the key to the change. To be sure, there were golden gains, particularly from petroleum, in the halcyon days before the OPEC cartel. If, however, one abstracts from that petroleum bonanza, then there is a profit differential, but it is not terribly dramatic. The profits averaged 11 percent in poor nations and 9.6 percent in the wealthy countries during 1965–1968. A more complicated truth may be at work in this area, and some liberal economists have noted it. The American corporations, they suggest, are not going abroad to get "superprofits" but simply to guard against a somewhat lower rate of profits at home.

More importantly, there is another mechanism that operates to send the American manufacturing to the periphery. Its fundamental character was identified long ago, and it has been explored in its contemporary setting by scholars from the Harvard Business School as well as by Third World and French Marxists. Since so many otherwise contradictory thinkers seem to share the insight, I assume that it has a certain authority.

Innovators, Karl Marx said—and the great conservative Joseph Schumpeter agreed—get a temporary monopoly and all of the special privileges—high profits—which result from it. But then those competitors who survive that first period buy or steal the new idea. As more and more firms are capable of getting into the business, the high returns—"technological rents," they are sometimes called—begin to diminish. In recent years, Raymond Vernon and a group of associates at the Harvard Business School have internationalized this theme in their theory of the "product cycle." And some of the more perceptive Marxists, like Samir Amin, have made similar analyses.

Innovation begins in the advanced country—as usual, the first are first again, because they were first to begin with. They have the science, the technology and the internal market to justify research and development. As a result, they also have an international advantage, and they export their product around the world. But the technology becomes routinized and producers appear, first in the other advanced countries, then, in some cases and to a limited extent, on the periphery. Thus it is that textiles, the classic industry of the first industrial revolution, have been migrating to the former colonies. So have consumer electronics, from a later stage in the evolution of capitalism. Even steel, Amin thinks, will make this transition. Meanwhile, back in the rich country, investment in the newest generation of sophisticated technology is the growing edge of the economy.

Paul Samuelson described this process in a dramatic metaphor borrowed from Max Weber. The United States, Samuelson said, is becoming a "cathedral economy." In Weber's analysis, a "cathedral town" was the administrative center, the Bishop's seat, which did not actually engage in production. Now, Samuelson held, the United States is becoming a "cathedral economy" in relation to the Third World. They will increasingly specialize in the laborious tasks of transforming raw materials into commodities; we will think, control, manage.

There is, however, a problem for the United States in this scenario. It began to surface even before the shift to the Third World but it was exacerbated by the latter, and by the OPEC cartel in particular. An understanding of it helps to deepen our view of recent American international economic policy.

Between 1945 and 1960, the United States was absolutely dominant in a Western camp in which the other nations had not yet recovered from the devastation of World War II and were, in any case, unified behind the nuclear superpower that protected the "Free World." During those years America spent billions on the reconstruction of European capitalism and not only tolerated, but encouraged, the revival of its defeated enemies, Germany and Japan. Washington in those days could finance its global military and political commitments by deficits; it could also live off its "technological rents." But by 1960, the Common Market and Japan had turned into competitors; and in many cases, like that of steel, their technology was superior to the American. (They had the "advantage" of losing much of their own plant during the War, and therefore they were starting from a very modern scratch.) By August 1971, the unthinkable happened. The once almighty dollar was devalued.

This country, then, had become somewhat chastened even before the problems of the new international division of labor penetrated its consciousness. Those problems, however, are not simply American; they touch the whole of the advanced capitalist system. Cathedral economies are particularly vulnerable to a strike on the part of the manual laborers of the planet, a fact that was brought home with painful clarity during the OPEC oil embargo of 1973–74. So it is that this explanation of the technological reasons for the shift to the Third World also emphasizes and amplifies a point made earlier: that access to the poor countries, security, an absence of surprises, all have become the more important to the United States. The good old days, when a Mossadegh could be punished for his nationalization of Iranian oil by means of a boycott and a little help from the CIA are gone. Thus, the new American tone of voice in the UN.

Still, couldn't one argue that all this is going to improve the position of the Third World? In absolute terms, yes, but a qualified yes; in relative terms, an unambiguous no. The whole point of this exercise, I assume it is now clear, is to preserve Western capitalist hegemony in a new form, under new conditions. Exactly what this means can be seen in summary form in an extraordinary analysis made by the UN Industrial Development Organization in 1974.

The developing countries, UNIDO commented, rely on the advanced powers for their technology, because their growing needs outstrip their domestic capacities for innovation. But then, even where there is success, the dependence on the giant capitalisms does not end. When a country gets to the upper level of the underdevelopment spectrum, reaching $800 to $900 per capita GNP, it finds it must turn to the same old sources for the newer technologies.

Though indigenous enterprises may have mastered the skills needed for the operation of textile mills, bakeries, sawmills and canneries, an array of newer and more difficult tasks emerges, tasks associated with the next wave of growth. The technical challenge thus moves from textiles to synthetic fibers, from canned goods to laminated metals.

For the poor countries, then, and even the least poor among them, the product cycle is a labor of Sisyphus. Every time they struggle up the mountain, they are pushed back down again by a wave of innovation that keeps them in their second-class place. Once, some time ago, a country did manage to break this pattern: Japan. But, as a sophisticated defender of the multinationals, Gustav Ranis, is forced to concede, no one wants that to happen again. It is within this context that I interpret America's conversion to sweeter reasonableness in 1975. The Secretary of State realized that a few judicious concessions, articulated in the utopian universals of Ricardo's theory, could help to maintain America's relative power at the head of the international pack. It was also a way of justifying the actions of a new institution with a very poor reputation in the Third World, the multinational corporation.[2]

III

In dealing with the subject of the multinationals, it is impossible for me to do more than treat of a few themes that bear on the central argument of this book. In doing this, I do not want to picture the multinationals as the agency of a diabolical conspiracy, or to suggest that they should be simply banished from the face of the earth. That is the kind of absolutism that can be so easily countered

by a Raymond Vernon. They unquestionably promote development—but in a skewed way. And they have pioneered certain
practices with a great potential when, but only when, they are
institutionally transformed into agencies of truly social and democratic impact.

Moreover, it should not be thought that the multinationals have
the power to do whatever they want in the underdeveloped countries. The very existence of their plants overseas means that they
are, in the words of a Shell International executive, "industrial
hostages." Even as I write this book, there are some signs that
multinationals have become more nervous about the insecurities of
the Third World than the State Department and that they are re-
treating from the periphery back to their secure homelands. So let
me grant all these ambiguities (and others which I do not have
time even to cite). I want to focus on the proposition that the multinational corporations are a positive instrument for the alleviation of the poverty of the world's South. That is the official
American position, under Carter as under Nixon-Ford. I dissent
from it.

To begin with, ironically the multinational delivers a *coup de
grâce* to whatever lives on of the Ricardian theory—that is, the
American corporate practice is doing a magnificent job of subverting the American government theory. In Ricardo's analysis, one of
the reasons that bad bargains were good deals in international
trade was that the factors of production (capital, labor and land)
were immobile, confined within the framework of a single nation.
Inside a single economy—in theory, but only in theory—investors
would be attracted by the advantages of backwardness, by low
wages in particular. Their competition would eventually bid the
regional prices up to the national average. Since the factors of
production could not move freely across borders, inefficiency could
survive on the world market, and even prosper, because of the
relative gains it permitted. Now, however, the world has become,
in Richard Barnet and Ronald Müller's excellent phrase, "a global
factory."

As the corporations leap over national walls, they can reap whatever comparative advantages there are by producing on the spot
and then taking the fruits of those advantages back home with
them. This is the source of a paradox noted by the neoclassical

economist Hyla Myint. The terms of trade can improve for a poor country, Myint reports, and the per capita income of the indigenous population can decline. The reason is that foreigners can capture, and repatriate, a good chunk of that advance. And so it is that Kaiser Aluminum finds it cheaper to ship raw materials to Ghana, where they are processed by government-subsidized power generated by a project financed by the World Bank, and to reship it to the States rather than to work on it in this country.

In economic theory, such things are defensible because they are "efficient"—that is, maximum production is being achieved with minimum inputs. Only, this "efficiency" is terribly inefficient from the point of view of the poor country that surrenders many of its natural advantages to a multinational. In a remarkably arch fashion, two Brookings economists even conceded this rather critical point: "There are many efficient solutions, and the choice will depend on income distribution within the society. In the face of existing extreme income disparities, both nationally and internationally, those who do not find efficiency and growth arguments by themselves compelling—particularly in relation to the underdeveloped countries—*may perhaps be forgiven.*" (Emphasis added.)

One would think that this was obvious. It is not. When the multinationals testified before the American Congress in opposition to protectionist legislation, they spoke, one commentator remarked, as if their profit drive was simply a means of maximizing "the welfare consequences of world trade." And a General Motors spokesperson before the UN's Group of Eminent Persons, who held hearings on the multinationals, said of such companies, "Their size arises not from power but from service—service to customers and markets. They have a broad constituency, which votes every day in the marketplace and determines their continuous success— or their decline or, at times, failure." This theory of "consumer sovereignty" does not work within the advanced economies themselves, because some people have a million (dollar) votes and others a thousand or less, and because hundreds of millions are spent annually to predetermine the "free" choice of the consumer. Moreover, it is not exactly an accident that the Harvard scholars discovered that the typical multinational is, precisely, a huge oligopoly firm that spends heavily on advertising—that is, is even more exempt from consumer sovereignty than most companies. It is surprising that GM permitted such crude ideas to be presented in its name before an international forum.

Other arguments in favor of the multinational in the Third World are more sophisticated. Giovanni Agnelli, the Chairman of Fiat and a rather imaginative industrialist, told the UN Group that "the network of multinational corporations represents in embryonic form the central nervous system of an emerging global order." This is not true; it assumes that the multinationals are, under their present control, dedicated to economic development. Yet it does contain a possible future truth. There is no question that the world needs global economic planning and that this idea, so seemingly utopian, has already been put into practice by the multi- • nationals. It will work positively, however, only when the multinationals are no longer agencies of private corporate purpose, when they are no longer multinationals.

Here, from an impeccably conservative source, the United States Tariff Commission, is a succinct statement of how radical the multinationals are in their pursuit of conservative goals:

In the largest and most sophisticated multinationals, planning and abstract monitoring of plan fulfillment have reached a scope and level of detail that, ironically, resembles more than superficially the national planning procedures of Communist countries. There are general goals set by top management, against which far-flung affiliates generate plans for a year's, 5 years' or 10 years' activity. These local plans then are fought out at the regional headquarters level, where goals, inputs, outputs and financial needs are recommended. The regional executive then carries "his" plan to a confrontation with his colleagues and top management at "the Kremlin" (U.S. headquarters), where still more recommendations and compromises are made.

At present, of course, this elaborate system of international planning is operated according to corporate profit-maximizing priorities.* As such, it is hostile to balanced economic development,

* There has been considerable academic debate as to whether the up-to-date corporation really "maximizes" profits or whether it now modifies that drive in the name of long-run considerations. Some have even talked of an emergent corporate "conscience." This has been, I think, a battle of straw men. Of course, corporations have become shrewd and Keynesian and even proplanning, which is a far cry from the days of the robber baron. What is being maximized is thus a profit defined in a new way, but a profit nevertheless.

even though it may promote unbalanced development—the development of underdevelopment—when that suits multinational purposes. But it is true that the techniques now being pioneered in order to rationalize the private exploitation of the planet could be turned to social use on a world scale, if there were a political movement with the power to do so.

And finally, the multinational is justified on the grounds that it spreads technology around the world. This, as a Vice-Chairman of DuPont told the UN, is its "unique role." The contradictions within this point of view are so well known that Mr. Kissinger publicly recognized them. It is not simply that the "product-cycle" pattern is, at its very best, a labor of Sisyphus. Beyond that, the R&D in the advanced countries is aimed at creating new wants, at differentiating products that are not so different, and at saving labor. So it was that Mr. Kissinger admitted in his speech to the UNCTAD meeting in Nairobi that "in many cases" the technology of the major capitalist powers is not adapted to Third World needs. And Raymond Vernon writes that "brand-new technologies, created to respond to the particular conditions of poor countries, have been rare."

But the multinationals come into the poor countries and create their enclaves, their "export platforms." They usually get special concessions, like tax breaks, from the host country, and they engage in "transfer pricing," evading local tax laws by taking profits in the form of the high prices that the Third World affiliate pays the home office (advanced nation) for supplies and management. Even nationalization is no guarantee that these practices will end. As Edith Penrose put this point, "foreigners may have *de facto* control even of nationalized enterprises whenever the expertise and knowledge they possess gives them the capacity to make decisions beyond the monitoring scope, as it were, of local partners." [3]

Thus the truth I assert in this chapter is, I am afraid, arrogant. I claim that most of America's brilliant economic minds, and all its policymakers, are in the spell of a utopia that has cruel consequences for the poor of the world. With enormous ingenuity they have polished and sharpened and mathematicized an idyl that has little or nothing to do with reality. It is not true that the Third World countries can follow in the American path, not least because we work hard to make that impossible; it is not true that economic growth in the South leads to self-sustaining development or that the world market furthers equality; it is not true that multinational corporations are a benevolent agency for the transfer of an appropriate technology to the periphery. These things are true only in that very functional utopia that commands the faith of powerful people who profit from their delusions of justice.

Chapter Three **Encounters: India**

[This chapter and Chapter Seven, which recounts a trip to Africa, are taken from a journal that I kept during the events it narrates. Since, as I explained earlier, I do not pretend to deep insights from a brief voyage but want to present the immediate impact of the Third World reality on a Western man, I have hardly edited the original text at all. In the notes on East Africa, I have even retained an error that resulted from reaching for significances that were simply not there. My point is to communicate a sense of spontaneous reactions that I hope will make the more formal analyses and statistics come alive. As the text shows, my trip to India occurred during some of the worst days of Indira Gandhi's Emergency. At the time, neither I, nor any other observer, expected that a free election in 1977 was going to permit the people to vote for democracy. I rejoice in the event, of course, and in the period between my return from India and that vote, I did some modest work with Indians in the United States who struggled against the repression. But I would add that the triumph of political democracy in India, as welcome as it is, does not mean that the economic and social problems which have bedeviled that country have been solved.

This is particularly so because the coalition which defeated Mrs. Gandhi encompassed movements from the free market Right to the socialist Left and was agreed on the issue of civil liberties but on nothing else. In a sense, the message of this chapter—and indeed, of the entire book—is now all the more urgent: the Indian people having magnificently asserted their commitment to the ideal of freedom must now have the chance to use that freedom to transform the intolerable conditions under which so many of them live. That requires that America do more than cheer election results. We must change those of our policies which help perpetuate misery in India.]

1/2/76—FRANKFURT AIRPORT EN ROUTE TO NEW DELHI

When I imagined making this flight, the part of it when I would begin this journal was much more pleasurable than, in fact, it is. What I omitted in anticipation was that I would be tired, headachy, grim, when the moment came. *Quand même.*

My feelings about the trip and the book are quite mixed. Above all, I am frightened. I was joking last night in the kitchen with Stephanie, waiting for the cab to come. I asked her, Do you think I'll be able to find any poor kids in India? But beneath the badinage there was—there is—a kind of physical and moral terror. Am I a tourist of misery who is going to Calcutta to look at a dying child, not to help, but to observe? And even if I can say that my observation may help—if not that particular child, then similar children in the future—is that enough of an excuse? Worst of all, will I be able to look at the child?

When I was young I thought and talked a lot about the problem of evil. As I somewhat vaguely remember, Ivan Karamazov rejected a God who would torment a child. So do I. But then, after those soaring philosophical discussions, I got caught up in the existential —but not existentialist—minutiae of life. And even though my minutiae involved political organizing to eliminate all needless human suffering, they were still minutiae. For the most part, I could reduce my anger to a rational, even if passionate, desire to master social reality, in theory and perhaps even in practice. There were times when the old, basic questions would assert themselves —particularly when I thought, rightly or wrongly, that my life was on the line in a few of my forays into the South as a civil-rights activist in the sixties—but for the most part I could escape into routine, even if that routine was a socialist-Marxist one that is not exactly commonplace in America.

But now I seem to be en route to a confrontation with the shattering outrages of existence. I am shy, a physical coward, and perhaps a moral one. I certainly agree with Eliot that mankind— or, more precisely, my frail fraction of it—cannot bear too much reality. So what will happen in this brief journey to a misery greater than any I have ever seen?

There is the anomaly of the tennis racket hovering over this. I will be going to a Fulbright seminar at Gopalpur-by-the-Sea, in the State of Orissa. That is how I am financing this trip. The seminar is being held at a resort and will be academic and middle class. There will be, I assume, a tennis court there and that gets at one of my abiding enthusiasms. But I could not see myself boarding a plane, carrying a tennis racket, on my way to what could be for me the heart of darkness, the horror. I would have felt too much a hypocrite and the occasional paranoid who dwells in my Id suspects that I would be photographed and presented to the world as a monster.

I didn't bring my racket, of course. But I packed tennis shorts and shoes and decided that I would borrow a racket if I could.

1/2—BETWEEN ISTANBUL AND KARACHI

My solution was the most blatant evasion possible. But I wonder if, without getting overly cosmic about it, my tennis predicament is not somehow paradigmatic. The capitalist Western advanced countries, including their socialists, feel embarrassed about their wealth in the face of the poverty of the underdeveloped nations. Or rather, the liberal and socialist Left does. Yet it is politically impossible, I think, to ask the workers or even the middle classes in those economies to give up the gains they have made—and for the worker those are both recent and quite modest. Perhaps more poignantly, the effect of such a renunciation would be problematic at best. Assuming that the Western world is still run basically on the principle of corporate capitalism, is there the least guarantee that a voluntary lowering of mass living standards would be transferred to the poor lands, raising their level?

When I visited Les Brown at the World Watch Foundation, an

organization concerned with anticipating global problems, like famines, I had put that question to him. If I ate less meat, I asked him, and thereby consumed less grain in that wasteful fashion, would that better the lot of the South Asians or of the Africans in the Sahel? Brown gave what was essentially a free-market answer. If a mass of consumers in the West voluntarily cut back, that would lower demand and therefore price. Then, all other things being equal, there would be more grain on the world market at a lower cost and the Asians and the Africans would be in a somewhat better position.

I wish that were true, but I am not at all sure. The agribusinessmen of America have typically responded to lowered demand by cutting production and getting a Federal subsidy to maintain income. And even if that didn't happen, wouldn't the main beneficiaries be the food-deficit rich countries—including Russia—which could then raise their own rate of wasting grain? But if I am right, then the best, the happiest and most possible answer to our problems doesn't work. If only we individuals could by moral decision dominate the economic and political structures of this age! If only my choice of not bringing a tennis racket could effect something other than my own sense of moral rectitude and even vanity.

Certainly the most unambiguous period of my political life was when I lived in voluntary poverty at the *Catholic Worker*. Only, I was young, without responsibility or family, and I didn't yet care about tennis. Is there some way that ordinary concerned people can make something more than a well-intended gesture toward the Third World? Or, do these ruminations en route to India lead to the bitter, or sectarian—or Stalinist—conclusions that only a sudden, utter and merciless tranformation of the economy, either within a Third World country or throughout the world market or both, can offer any hope to the starving, twisted children who persist in the midst of mankind's most developed century?

The Stalinist temptation. It is strange that such a theme has haunted me from time to time. In the American radical movement I have been known for some twenty-five years—and it was nearly twenty-five years ago to the day that I decided to join the *Catholic Worker* and thereby the organized, full-time Left—as being implacably anti-Stalinist. That issue was one of the sources of my painful, and partly stupid, break with the founding sons and daughters of Students for a Democratic Society in 1962. It was a major determinant of my position within the antiwar campaign of the middle and late sixties, when I refused to associate myself on occasion with those with whom I agreed on the immediate issue of getting America out of Vietnam, but who had illusions or even just naïveté on the character (the Stalinist character) of the Viet Cong. I remember in April 1967 literally sneaking into an antiwar march in New York that I could not endorse because of the soft-headedness of some of its leaders on the Stalinist problem, but could not miss because of its basic purpose. So, for once I was an anonymous rank-and-filer.

How, then, can I talk of a Stalinist "temptation"?

Because from time to time, and particularly when I have thought about the Third World, the cruelty of the unnecessary suffering there has raised a voice within me that says, Let us forget the democratic niceties for a decade or two; let us without stint do whatever it is that is necessary to shatter these vicious, ancient ways and social classes; let us, yes, force the people to the sacrifices they do not want to make in order to make life tolerable for their progeny. I have never been overwhelmed by that thought, but I have been tempted by it. Bertolt Brecht was perhaps the most brilliant exponent of the theme in Von Armen B.B.—"For even hatred against injustice makes the brow grow stern"—and it reached me even if it did not convince me.

It did not convince me, first of all, because it is so utterly, in the worst sense of the word, "economistic." The white racist South Africans have, out of no motive more noble than the search for their own profits, raised the living standards of the blacks in their country to a higher level than is to be found in all of sub-Saharan Africa. Does that make them "progressive"? And if it does not, what is left of the claims of Stalin and Mao? They, of course, carry out their repression in the name of the most emancipating ideology the world has ever known, and that is a significant difference. It means, among other things, that when the people revolt, they do so in the name of ideals that the society proclaimed and betrayed—they seek "socialism with a human face." But still, the bureaucrats of Communist nations have a stake—a class commitment once the bureaucracy becomes a truly privileged elite—in both antifreedom and inefficiency. And finally, there is that most basic of Western (I would say, human) values: that, as Kant would put it, you cannot treat people as mere means.

I know all these things; I am persuaded by them, even if I feel an angry velleity to the contrary from time to time. But now—and right now we are sitting in the Karachi airport in the middle of the night—I will have to face that temptation, not as a possible theory, but as an existential response to an immediate and unconscionable reality. Being in Pakistan in transit evokes that irrational aspect of life in a disturbing way.

I have just finished *Freedom at Midnight*, the quite interesting pop-history of the liberation of the subcontinent from the rule of the British raj after World War II. Part of the book depicted the unbelievably savage communal massacre by Hindus, Moslems and Sikhs that took place in those days. In a brief span of time a number equal to half the Americans killed during the four years of the Second War lost their lives, many of them most cruelly. So I am arriving in a place where life for so long has been, in fact and attitude, so cheap. I come from a society whose level of affluence allowed it to develop—not mechanistically as the mere and inevitable outcome of the means of production, but complexly, in a cultural, political and economic interaction—certain ethical values. I have never joined in the praise of the mysterious East, not least because I have long thought that much of the mystery is based, in an intricate way, on a lack of food and consequently even of energy, of sheer human vitality. But if I think these things, how do I respond, not simply intellectually, but also emotionally, when I confront them in the tormented person of an innocent, twisted child?

New Delhi, 1/4—5:30 a.m.

The arrival yesterday was pretty much as I imagined it. (I have "lost" a day, having gone through two nights on a flight of twenty-five hours.) After the bureaucratic inefficiencies of the airport, which took two hours, and with the accumulated fatigue and disorientation of the trip itself, I walked out of the terminal door into India.

The first thing I noticed on that Delhi morning was the scent. I remembered it well from my brief visit during the Bangladesh crisis of 1971—a pungent, rather pleasant odor, carried by a low-lying mist. It is, I was told that earlier time, the odor of the dung

fires. I had seen the people, sitting by the side of the road, shaping
the dung into fire bricks and setting them out to dry in the sun. It
had struck me then how incongruous it was that the romantic haze
over the city in the morning and the evening came from manure.
Marx would have had Homeric fun with a metaphor like that.

Now the smell was a welcome one, assuring me that there was
rhythm, repetition, persistence in my half-sleepless, continent-
leaping life. But that was the only solid certitude of the arrival,
that haze. All the rest was a discombobulated, cacophonous warning about how dangerous—and pretentious—this two-week project,
with its journal, is. Seeing the bullock carts bobbing down the road
as we sped by in a Fulbright Foundation car with its horn, in standard Delhi fashion, playing a tattoo, looking at the ragged people,
the barefoot, dirty children on the road's edge—*and* the neatly
dressed young men in ties and turbans on motor bikes, or the
unexotic crowds waiting for buses; seeing these things and so much
more that was confusing and contradictory, I was utterly troubled.
I have known for a long time that it takes years for a foreigner to
even begin to get on the inside of a culture. The nearly one year
I had spent in Paris in 1963 had convinced me that I knew very
little about France. This was the greatest positive knowledge I
had won.

But France was already inside my head before I got there. It is
part of my culture, even of my language. But India—nothing in
my experience prepares me for it. As I ride into the city, it occurs
to me that I don't know which of the people along the side of the
road are really poor. In New York, to go barefoot on a public road
in the fall—unless you are part of the counterculture, which any
experienced observer can spot at a block's distance—is to be poor.
But is it here? And the men in the dirty white wraparounds—I am
not even sure of the Indian name—are they thereby proclaiming
that they are hard-working and honest, wearing soiled work clothes,
or have they been sleeping in the streets?

The last time I was here I had taken a little solace from my
ignorance as well as being chastened by it. I wonder if that thought
might not justify what I am doing now. In four days in Delhi on
that occasion—an international conference in solidarity with the
struggle then being waged in Bangladesh for nationhood—I had
not discovered a single profound thing about India, of course. But,

I thought to myself then, I had achieved the one thing possible short of ten years' immersion in the country and its culture: an utterly superficial, yet still unique and haunting sense of what the surface of life looked like. If there is a quantum leap between four days—or sixteen days this time—and ten years, there is a bottomless chasm between never having been here at all and four, or sixteen, days. At best I will get a personal and, I hope, communicable sense of the Third Worldness of India and particularly of its children. If I am careful not to pretend that there is too much, then it will indeed count for something of value.

A thought and an experience and then to morning tea, that blessing imparted, I assume, by the British raj, which comforts the insomniac traveler.

Thought: Even if there are enormous relativities to be faced here, and even though I will not understand most of them, there are some absolutes too. Dying is one—infant mortality, early death. Disease and twisted limbs are others. One of the defenses the affluent Westerner builds in the presence of a country like India is the myth of its exotic holiness. "They" must like to live at low levels of consumption and energy; we must not disturb the culture they have built out of their suffering and misery. That is true in part, and nonsense in part, pernicious nonsense. Yes, a people who make a culture out of their limitations, out of their deaths and famines, have thereby asserted their freedom and transcended those limits by the very fact of having been able to turn them into symbols. Malraux said that well in *The Voices of Silence*. He understood that the culture evoked by a cruel existence was not itself cruel, but the release from cruelty, its sublimation.

But all that is justified only so long as it is inevitable. To honor the stoic acceptance of the death of babies in an age when medicine might save them is criminal, not cultural. On a much less dramatic level, I long ago realized in the United States that black "soul" was not genetic but the expression of a people who had not been subjected to the Protestant ethic (even though they were nominally Protestant) and the capitalist economy. The Irish had a similar "soul" in the middle of the nineteenth century, both in England and in America, and were loved (by radicals like Engels and Marx's daughter) and hated (by most others) for that fact. With industrialization, modernity—with a decline in infant mortality—

came a loss of soul. Something is lost, of course; but something greater is gained. (And maybe, on the other side of capitalism, if it is socialist and not bureaucratic-collectivist, soul—a different kind of soul, but soul nevertheless—will once again become possible.) In looking at, in trying to feel, however inadequately, the plight of the children of India, I will not forget this absolute. On this count I am, like Nehru, that rationalist leader of a mystic liberation movement, in favor of science in the service of man and against the outrageous holiness of unnecessary human suffering, however nobly it may be borne.

An experience. Yesterday was, as I expected, a frustrating, disappointing day of trying to make some contacts on a Saturday and in a city where one must now be more politic than when I was here before. The details are irrelevant to this journal: one incident is not. I was walking through Connaught Circus, when one of the shoeshine kids pointed at my shoes. I turned him down, but he kept pointing until I saw a big white glob on my shoe. It was, I realized later, as I remembered my first time in the Circus under the tutelage of Stanley Plastrik, probably put there by its discoverer or one of his friends. Three boys surrounded me, took off that shoe, put down a rag for me to stand on and started polishing; a local hustler, seeing me thus immobilized and perhaps intuiting how embarrassed and vulnerable the whole scene made me feel, came over and started a con game in which he wrote some things on a folded paper, which he gave me to hold and then elicited, by a series of transparent guises, answers which led back to the three things on the paper! This all lasted two or three minutes, and I fled having paid the shoeshine boys "too much" and, out of sheer anger at being so inexpertly conned, giving the hustler nothing.

Thus it was that my first contact with the children of India was with children whom the society had made into artful dodgers; and the first emotion they evoked in me was hostility. Walking away, I could rationalize all those ironies out of existence. But, a Westerner steeped in the commercial calculus of advanced capitalism, where haggling and hustling are on the periphery, was I not a cousin of that snob of a British genius, Keynes, who tipped a North African kid practically nothing because he didn't want to "debauch" the currency? And wasn't it depressingly revealing that every beggar or con man at Connaught Circus seeing me recognized, not a friend of the Third World and of its children, but a mark, a sucker, a well-meaning foreigner to be fleeced by the enterprising poor?

NEW DELHI, 1/5—5:15 A.M.

Yesterday began with considerable frustration, and it seemed that I was going to waste an entire and precious day without making more than the most superficial contact with the India that I had come to see. Then, what I suspect is an important lesson was taught to me in four sudden, overwhelming hours. I learned that that India is always just around the corner, even though it is possible for the tourist to only brush by it.

I left my hotel in the morning in search of some foreign newspaper which, I was told, I would find at the Janpath Hotel. That was where I stayed in 1971; so, when I discovered that I had been wrongly advised, I decided to kill the hour and a half before an appointment by walking around a neighborhood that I remembered. The stretch on Janpath Road down toward Connaught Circus is *touristy* in the worst sense of the word. It is crowded with cheap shops selling mostly shoddy merchandise at high prices. I saw some of the ugliest most degraded batiks—a process of painting on cloth that is one of the glories of the culture—with busty pinups rendered in a caricature of a traditional art. There were, of course, the various hustlers who wanted to change money and at Connaught Circus yesterday's con man took another shot at me, having forgotten my face.

Every so often there was a reminder of the realities behind the bazaar. I passed a group of men and women in soiled cotton dress, clawing at a construction site with hands and picks, and "labor-intense" investments became something more than a phrase of economic jargon. And there were the little girl beggars, ragged, dirty, insistent, one following me with a tin cup pushing it at my leg, disregarding my litany of No's. I have always been at a loss in this situation, but more so here. In New York I usually give to alcoholics who panhandle me but—out of an old-fashioned puritanism—not to the hippies who used to throng the Village asking for "spare change." I had given a coin to one girl on Janpath, but the second time I was confused. It was not that I grudged the money. Rather, it was that the whole scene once again cast me in the role of the white and privileged band. If I were generous it would be to act out a *noblesse oblige*, which I detested. I don't want noblesse; I want justice.

I thought of a time in the fifties when I went to Tiajuana, just across the Mexican border from San Diego. In the bars, I was offered women—or, more precisely, young Mexican girls—by an army of pimps and by the girls themselves. "We got French girls, Russian girls, American girls, Mexican girls," the pimps would say. But all I could see were terribly young Mexican girls who, I imagined, had fled some hell-hole somewhere to come here to work as whores. And I thought to myself that if I were even to consider touching one of them, it would be an act of personal imperialism as hateful as a master abusing his slaves in times that are better forgotten.

It is, I suppose, preposterously finicky of me, but it seemed there on Janpath that my tourist "charity," if I gave it, would put me in a similar position. But then so did my refusal. All this was made more maddening by the fact that the scene mocked my very coming to India. I had not, after all, traveled here to play the role of tourist. And yet, in my anger, I felt another layer of ambiguity. Was I here as a tourist of horror looking only for the misery, for the misshapen lives, and ignoring the traditional sights? Earlier I had found out that the square outside my hotel was a place where poor workers shaped up, waiting to be picked up by trucks for a day of casual work. The men and women were clumped at a broad intersection, some of them sitting in a stoop. There was a little canteen of some kind in a broken-down structure, and I edged toward the scene with a camera, hating myself for the spectator I was in the presence of human suffering.

So, was there no way out of the tangle of ambiguities and ironies? If not a way, then a glimpse of a way, opened up suddenly.

In 1971, I met an Indian batik artist, a shy, rather classically beautiful woman by the name of Saavitri Sristava. She had come with her brother to meet Stanley Plastrik, who knew her, and me at our hotel. I bought a magnificent batik from her. Now I had called her, since she was one of the few people I knew in New Delhi. The day before, I had gone out to find her at Bal Bhavan, the children's museum where she worked. She invited me to lunch and we arranged that a colleague of hers, a pleasant man whose name escaped me, would take me to her place today.

I met him at Bal Bhavan, where I discovered another one of those contrasts that abound in this city. There, in a pleasant neighborhood of big houses and institutions, right across from the children's museum, was the headquarters of the Communist Party of India, the fanatically pro-Russian wing of an Indian Communist movement that is split in three. The building was modern and prosperous—but with no windows that I could see at the lower level—and flew a bright-red hammer-and-sickle banner. Beggars and construction workers in bare feet, Communists with a modern office building. But such contrasts are routine here. The moment was an amusement and not an epiphany.

Then Saavitri's friend and I got into a cab and an extraordinary journey began. We turned into Old Delhi—which I had seen in 1971—and suddenly the streets were choked with people, with motorcycle and bicycle cabs rather than taxis the rule. We came to a secondhand-goods market, which stretched for at least a mile near the Red Fort.

The driver stopped to get some gas and suddenly a tall, wild-eyed and frightened young man bounded by, pursued first of all by a policeman with a wooden baton that must have been a yard long, and then by a crowd of gesticulating people. The policeman got close to his quarry just after they passed our cab and began to beat him. The young man slipped and was dragged down the road by the cop, escorted by the crowd. The driver and Saavitri's friend asked passersby what had happened. There had been an accident a hundred or so feet away, the youth had been involved in some way, only it turned out that he was a deaf-mute and mentally deranged. All this was related by the passersby with what seemed to me to be amused good humor.

I thought of a passage from O'Casey that I had quoted in *The Other America*: that for the poor, fights and tragedies and death are sometimes a great diversion from their own misery; that, O'Casey said, was true in Ireland; I had seen it in America. But here—or so the sudden shocking incident suggested—it was true to a degree that boggled the mind. In that crowd there must have been some who had been moved by Gandhi (whose death had been mourned by an immense throng at the funeral pyre by the Raj

Ghat, only a short distance away). And yet, the same society that could be so profoundly responsive to a saint could enjoy the casual, unwitting cruelty of the scene I had just witnessed.

We moved on down the marked road in the midst of a cacophony of people, motorcycles, cars, bikes, honking horns. Then we came out on a broad road that led toward the river and a colony of huts and tents, where everything, even the people, seemed to be the color of dirt. There were naked children roaming around, and people of all ages were to be glimpsed relieving themselves wherever they were. It looked like a village of perhaps three or four hundred lean-tos and several thousand people. A "real" reality only a ten-rupee ride from the tourist market on the Janpath.

But was it? In 1971 a friend at the Embassy, Murray Weiss, got a car one day and took me out to a village where people who had slept in the streets of New Delhi had been resettled. To me, it was an appalling place. Above all, it assaulted the nostrils with the stench of the open sewage ditches. There were naked children and skeletal animals everywhere, and I decided that I had looked into the abyss of Indian poverty. Murray explained with enthusiasm that I was looking at a real success story, that he could not believe the improvements. The noisome sewage ditches were one of the recent gains; a short time earlier there had been none.

So I decided that I could not interpret the meaning of my own appalled senses as I looked at the colony in New Delhi. But it turned out that I was right. Saavitri and her friend later told me that this was an area for some of the poorest laborers and beggars of the city. I did not, however, get the chance to ask them about another impression: that there is a correlation between social class and skin color. The untouchable family I saw living on the Janpath sidewalk in 1971 were the blackest of the black people I encountered on that trip. Now, in this miserable slum by the river, it seemed to me that the skin of the people under that ubiquitous mantle of dirt was black. I must find out.

BOMBAY, 1/7—7 A.M. NOTES ON SUNDAY 1/4 CT'D.

We went on down a market street toward Saavitri's. It was teeming, raucous, jammed with pedestrians, motorcycle (three-wheel) cabs. A woman perched on a roof calling down with great gusto, and though she probably was out there for some utterly rational purpose, the sight reaffirmed the unreality—the *surreality*—of the scene, turning it into a Chagall. We got out of the cab and walked down some narrow alleys toward Saavitri's. There were naked children playing in the streets; animals, including cows, wandering about; and as we passed one house a gush of waste water tumbled into the gutter of the street. This was, Saavitri and her friend later told me, a middle-class neighborhood.

We entered Saavitri's house—actually, I think it belongs to her brother, a lawyer—through a courtyard and then into a small room that looked out on the narrow alley we had just walked and was separated from it, now that the shutters were drawn back, only by a braided (bamboo? wood?) curtain, which flapped in the pleasant Delhi winter breeze. We stayed in that room the whole time I was there. Saavitri served an elaborate meal of various rices, spices and sauces; and I, with my timid Western stomach, tried to navigate my eating between politeness and survival.

Saavitri brought out some batiks and described their symbolism to me. She is, I think, an artist of real power. But one of the things that struck me as she explained her work—particularly one that based itself on the myth of Kali—was that death and destruction are not simply accepted, but worshiped. (Stranger yet, given my Western—or is it?—aversion to snakes, that animal, especially in the form of a cobra, is apparently a sign of happiness.) I will not try any instant anthropology. Suffice it to say that I wonder if the difficulty of life in this country, which is also to say the omnipresence of death and cruelty in everyday existence, might not be related, complexly I am sure, to those symbols. In several of his books, Malraux talks of the East "discovering" the individuality—the personality, so to speak—of death.

And yet, this morning in Bombay, writing these notes about Sunday, I took out the batik I bought from Saavitri. There is a figure—he is, I think, a village holy man or saint (Saavitri's English was less than perfect; my Hindi nonexistent)—that is buoyant, and he is surrounded by the symbols of a fish, a flower, a snake and the sun. The effect of the whole is a celebration of life; it is anything but lugubrious. (The cloth of the batik seems impregnated with that Delhi odor, which is fast becoming my tea-and-madeleine for this trip.) I am also struck when Saavitri and her friend speak of how Homeric the Gods of India are—that is, how human, raunchy, angry, jealous, et cetera, they are.

I rode back to the hotel on an open-air, bumpy, jerky motorcycle cab. We had gone over on a pontoon bridge that was scarcely two cars wide. I went back across a more conventional bridge, in the midst of what seemed to be a permanent, raucous, but good-humored traffic jam. When I got back to the hotel I found myself emotionally and physically exhausted, yet I had been gone—from the cab ride to the Janpath to my return, when the three-wheeler let me off at the edge of the entrance—only about five and a half hours. But in that brief span, the place had begun to overwhelm and frighten me.

BOMBAY, 1/7—3 P.M.

I arrived in Bombay early in the morning on Tuesday, the 6th. Coming into the airport, one looked down on crowds of people walking along roads to work. More than that, we flew over compact little slums, like villages of urban poverty. They were mud- or dust-colored and—I now add details that I couldn't see as I was coming in—jerry-built out of all kinds of material: old bricks, stones, canvas (or something like it), thatch. They were very much like the colony I had seen Sunday in New Delhi on the way to Saavitri's. But then some of them have flags out front—either in honor of Lord Shiva or, as I learned from two friends, as pennants of a Maharashtra political movement with deep roots in the slums. The party protests the fact that the Maharashtrans are a minority in the main city of their own province (where they are literally a numerical, as well as a sociological, minority) and demand better jobs for themselves at the expense of the other Indian ethnic groups. But what fascinated me at the airport and later, peeking into these hamlets of misery with their ubiquitous fires and naked children playing in the refuse, was that they had these flags, sometimes even a garland. More than that—and this is the horror of it— the children as I glimpsed them seemed to be childlike, even under these appalling circumstances, playing, posturing and often bright-eyed and inquisitive. They had, that is, survived the passage into the world better than I could have imagined; they were to be ground down later on. All this is wild speculation, and perhaps it is not the Indian reality at all; but it is what that reality seemed to be, which made it heartbreaking for this Western father who thought often of his sons, Alexander and Teddy.

But before getting to the much more violent emotions that the day and a half in Bombay have evoked in me, it would be better to begin with the setting. The contrast with Delhi is as subtle as a thunderclap. Delhi, as a friend here told me later on, is nothing but an overgrown village. Bombay is a bustling, aggressive city, a metropolis whose contrasts make the ones in New Delhi mild by comparison. The main streets are clogged with cars, some of them expensive, all driven in the best Roman manner at breakneck speed, with the horn in almost continuous operation. There is a dynamism that reminds me of New York. Even stranger, the waterfront along the magnificent bay looks at first like the decayed section of Miami Beach, down toward the south, and then, when you come to the Oberoi Hotel, where I am staying, like Miami Beach, period. From my room I can see an impressive skyline dominated by huge modern buildings, with the power and density of, say, downtown St. Louis, or sometimes even reminiscent of that incredible Chicago on the Lake Michigan fringe.

And yet, in the heart of this modern, vibrant city one keeps coming to the slum sections, or suddenly a soft-voiced little girl will be standing by the window of our stopped cab, begging, and you will not even have seen her. The Oberoi is a fancy hotel. I came here without any room reservation and was told by someone at the airport to go to the "Sheraton." And thus I blundered into grande luxe on a trip which is totally absorbed with poverty. At the very front of the Oberoi, there is an excavation, which apparently is not completed, and in it, right there at the very base of thirty-two floors of wealth and dining rooms and a third- or fourth-floor pool, with a view of the bay—right there is a lean-to, with a clothesline strung up and a woman chatting with some passersby as if she were on a suburban porch.

I made some phone calls and then walked out, thinking I would stroll over to the Gateway of India and act the role of plain tourist. But I was pursued by insistent begging children racing along like a band of furies. And when I passed a mud-colored slum a few blocks from this luxury hotel, a group of children who had been playing in a refuse-strewn lot saw me, this obvious Northerner with his Instamatic Kodak dangling from his wrist. They broke up the game in an instant and set off in pursuit of me. I have tried every strategy I know to deal with them—to give, which brings a new line of suppliants; to say no, which means that they would follow, pleading in a kind of singsong chant. Finally I took a cab over to the Gateway and once again I was assailed by a motley army of the deformed, the hustling, the rickety and spindly-legged, including a man who offered to open his wicker basket and show me his cobra—for a price. So I fled into the Taj Hotel which is right there and which is of even higher status than the Oberoi. It was as if I had been locked up by that militant, counterrevolutionary poverty that, on its knees to the West, waited just outside the door, and frightened and sickened me and reached out to my heart.

I think it was then that I began to feel a monstrous emotion somewhat similar to a reaction that Gandhi's nonviolence used to have on the British troops. It is said that when they were ordered to attack the unresisting satyagrahees—this story dates, I think, from the Salt March—the soldiers at first struck at them half-heartedly, gingerly. But then the very steadfastness of the demonstrators, this willingness to be beaten, got to the troops and they became more furious, more brutal, trying to beat the nonviolent foe into an act of violent resistance. And sometimes this wheedling misery, this demanding vulnerability of the child beggars, makes me angry even as I have to suppress the instinct to weep.

BOMBAY, 1/7

This morning I took some casually offered advice. I had phoned the local Fulbright representative yesterday and, in what I now suspect was a horrid American gaucherie, I asked him if anyone there could guide me to some of the Bombay slums. I think I might as well have asked if I could borrow his wife for the night. The answer was a cool No. But then he advised that I take a commuter train that would take me past the hovels.

So about nine this morning, I set out in a cab. The driver got lost—he, like many of his fellows, really understood no English—and we roamed aimlessly (or I should say dashed aimlessly) around, passing by families who lived in lean-tos on the sidewalk. Finally, we came to Victoria Terminal, where a vast press of people streamed out and almost engulfed me. I sat down in a second-class carriage, which was almost empty. That made me happy enough, in part because I didn't have much emotional strength left for coping with a crowded train, jammed with riders, in part because I wanted to take some photographs. I think I felt—and still feel— that taking pictures of misery is like being a pornographer. I know that that is absurd and illogical; Walker Evans's photos for *Let Us Now Praise Famous Men* have had a tremendous impact, and photographers that I have met, like John Vashon or Bob Adelman, have done much, much good. Perhaps it was not photography that I was accusing, but myself, the spectator, the camera's eye clicking away at all this tortured humanity.

But soon the car filled up and there I was, jammed against the window, surrounded by jostling workers, looking at people eating in hovels or pissing against the walls, at children playing with refuse, observing an intolerable, unconscionable world. Up and back, it lasted about two and a half hours; near the end of the return I was numb, and the sight of a mud-colored slum that had had me on the brink of tears an hour or so before did not even move me now.

I am tired of my conscience. It is a wheedling, jesuitical conscience; a sloppy, sentimental, pathetic conscience; it is a hypocritical conscience. I am tired of it or, rather, of all of them. And perhaps that is a psychological secret of why we Northerners can be as callous as we are. We can't really contemplate these things, or else we would be driven to some wild kind of holiness, or else we would go crazy. But then that's nonsense. Most people are locked up in a routine anyway; they don't come to India to tour man's inhumanity to man. But even those of us who do can't stay focused on these things. I remember at the *Catholic Worker* we had the impossible ideal of never letting the scab develop, of always being personally available to every person who made a demand on us. We even used to say we wanted to be saints, and some of the people there, Dorothy Day above all, are still trying. I don't want to be a saint. I want to change the world and maybe I can—maybe I even have—just a tiny bit. But this afternoon in Bombay, I am dog-tired of empathy, especially empathy at an impotent, passive, Northern distance.

BOMBAY AIRPORT, 1/8—5:20 P.M.

I should add that I came back yesterday morning in a first-class compartment to see what it was like. The first-class compartment had some kind of stuffing in the seat; it was cleaner than second; but it fairly quickly became crowded—only, with a different kind of people. Going up on second there may have been one person reading an English-language newspaper, a few reading Hindi papers, and most just sitting. Beggars came through the compartment, chanting, and poor people (or people who seemed to me to be poor) gave them money. The whole scene was dominated by a kind of Mediterranean exuberance, with people hanging out of the door and much gesticulating to friends in the station.

First class was, of course, quite different. Most of the people —they were all men; there are special compartments for women— were reading English-language papers. Many of them wore Gujarati dress—white dhoti and tunic, and the white hat that is associated with the leaders of the Congress Party—and their clothes were blindingly clean and crisp. Many carried attaché cases and had the solid, self-confident look of businessmen on their way to the office. The mood was not too different from that of a Westchester commuter train heading for Grand Central.

All of which raises an extremely important, obvious truth, one which can be ignored if one focuses solely on suffering India. This is a society of social classes, of the wealthy, like the Tatas, and the middle class and the workers as well as of the destitute and outcast. It is not one thing, as the populist image of the Third World suggests, not merely poverty; neither is it a place, as some simplistic Marxists have it, that counterposes a vast mass to a tiny bourgeois elite. It is on the very surface a complex infrastructure that is somehow, and not so obviously, functional, at the same time as it is outrageously and unconscionably dysfunctional for the people who sleep in its streets.

Last night that point impressed itself on me again. I went with two young friends and walked for better than an hour through a Bombay market area. The place was bursting with a mob of amazingly good-natured humanity, taxis, horse-drawn carriages, hawking merchants. The sides of the jammed streets were covered with shop after shop, usually grouped according to a certain commodity: jewelry, cotton, and so on. We went into one arcade that was a narrow passageway between endless stalls that seemed to stretch for several blocks. Almost all of the people there, I was told, were Gujarati and some of them were fairly well off. In their narrow little cubicles men lounged with phones on their shoulders or else engaged in casual talk. Above this turbulent scene were apartments that were, I was told, middle class and quite desirable, despite the teeming bazaar at their very doorstep. And in the midst of the fervid buying and selling, there were temples, Hindu or Moslem, according to the neighborhood.

BOMBAY, 1/9—8 A.M.

We went into one temple. My woman friend, who rightly did not like it one bit, was not allowed to proceed beyond a foyer. Women, it turned out, could penetrate into the temple proper only at certain restricted times. Her husband and I walked around a gallery that looked onto a central room with a very high, domed ceiling covered with murals recording the history of this particular sect, which had been founded by a holy man, an incarnation of God who adopts more than one human form—about two hundred years ago. In the center of the bare floor of the room a monk sat, chanting endlessly. I heard snatches of his prayer, the word *Ram*, "God," punctuating it like a tolling bell. In the front of the big chamber was a walkway and in the rear of it three altars, each enclosed and containing statues. The latter were of surprisingly low artistic quality, having that vulgar look of some of the Madonnas and saints one encounters in the churches of the South Village in New York. Our coming caused something of a commotion, and we were escorted around the altar—two times, according to some tradition—and saw the monks' quarters behind it.

A handsome, earnest-faced man appeared back in the main chamber. My friend recognized him as a lawyer at the High Court in Bombay. Here he was a devotee, and he recounted some of the history and theology of the place with evident enthusiasm and reverence. The experience surprised me. The faith I saw around me seemed quite superstitious, a phenomenon of the masses' backwardness, once again much like some the simplistic versions of

Christianity I have observed. But this lawyer, obviously intelligent and apparently very much his own man, was a part of it. I was tempted to make some more superficial generalizations about mysterious India, but resisted.

We left the temple, threaded our way through packed, dense streets, passed through a Moslem section that was poorer than the Hindu area, and finally made our way to a Gujarati restaurant. Talking there with my guides, I realized something I had known but not known. They had been at pains to show me a part of Bombay that might have seemed poor, but was not. In a sense, they were pointing out how, contrary to appearances as they strike a Northern eye, people in this human maelstrom were leading relatively comfortable and happy lives. Why should my Bombay friends, committed, idealistic, secular and democratic, want to strike that optimistic note? (I heard it in various ways from other people during this first week of my stay.)

One answer contains, I think, a most important truth. If one dwells on the poverty of India alone—on its families living out their lives on the pavement, its beggars, its obvious and lacerating misery—then it is easy to slip into a kind of despair. If that is the only India, then what hope for development, for change? Why seek to get American aid for a hopeless situation? At this point, compassion can become reactionary. It produces a new edition of an ancient myth: the eternal, self-contained and unchanging East. So it is a grave injustice to do what I inadvertently began to do, to set out in search for suffering India and suffering India alone.

Gopalpur, 1/11

Indira Gandhi had declared the Emergency last June and many politicals—including some of those I had met on my brief trip in 1971—were imprisoned. But in June, the measures were taken, in theory at least, as temporary responses to a chaotic situation allegedly created by Jayaprakash ("J.P.") Narayan's opposition movement. Now, however, these measures are looking more and more like a permanent, structural change in Indian life, a shift to a formally authoritarian structure. On Thursday, for instance, the President formally suspended Article 19 of the Constitution, which states the "seven freedoms" of India—the right to free speech, assembly, organization, movement within India, private property, choice of residence and practice of a profession. In the courts, the government has argued that the right to personal liberty and to fair procedures before arrest or detention is no longer a common-law right, but is only a constitutional right, which has now been suspended.

The rationale for these actions bears very much on the issue of economic development. Mrs. Gandhi argues that discipline—a virtue that is constantly proclaimed on billboards throughout the country—is necessary if foreign enemies are to be repulsed (the United States is obviously intended, along with Pakistan and China) and if "socialism," secularism and industrialization are to triumph. The "Stalinist temptation," which I thought about on the flight, seems to have seduced the leaders of the most populous democracy human history has ever known. Only it is worse than that, or at least so it seems to me.

Before the Emergency, Mrs. G. was in a commanding position and had all the means to carry out the "socialist" programs for which she so vigorously argued during election campaigns. It is true that immediately prior to her new term she was menaced by a court decision that could have deprived her of the Prime Ministership; and some here argue that she was also threatened from within the Congress Party itself. These political aspects of the situation, so crucial in other respects, are beyond my knowledge and analytic competence. But it is a fact that when Mrs. G. was in complete and quite democratic control (say in the period right after the triumph of her Bangladesh policy), she could have moved if she had wanted to, and could have done so with full respect for Article 19 of the Constitution. She did not.

This raises the suspicion that she has moved now, not so much to gain the possibility of leading India to "socialism" without having to observe democratic niceties, but for other reasons, which have to do with the maintenance of power, that she turned against democracy simply to save her political skin, which was endangered by a court suit. Certainly, one of the main targets of the new authoritarianism is the judiciary. The decree abrogating the "seven freedoms" strikes against the right to a profession, and that means that a lawyer can be disbarred for political reasons, without due process or even cause, except the cause that he or she has angered the government by, say, defending a person accused of disloyalty or subversion. When it may be a crime to defend an alleged criminal, particularly an alleged political criminal, any semblance of democratic legality has vanished.

If, to return to the main argument, I am right and the "Stalinist" rationale—that authoritarianism is necessary to achieve that discipline that alone permits real economic development—is only a cover for much more traditional power grabbing, then India has embarked on the worse of two different worlds. It will have the antifreedom institutions characteristic of Stalinism, but the corruption and lack of mass mobilization that were typical of India's "soft" capitalist democracy.

All of this is an enormous blow to me, and if I am not as personally shattered as the Indian intellectuals I have met here—they, after all, must now look over their shoulders when they say what they think—it is an extremely depressing moment for me. For years I have argued, in books and articles and speeches, that Stalinism is not socialist, even though it modernizes and industrializes, and that there are alternatives to it. And I have said that India, with all its manifest inadequacies and all but overwhelming problems, was at least trying to find a democratic path out of poverty. Now that is over, at least for the time being. And if I am right, this great experiment has fallen not because of the cruel necessities of economic development, but rather to a choice made by some individuals who will not even attack that poverty, who will use authoritarian measures to maintain, not to revolutionize, the status quo. And by an accident, a complete and utter accident, of history, I came to India in the two weeks that may well have been the two weeks in which everything that democrats and socialists here and throughout the world hoped for in India was destroyed. Enough of me.

(In what follows, I have jumbled conversations together out of chronological sequence. One reason is that the voicing of opposition sentiments in post-Emergency India can lead to harassment, the loss of a job, or even jail. None of the people to whom I talked was in favor of armed struggle against the government, or anything like it, but there is no point of identifying them to a government that regards much more moderate—democratic—modes of criticism as subversion. I should also add a fact that, because it might be read by the police, I did not include in the journal. I was contacted

by a person who claimed to be, and, for all I know *was,* a representative of the underground. I was asked whether I wanted to go
and meet George Fernandes, who was then in hiding and has since
been imprisoned. I had anticipated such an eventuality and discussed it with political associates in New York before I left. We
decided that this would be a situation in which it would be impossible to tell an *agent provocateur* from a real member of the underground. I told the person who contacted me that I did not want to
go underground to talk with Fernandes, that I would, however, like
to talk to someone in an open, public place. We agreed to meet
again, but no one ever came back to talk with me. In the India of
1976, one was not sure exactly what all this meant.)

GOPALPUR, 1/12—7 A.M.

Over tea: One intellectual says that he thinks the Emergency
will last for a long time and that India is going to become like
Franco Spain. He quotes from an underground circular—they
appear, I am told, under doors at the universities with a note to
read it and pass it on—that there are 100,000 people in jail. But
then he adds that his figure includes Naxalites, members of an
insurrectionary Communist tendency, many of whom must have
been imprisoned long before the Emergency. The problem is, of
course, that the newspapers here are now totally devoid of any
information on Indian politics other than what are, in effect, government handouts. (A scholar: "When there is external censorship,
someone else has to take responsibility for what you publish; when
there is internal censorship, that is much worse, because you have
to censor yourself and you are not sure of the rules.")

Both of the people with whom I talk are rather negative about
alternatives and opposition. There is, they say, no coherent program, no group that offers a clear and politically relevant option
as against Mrs. Gandhi. Her foes and critics are divided, uncertain
and unclear. She for the moment seems to be in complete control.
We gossip about her son, Sanjay, who is the talk of India right
now, having made an important and dramatic appearance at a
Congress Party convention just before the New Year. He is a businessman, engaged in a project to build cars, and it is widely believed that he has not suffered in his personal business from his

blood relationship to power. But now, he is coming forth as a political, indeed, some think as a Dauphin.

All of this is utterly depressing. But then one of these new acquaintances shifts to a somewhat different line. It is not quite progovernment, but it uses analogy—particularly cases taken from American history—to put the Emergency in a long-term perspective. At least part of the motivation for the talk is a defensiveness about India that I have perceived in every intellectual with whom I have talked here. Even the most bitter foe of Mrs. G. does not want to be understood as denigrating India. Therefore, criticism must be put in a context where what is happening, even if it is seen as a basic and long-lasting structural innovation, will be analyzed as a deviation.

My friend's analogies are serious. What about you Americans, he asks? You had the Alien and Sedition laws, the criminal-syndicalism statues, the Palmer Raids and the hysteria directed against opponents of the First World War. And during the McCarthy period, he continued, you foolishly perceived the internal Communist threat out of all proportion, and in the Smith Act persecutions, the loyalty and security programs, and all the rest of the repressive measures, you had an effective Emergency of your own. He concluded: "Don't sell India short; allow us the right to behave as badly as Americans; allow us the hope that we, like you, will recover from the miserable period."

There is much that is compelling in that argument, and part of it is obviously true. But ultimately, I think, it fails. I tried to explain my negative judgment to my friends. At the height of the McCarthy period, which was when I became politically active, there were still freedom of speech, of press, of assembly, even if they were under assault. Our liberties were outrageously infringed, no doubt about it. I had my own experience in that regard and know of these things personally, not as a matter of history. Still, the channels of protest, of appeal and change, remained open. We had newspapers like the *New York Post* and the *Washington Post*, organizations like the American Civil Liberties Union, and so on. We fought back, and eventually we prevailed. That victory, to be sure, probably had more to do with a Republican President ending the Korean War and thereby depriving the Right of its most emotional issue—how can you defend Communists' freedoms when their comrades are killing American boys?—and with the Warren Court than with the might of the civil-liberties forces. Yet we, and America's democratic institutions, made a contribution.

What is so frightening in India now is that there is not a single newspaper that prints domestic news. A Bombay edition of one paper, for instance, reported on the debate in the Parliament by quoting government statements at fulsome length and then cryptically noting that Mr. So-and-so of the Communist Party (Marxist) had "bitterly criticized" Mrs. G's policies. Only, there was not a word of the content of that bitter criticism, and one wonders whether it will even be alluded to in the future. The same holds for assembly and speech. I have the strong impression that people here are very circumspect in what they say. I would be, under similar conditions.

Another conversation, a related point. I talk to young friends, and they tell me with pride that the judges and the lawyers are upholding the rule of law and countering the arbitrary actions of the government, or at least trying to do so. They are an appealing pair, deeply committed to democracy and to India. They know that the courts are under assault, but they have hopes. A few days later I read that the "right to a profession" has been suspended, and that the authorities are now able to move against any lawyer who opposes them.

Earlier, a very perceptive intellectual: "The trouble is," he says, "that the opposition led by Narayan based its program strictly on a protest against corruption. It had good points, but it was basically middle class and it had no economic and social solutions for the miseries of this subcontinent. But then that point," he goes on, "also applies to Mrs. G. She has had the great good luck of an excellent harvest coinciding with the Emergency. So, the great mass of the people are content and the educated elite, which is hit most by the antilibertarian measures, is isolated and confused. However, this situation will not last forever, since the government, for all its assertions that it has suspended freedom in order to get on with the work of socialist construction, has nothing new to offer."

What, I asked him and everyone else I talked to, would come after Mrs. G., supposing that the Emergency ended or was ended? "Anarchy," a few said. "We don't have the least idea," was what most answered.

GOPALPUR, 1/13

This is being written in Gopalpur, a hamlet on the Bay of Bengal, a good distance south of Calcutta. As I have been sitting here in what is thought of as a luxury hotel—but in which the toilets function indifferently and the relative poverty of Indian affluence asserts itself—the fishermen down on the beach have been returning with their catch in primitive wooden boats crafted together, as far as I can tell, without the use of a single nail. There are smaller, canoelike craft with two men in them, both standing up as they negotiate the surf to the beach. On the beach itself there is a vibrant social life. The fishermen are apparently from one ethnic group. The women who come to buy their catch from another. There are children running around, and the whole place is used as a vast outdoor privy; I watch an adolescent standing happily, even proudly, and pissing into the surf. The sand is littered with human feces. There are even little shrines, and one evening I passed a family group at its devotions there.

In *Remembrance of Things Past,* Proust writes of the resort hotel and how the rich within it must have seemed, through the window, like an aquarium of exotic, marvelous fish. But the differences between the worlds at that hotel and those at this one in India are enormous. Proust's privileged people were separated from the spectators by barriers of social class, but here there are two ages, two cultures, two worlds, counterposed to each other. Proust had wondered when the people watching would burst into the aquarium of the rich. What is striking here is that the enormous inequality—in which I, alas, participate—has provoked only sporadic, periodic protests, not a nationwide revulsion.

Yesterday, for instance, we went on an afternoon excursion to a nearby lake. There were about twenty-five of us, roughly twenty Indians and five Americans. At the lakeside inn, we chipped in 10 rupees apiece for beer (the official rate would make that about $1.50). So we had more than 200 rupees. The group was prodigiously thirsty and fast-drinking, and the beer disappeared in about twenty minutes as the porters—the "bearers"—of the place looked on. Later, some of the Indian scholars commented that those porters made between 100 and 150 rupees a month. They had seen a group of people consume about—in some cases *more than*—twice their monthly income in the twinkling of an eye. Henry Teune, a political scientist from Philadelphia, with whom I share a room, remarked to me that it would be like an American worker watching twenty-five people drink more than a thousand dollars' worth of fine wine in less than half an hour.

Or would it? There are notorious statistical problems in comparing different national currencies in terms of buying power. But more than that, there is the utterly different mode of economic-social integration in different societies. On the way to and from the lake, for instance, we proceeded along a road with a number of small towns and roadside shops. Coming back at night, I was struck by how poverty-stricken the locale seemed by American standards—dust everywhere, holes in the wall, pathetic little displays of soft drinks and cigarettes and occasionally interrupted by a rich flash of saris—and how prosperous by what I guess to be Indian standards, the standards by which (beware of oversimplification) the people judge their lives. There were electric lights in fair profusion (and remember, rural electrification is only a generation old in the United States), bicycles everywhere (they cost between 200 and 450 rupees), but most important of all, a sense of life, of bustle, of society.

Obviously this is not a justification of the outrageous maldistribution of the world's wealth that is incarnate here. Indeed, the opposite: if there is a kind of equilibrium here that is self-contained and "normal" for the people—that is, that does not weigh upon them as a brute force but asserts itself from within their lives naturally—if there is such an equilibrium, it is purchased at a price of enormous lost human potential. These fellow men and women of mine could be so much better than they are—as persons, as members of a society—if only they did not have to exist at this level of life.

1/13 (1/15)

The evening of the thirteenth, the conference at Gopalpur went to a special "cultural event" in Berhampur. There was something pathetic about the eagerness of the Berhampur College faculty members, a mood of boosterism that most Americans have become too sophisticated to act upon, even though I suspect they still feel it. We went on a bus and arrived at a barnlike building just off a dusty, teeming road. It was the cultural center. The audience had been assembled before the guests arrived, and we were escorted like VIP's to reserved seats in the front row.

The curtain rose on a play that, were it not a classic of its kind, would have been impossibly embarrassing. It was staged by the women from a local college who played all the roles and it was about Queen Elizabeth I visiting Mr. William Shakespeare. Shakespeare was persuaded to drop work on *Hamlet* and to start on a lighter play for the Queen, because she threatened to go to Ben Jonson if he refused. All this was done in pantaloons and doublets and gowns, and in that curiously accented English that some of the less—but nevertheless—educated seem to speak. I assume that the point was to prove to us that an English-language culture and gentility still flourish in a provincial backwater on the Orissa coast. But what came after was neither amusing nor embarrassing.

A group of children, marvelously made up, danced a charming local folk dance; two male singers and some instrumentalists performed several haunting chants; and there was a full-scale ballet about how Konarak came to build his famous temple. One young girl—perhaps thirteen—and four girls who were slightly older performed. They were made up beautifully with the eyes drawn wide, and they moved with a ritual kind of precision that had power as well as charm, even though the dance was being performed by children and adolescents. The experience moved me aesthetically as well as sociologically. I responded with emotion as well as with interest. Afterward, the visitors were asked backstage to meet the cast, and a few Americans who felt comfortable with the symbolism answered that marvelous salutation of the praying hands in kind.

What struck me in this experience was something I had known in theory for some time: that an underdeveloped economy can exist in, and even feed upon, a developed society, a coherence, a culture. It is so simple to see on the very surface of life: children dancing wearing makeup and using gestures that are centuries old; the ubiquity of the ritual of bathing. And it is a ritual. This morning we watched a group of men by a pump just a few feet from the road. There was a drainage ditch between them and the cars and the crowd; that was all. They splashed themselves and scrubbed as solemnly as the participants in a liturgy.

But the coherence of these songs and gestures and movements derives from an ancient society, which stabilized itself on a certain ecology and equilibrium that, by the cultural, social and economic standards of those times, were developed. Indeed, until modern times—I think John Strachey puts it as late as the early eighteenth century—it was not "underdeveloped" at all, even by comparison with Europe and certainly by comparison with the United States. Now, however, these rituals and liturgies exist within a modern world, one that moves to the rhythms of urban clocks and machines, not to those of the seasons, or even of sunrise and sunset.

At lunch today in the Bubeneswar Airport we ran into a Dutch agricultural specialist who has been working for twenty-one years on the problem of food production in the Third World, particularly in Africa, but also in Asia. He tells us that the Chinese, whose methods he detests, have succeeded in achieving a certain discipline. In the thirties, he says, one famine in China—which was not very much remarked in the Western press—wiped out forty million people. Now such apocalypses are possible in India—unless the nation finds new ways to produce much more. But can they if the ancient ways persist? It is that problem of "soul," which I mentioned before. The difficult questions surfaced again. Is soul worth a life? Two lives? A hundred million lives?

I am not really sure that you must destroy—nonviolently—this charm and beauty to modernize. Henry Teune, who knows much more of the scholarly literature than I, says no. Only, as an urban, modern man who responds lovingly to children doing dances ancient with wisdom, I intuitively suspect that Teune is wrong.

A few minutes ago, a conversation with a scholar. I was telling him of the curious quiescence of the students at Jawaharlal Nehru University when I kicked up a storm over themes like Marxism, imperialism and the Third World. Perhaps, he said, they were concerned about the Emergency situation. A faculty member, he tells me, can be fired without cause or appeal, his professional life ended by an edict and three months' salary. It can be said, But these are only an elite stratum of intellectuals. They and their students are but a minute fraction of Indian society. What is their freedom worth? Is it more or less valuable than a dance tradition? I don't know how to make such an evaluation—how to quantify and weigh such spiritual imponderables. I do know for certain that a society without intellectuals, without competent criticism, will in the long run penalize itself. It will, of course, institutionalize a new ruling class; but it also may well become bureaucratically inefficient, as the Russians have.

I am back at the Stalinist temptation theme. Let me just summarize it in one last visual image from this morning. (As I write, schoolchildren race through the waiting room of this seedy airport to witness a great event: a four-motored jet from Singapore taking off.) We were in Puri, one of the holy cities of India, having driven there past endless dusty villages, passing bullock carts, bicycles, women walking in that curious heel and toe gait which seems to permit them to better balance their bundles of wood on their heads. There is a huge temple in Puri, a monument to the god Jaganath. Non-Hindus are forbidden to enter, so the standard way to get a glimpse of it is to go to a nearby roof; the best vantage point, a three-story building housing a library right near the temple, was not open. One of the ubiquitous hustlers of the place takes us to another rooftop.

There is, for me, an oceanic sense of the scene: the intricately carved temple with its red pennants at the top, the awakening swirl of life in the squeal of merchants, of people bathing, of beggars and lepers, the chanting that is broadcast—from tape? live?—from the temple. It is preposterous that this suffering and agony should blend into a pleasing whole, that the lame and hurt and hungry should play a part in an aesthetic scene for the Northerners. It is preposterous; it is true; it is wrong. This music, this aura, this dusty, ancient and cruel serenity must give way to the superior claim of life, of children, of babies I see in their parents' arms, with their eyes still bright and inquisitive and delighted. It must go, I think. But how?

1/16 CALCUTTA

I arrived last evening from Puri via Bubeneswar on a delayed flight. So it was evening when we walked through the picket line of begging, insistent children and then made our way by car into what has been called "The City of Dreadful Night."

The one thing I did not expect was the smoke. The haze at Delhi has a characteristic and, to me, not at all unpleasant odor. But this is a choking, irritating smoke that could be mixed with coastal fog. In part, of course, it comes from the myriad fires that burn on the streets. As we came into the city proper those streets were tumultuous with a jostling, often laughing, not tragic-looking, humanity. I also saw the clumps of figures around the sidewalk fires, or the people who had even gone to sleep already. (It was about 7:30 P.M.) My reaction surprised me.

Ever since I began this trip, I have been fearful of the very sight of Calcutta. Its horror is legendary. A Bengali intellectual whom I met in Delhi had said to me that the place was "shocking," and that had been a signal, for most such people in India tend to play down, not dramatize, the miseries of their homeland. And I had read Ved Mehta's account of Calcutta in his *Portrait of India,* and it too had expressed a near despair over what one can see here. But, in my first impression at least, I did not feel that (and all that I will have here is a first impression). The sight was, no mistake, appalling. The people rushed and pushed, the cars perpetually honked in a maniacal din, the buses and streetcars were all packed more solidly than any New York subway, and all of this convulsive human motion undulated in and out of a nearly asphyxiating cloud of smoke. The moment could have easily passed for a backdrop in a surrealist version of the Inferno.

Only I was somewhat numbed. Perhaps it was sheer physical exhaustion. I had risen at six in a most spare tourist bungalow on the ocean at Puri—it was complete with a lizard on the water pipe in the bathroom, and a mangy, malformed one-eyed dog that looked at me hopefully when I opened the door that looked out toward the beach. And there had been a long day of jolting over the back roads—actually main roads; only, they are like back roads in America—to Bubeneswar, then a long wait for a delayed plane at the airport, and finally our arrival. But I think my reaction was more than a result of the fatigue I felt.

In Delhi the sight of the huts and the dust-colored people had almost made me sob aloud; so did the misery of Bombay, though by then I was also feeling oppressed by the begging. But time passed, and during the last two weeks in India I have seen more poverty than in a lifetime in the United States. Riding the other day from Gopalpur to Puri and yesterday from Puri to Bubeneswar was like floating on an endless river of men, women and children, of life at intolerable levels. Soon one became incredibly relativistic.

If a battered, dilapidated hut by the side of the road had a bike in front, if a miserable little shop whose total inventory of cigarettes or soda was not worth what a tourist would spend on a good meal also had a harsh, naked light bulb, one thought, this is not so bad. Had I seen those things the day after I arrived, I would have wanted to throw myself on the ground and beg forgiveness of these people. Not now. This is not to say that I have become indifferent to them. Quite the contrary. I am more determined than ever before that I will work however best I can to alleviate—to eradicate—this intolerable agony.

Only, now, I am—or at least, coming into Calcutta last evening, I was—too drained, too tired of empathy, to respond to each individual. I think of Dorothy Day's impossible motto: to see Christ in every man, never to develop a scab, never to become clinical, always to react one to one, even to the most ugly and deformed of people. I couldn't do it at the *Catholic Worker,* at least not for long; I can't do it now. I am little different from, perilously close to, the average rank-and-file citizen of the affluent societies who simply does not want to hear about these distant, incomprehensibly huge, tragedies. (We flew yesterday over an area in Orissa that is often flooded. I was told that a few years back twenty thousand had lost their lives in such an incident. It was not, as I remember, reported in the American press; if it was, I forgot it the moment I read it. Twenty thousand!) I am like them in that I, too, cannot bear this reality—cannot, rather, stand to keep my gaze fixed upon it and my heart open to it—and I retreat back into the oasis of a hotel. At Bubeneswar at a temple I even felt an anger toward the pathetic whining women, the misshapen women, who came to beg from me. So I must understand the callousness of the West, since it is in my soul as well. Yet, I am unlike them, for this country excites in me a passion to change the world, and it reaches down into the center of my being, which sometimes overwhelms me with a tenderness, like a woman with whom you are in love. But, as I thought yesterday sitting at the airport at Bubeneswar, How? How? How?

CALCUTTA, 1/16—11:20 A.M.

Walked around the city for a couple of hours with Henry Teune. Some impressions and thoughts.

First, broad, bustling avenues; not as many beggars as in Bombay; sense of urban pace. Then into winding, muddy, crowded, crooked back streets with little shops on the side. Like Bombay market. Thought: since a person can go into business here with such a tiny capital, the underemployment is enormous. Dead rat in street. Why don't these people assault us well-dressed, well-fed, camera-carrying tourists? Why don't they scream "unfair" and set upon us? In part, because they are decent people, though poor; in part, because a society holds together precisely because those on the bottom are socialized, ideologized and repressed into accepting the intolerable. The streets remind me of some Algerian slums back of Notre Dame in Paris in 1959, but by now I have two entire weeks of sophistication. I see that the apartments above the scene are crumbling but intact, and I assume that they are dwellings of the lower or even middle-middle class. I note that these shopkeepers have saris or watches or jute to sell; their capital is more than a pile of peanuts or some betel leaves and the makings of "Pan." Thought: this country seems commercialized from the top down, but in small units. Henry comments: This is functional in a country that has an enormous excess of human labor. That is absolutely right. But then I say to Henry that functionalism can become the worst rationale for any status quo. There was, I suppose, an equilibrium in a German concentration camp; an evolved set of behavior patterns, which allowed the hardy to adapt to the monstrous. Henry agrees.

To broad avenues and what I think is the discovery of the obvious. The people who live on the streets here do not bed down in the market lanes in the center of the city, for they are used from wall to wall. Rather they camp out in the boulevards where there are sidewalks to shelter them from the traffic. My scab, alas, is still in place. I walk by sleeping people, stooped people, without shedding tears. (The stoop is something I do not understand. They go down on their haunches until their rump almost, but only almost, touches the ground. It strikes me as anatomically and mechanically impossible. It happens constantly.) Two disturbing epiphanies: a mother washing a little baby with soap on a sidewalk, using water from a pool collected there, the two of them acting out a stereotype of maternal affection and baby crying, so much so, that a soap company would do well to photograph them for an ad; only, they play the charming scene on an open street where they live. Another mother cradles a baby and his sister gives him "blubber" kisses on the belly, laughing happily; this too on a sidewalk. One more epiphany: everywhere people are washing themselves, their dishes, their vegetable wares. They stand in the street at the pump and perform the ritual ablutions. I see hunger, passivity, despondence; I see laughter, love and ordinary existence. It makes me think of Mann in *The Magic Mountain*, of how life, pulsating, vulgar, rotten, creative, assertive life thrusts forward. It is a depressing thought, for it makes life compatible with such indignity; it is a beautiful thought, for it states an indomitableness that can even reveal itself on a Calcutta street.

JAMSHEDPUR, 1/17—6:05 A.M.

I spoke yesterday afternoon at a center in Calcutta. The participants—about ten people—were economists and social scientists, postdoctoral, almost all of them Marxists of one kind or another. I talked about poverty in the United States, which might seem a bizarre thing to do in India. They were interested in my facts and figures but upset by a distinction I regularly make between poverty, defined as a deficit in the necessities of life as those necessities are determined in a given society, and inequality, which may or may not include poverty at its lower limit. There could be, I said, a society in which no one lacked necessities, but in which there was a terrible maldistribution of luxuries. Furthermore, I argued, capitalism requires inequality, because there must be a profit, an excess, a surplus, to motivate the capitalist and to provide him with funds for investment and expanded reproduction, but it does not need poverty as a systemic precondition of its existence.

This set off quite a furor. The details are not important, but the underlying attitude is. They were disturbed that I seemed to be saying something nice about capitalism—that it did not need poverty. They hankered, even though they were sophisticated, for the consoling simplicities of the theory of impoverishment. And they wanted to make the working-class gains under the welfare state either nonexistent or explicable as a shrewd bribe conspiratorially handed out by the bourgeoisie. Most basic, they tended in the direction of a mechanical "base-superstructure" model of Marxism in which the political and economic are always in phase with one another, because the economic "determines" the political. In that perspective, the capitalist welfare state is, and can be, only a capitalist strategy. That it is also a working-class triumph is too intricate a theoretical truth to fit in the base-superstructure model.

I don't want to go into this issue, which is treated at length in *The Twilight of Capitalism*. What concerns me is that for these thinkers, and for other Marxist intellectuals whom I met on this trip, Marxism is a morality play, a drama, as much as a methodology. They are the victims of the systematic misrepresentation of Marxism that has been going on for about a century; but they are also influenced by their positions as intellectuals in a country of such desperate poverty. Even though I made some headway when I criticized the neo-Leninist theory of imperialism, they cannot view the role of the United States academically. They respond angrily, as I would if I lived here. There is a black-and-white aspect to their thought, because the world in which they have been unconscionably thrust *is* black and white.

I left with a USEFI staffer, and we drove through the dense streets toward the railroad station. Once again the pollution was overwhelming, a choking incarnation of something Marxists call "the law of combined and uneven development." For on closer examination I realized that it was compounded of automobile fumes and the fires the poor people made on the sidewalk; of twentieth century and paleolithic forms of energy brought together in this incredible society.

We moved toward the bridge, and I became aware of the pilgrims. They had come to bathe at the confluence of the Ganges and the Bay of Bengal on Wednesday, which was a holy day (connected, Henry said, with the winter solstice). They moved in clumps, obviously country people plodding down alien streets. Then when we arrived at the station there were still more of them, a river, a tide, of people. I accused myself of romanticism; there are crowds in New York, I thought, and these people seem so exotic, so significant only because they are wearing different—to me, strange—clothes. But on second sight and thought, I absolved myself of the charge. In New York the people do not squat, or even lie down and sleep, on the floor of Grand Central Station; and they do not have these faces. I don't know whether it is physiological or only a matter of mien, of attitude, of learned gestures, but peasants look and talk differently from urban folk. And these people have a quality in their faces—a stolidity that mixes strangely with a haunted, almost demented air—which you do not see in New York. It is even different from that slow-moving, guttural-speaking style I encountered in France among peasants when I stayed at a rural community near Tours for three weeks. Moreover, as any student of Hegel knows, the sheer quantities of this place are its quality.

I criticized and analyzed my romanticism. I did not shake it off. I have often thought—under Augustine's influence, I assume—of humanity as a pilgrimage. At my most optimistic moments, I think that the pilgrimage leads, not to the City of God, but to the City of Man. Now, for the first time in my life, I see a pilgrimage—only, it is inspired by the past, by what I take to be a superstition, and I am divided in myself, for my heart goes out to these God-driven people even as my head puzzles about them.

Darkness at Noon by Arthur Koestler is widely known as an anti-Communist novel. When I was working on the Fund for the Republic study of the blacklist in the entertainment industry in the fifties, I found out that actors who couldn't work because of real or alleged, present or past, Communist associations often vied with one another to get parts in productions of the play (or television drama) based on the book. That would prove that they were anti-Communist. I have always thought Koestler's work the most persuasive case for Stalinism I have ever read. The sophisticated interrogator who finally breaks the Bolshevik, Rubashov, is named Gletkin. In one exchange he tells Rubashov that the peasants would go to the train station and wait. If the train came in five minutes, or twenty-four hours or two days, it was all the same to them. They had no sense of clocks and schedules. These people, Gletkin said, had to be turned into industrial workers. To do so required force, brutal force, but that was the only way to take Russia by the scruff of its peasant neck and to drag it into the twentieth century.

Does that apply here? Would an Indian totalitarianism dragoon these pilgrims into the modern world? I am not sure. Before coming here on this trip, I had some secure abstractions—Aid, Stalinism, Development—but now, with only two weeks of learning, I am much more skeptical. It is not just that I am politically and temperamentally a passionate democrat, though that has something to do with it; it is not even only a moral revulsion against totalitarianism, though it is certainly that. It is also a suspicion, a growing suspicion that the peculiarities and intractabilities of this society are such that perhaps you simply could not totalitarianize it even if you wanted to.

Am I becoming a Gaullist? In 1963 in Paris, Stephanie and I went to one of De Gaulle's press conferences at the Elysée Palace. Someone asked him what he thought of the Sino-Soviet ideological dispute. In his summary he answered that he knew nothing of the ideological quarrel and was not interested in it. But, he went on, if you ask me about the enmity between two ancient empires with miles of common border, that I know something about. Now, my Marxist structural analysis is being tempered by a vivid impression of the tremendous force of history, of the gigantic psychological and intellectual lacunae left over from much more than a thousand years of cultural history. Structure, God knows, is profoundly important, and India is cruelly used every day because of its systematically inferior position in the world economy. But even in the utterly unlikely event that we could remove those institutional negativities (and iniquities), the ancient India of the pilgrim in the railroad station would remain. Or more, even if there were a Stalinist government, would it become a power able to force six hundred million people into the modern world? Not just six hundred million people, which is a number; six hundred million Indians, which is a complex, resistant fact.

After an uneventful train ride of four hours, I arrive at Jamshedpur, a steel town owned by the Tata Company. I am met at the station—where a deformed beggar crawls after me, the most affluent-looking person in the place, on the stumps of his legs, and I flee—by Father O'Leary, a Jesuit. I am taken to the Institute, where I will speak tomorrow, and O'Leary and Father Tome and I chat while I drink a little Scotch and here, in the state of Bihar, I am transported back to the days of my Jesuit-educated youth in St. Louis, Missouri, and Worcester, Massachusetts.

This is the other India. In the United States, affluence is visually obvious, and it takes an act of the imagination and will to see poverty. In India, poverty is obvious—insistent, overwhelming—and what is difficult is to see that which is not poor. Only here there is no real problem.

Jamshedpur is a company town, dominated by TISCO—the Tata Iron & Steel Company—and four or five other corporations, several of them also involving the Tatas, the Parsee family, India's richest, headquartered in Bombay. It was laid out just after the turn of the century in Bihar, the poorest of the present Indian states, a place that is nonetheless blessed with major natural resources, like coal. The Tatas had a paternalistic attitude from the very start, believing, if the current employees I talked to have their history straight, that happy workers would produce more. In the twenties they made concessions, and today the people who work in the huge plants that dominate this city are a kind of labor aristocracy, making, I am told, about 450 rupees on the average per month. That is, according to the official exchange rate, about fifty dollars a month—only that rate is next to useless in measuring social well-being in this city. In any case, they get twice or three times as much as casual labor in this country and they have access to company housing as well.

This raises a disturbing question, one originally posed to me by a Gandhian intellectual on a sun-swept terrace in New Delhi: Are the industrial workers a "middle" class in this country, enjoying the benefits of the high production and technology of the factory enclaves, lording it over the peasants, who are trapped in the immemorial traditional economy? Strangely enough both my New Delhi friend and Mrs. Gandhi—who, among other things, successfully broke a major rail strike—have this point of view. I can't buy it. Certainly the sociological assumptions of American society don't apply neatly—or any other way—here. The most outcast are, to be sure, the rural poor and the urban unemployed. But without getting into high theory, these workers are still going into dark Satanic mills. They are exploited by rich families like the Tatas; and when one calls them an "aristocracy," that is a term that is relative to the poverty of the surrounding countryside.

Moreover, even though Jamshedpur looks better than any city I've seen in India—how much more sophisticated my eyes are now than two weeks ago!—it still has its huts and its beggars. Yesterday, when I was riding around town with one of the Jesuits, I became aware of a band of humanity clinging to a hill (or was it a slag heap?). It was, I was told, a company of women who were out scavenging for any little piece of coal that got dropped by the wayside. And there are other tensions here: between members of some tribes from the area, Biharis (nontribal people from the state) and the other Indians who came here to work. A priest tells me of the tremendous competition to get a job at these plants, and of the graft that sometimes goes with it. There are unions in the shops, but they are quiet now, apparently cowed by the Emergency measures taken by Mrs. G.

We drive through a small bit of bloody history. Here, my Jesuit friend tells me, is where the Moslems live on one side of the road, the Hindus on the other. In rioting that took place in the sixties, at least a thousand were killed, 500 in a single afternoon. In a communal frenzy, people were knifed, clubbed and attacked with rocks, primarily because of rumors from some refugees from East Pakistan (which is now Bangladesh). The ancient passions brooded in the midst of this Pittsburgh of a place.

But still, there is something important to be understood here. The Indians can obviously enter the modern world and have done so in great numbers—only, in a society where the total population is so huge that the percentages are low. The point is that timeless and unchanging India of the imagination—and sometimes of the Indian's own mythology—can enter time. That is clearly a mixed blessing—the mills here are lowering and spew their smoke over a lovely countryside—but it is, on balance, clearly a blessing. And, I am told by the Jesuits, the conditions at the nationally owned steel plants are as good as here.

The Jesuits themselves are in something of a bind. They are a nice, deeply dedicated bunch of men who have been working in this country for twenty or twenty-five years. They came to be with the workers, establishing the Xavier Labor Relations Institute (XLRI) in the early fifties. Only, they ran into union problems— the federation that is strongest in Jamshedpur has ties with the Congress Party and did not want the priests to deal with any other group—and they wound up creating a business school. During the day I watch the students at cricket, some of them wearing tennis sweaters. In the evening before my talk there is tea on the lawn. Two men who came up in the train with me are executives of the Asian Paint Company doing interviews on a recruiting swing. And at my talk last night, the chair was the most important person present: the plant manager of the TISCO operation.

The students, aspiring businessmen though they may be, were clearly fascinated by my radical analysis, and I was introduced by a Jesuit who spoke of me, with a sort of bewildered pride, as one of the most informed Marxists in the world. The plant manager himself was surprisingly affable, even after I spent one third of my evening lecture carefully explaining why capitalism is a contradictory system that deserves the earliest possible death. He could not resist a small remark—that in a socialist society where everyone will have enough, where will the drive for action and change come from? I thought it was a marvelous paradox that we were discussing this classic Adam Smith point in the midst of a society that is desperately trying to claw a subsistence living out of a reluctant soil. But, then, there has been nothing but anomaly these last fifteen days.

1/18—4:45 P.M.

I came down this morning on the Steel Express, leaving Jamshedpur at 6:20 A.M. The countryside I watched roll by looked idyllic, as if it were posing for a picture postcard. Rich fields, some of them an incredible splash of green on the landscape, houses, not huts, thatched roofs sometimes, tall wooden structures for pumping water from a pool into a field. With my two-week-old eyes it did not look at all bad.

Then Hourah terminal. Two porters fought over my bag. The "First-Class Waiting Room for Gents" is a seedy place with some people sleeping, wrapped in their robes. I decided to go to the airport, even though it would be hours before my scheduled departure. A young man from USEFI escorted me out of the station.

Then there began the Via Dolorosa of Calcutta, the stations of its cross. Friday night, when I arrived, the scene was numbing with night and smoke; Saturday when I walked around, my path was random. Now I was led down a logical route from railroad station to airport, a tourist's route, and therefore a beggar's route.

I can only evoke the miseries and infirmities I saw. The man with legs so misshapen that he walked on fours; another with wads of flesh hanging from his cheek; piteous, mumbling, muttering, dirty children; haggling cab drivers; people picking at garbage; bright-faced babies who have not yet understood that they were born condemned, convicted, sentenced; and on and on, a vast wheedling,

suppurating army of the halt and the maimed. They finally led me
to think blasphemies about Christ.

Though I left the Catholic Church long ago, I have always had
an affection for Christ—which is to say the Christ of the *Catholic
Worker*, of the Sermon on the Mount, of compassion and gentle
love. But now I want to curse him. Who is he to set up his anguish
as a model of meditation for the centuries? He was crucified only
once, that is all. If you assume that he was God, which I do not,
then you can say that he must have felt a terrible psychological
loss as they nailed his divinity to the cross. But only one time; only
for a matter of hours. Just one excruciating struggle up the hill with
the means of his death on his back; just one crown of thorns. Terrible, but just once. In Calcutta, I think, people are crucified by the
thousands every day, and then those who have not died are crucified again and again and again. If he were half the God he claims
to be, he would leave his heaven and come here to do penance in
the presence of a suffering so much greater than his own, a suffering
that he, as God, obscenely permits. But he does not exist. There is
no easy transcendental answer to this agony. There is only our
fallible, failing, necessary fight. And if we were to win it, the happiness of numberless generations would not pay these people back
for a single day of their suffering.

PA FLT. 1 BETWEEN DELHI AND TEHERAN, 1/19

PA FLT. 1 BETWEEN LONDON AND N.Y., 1/20—12 NOON DELHI TIME
1:30 A.M. N.Y.

So what have I learned?
In fact, absolutely nothing. It is like when I went to Hollywood
in the middle fifties to work on the blacklist project. My first stay
there was about three weeks, and when I came back my friends
wanted to know what the "real" Hollywood was like, the Hollywood beneath the tinsel and the glitter and all the stories about
casting couches and vulgarity with millions of dollars. And I told
them what seemed to me to be the truth (and still did more than
a year later, after several more-lengthy trips and extensive interviews with people from every walk of life there): Hollywood's
depth is skin deep, its ultimate secret is that there is nothing beneath the obviousness.

So, too, with India—in part. If you arrive at the Calcutta airport and take a cab to the Hourah terminal; if you ride down a single country road in Orissa or Bihar for one hour; if you stumble on to a single hut colony in the very heart of Bombay; if you have the most unperceptive unseeing mirrorlike eyes; you will have understood an aspect of the deepest essence of India. It is poor. That is the overwhelming, basic, inescapable fact that underlies every analysis; the tourist impression is a sophisticated insight.

Only it can't be that simple.

First of all, it is not simply an appalling poverty that one encounters in India, but a poverty that inheres in a rich, differentiated structure, a poverty that in many ways is a part of a coherent social whole. That whole includes family life, religion, the caste system, the ancient way of doing agricultural and handcraft things, and so much more. Yesterday, for instance, when I got on the plane, the USEFI people had sent copies of two newspapers that carried interviews with me. One of them was the *Hindustan Times* for Sunday, January 11. In it I found pages of small-type ads for marriages —ads that came from college graduates, representatives of the most sophisticated and advanced people in the society. I don't want to be smug. Perhaps it is true—as many Indians and the Jesuits at Jamshedpur told me—that arranged weddings have more stability and durability than the love matches of the West. And yet, I am not persuaded. I do not see mating a woman to a man on a commercial (dowry) basis, of denying freedom of choice in the most intimate of relationships. And from what I have heard from Indians and others, of the role of the Indian wife—passive, silent, subservient—if there is a high rate of intact marriages, then it is maintained at much too high a price.

But my point is not to argue the pros and cons of the marriage issue. It is to assert the broader proposition of how India's under-development is not a misery on the order of an enemy occupation of the land, a level of life that is imposed from without. In part, it springs from within, it is a product of a way of life that has the approbation of the very people whom it wracks with so much pain. It is "freely chosen"—in quotes because the voluntarism is, in considerable measure, determined.

Two related thoughts:

First, the knowledge convinces me anew of something I have been persuaded of before: that talk—Nathan Glazer's neoconservative article some time ago in *Commentary*, for instance—about the great value of traditional society is often terribly, terribly wrong and romantic and elitist. Do people find a certain meaningfulness, an equilibrium in which their suffering is somehow made less horrible by the fact that they do not know it is suffering? Are we to compare this order—and an order it is—to the deracinated, aberrant, anomic life of the "advanced" countries, and then to mourn the passing of the immemorial—even if false—certitudes? Are we men and women of the world, who would not, it should go without saying, ourselves enter into an arranged marriage but approve such an institution for "them"? I am truly unfair to Glazer, since I am reducing his attitude to an absurdity. But what about that absurdity? It raises one of the profound moral problems of our time. Dare we shatter these ancient adaptations of life to environment, purchased at a price of human deformity, which may once have been, given the possible alternatives, cheap—shatter them in the name of the possibility that what will come after will be better?

Yes, yes and yes! Humankind cannot in Machiavellian fashion accept, count and use its own agony. It may be forced by implacable circumstances to accept that agony for a millennium or two. But its genius, its success, its hope, its morality, have been precisely the Faustian insistence on challenging and changing those horrible limits at the first possible moment.

What I am saying—and let me put it excessively, so as to be unmistakable about the basic point, and then make the necessary qualifications—is that many of the truly holy and profound institutions of India should be, must be, smashed. Nonviolently, persuasively, rationally smashed; but smashed. At Gopalpur, for instance, there was a wholeness to the life of the fishermen in their boats and the women and children on the beach, the pissing and the shitting in the sand and surf, the traditional rhythms. There is a beauty to some of it, of course; yet, ultimately it is abominable. I want India to transcend its quaintness and its charm—and yes, even its mystery—because some, perhaps many, of its traditions stunt the human potential. And I say this despite the terrible risk I take—for it would take a fool to be certain that what will follow upon the destruction of those integral customs will be necessarily humane—because that way lies the only *possibility* of humanity for these millions, hundreds of millions.

Am I talking like a Stalinist? Has this vivid existentialist knowledge of what is, after all, only a banality known to any social scientist who thought about it for a second—that the culture of underdeveloped societies is a bar to the modernization—turned me into Gletkin? No, not at all. Indeed, one of the things that struck me at Gopalpur was the depth of the commitment of the intellectuals there—some of the more important social-science scholars among them—to democracy. None of us mentioned Mrs. Gandhi and the Emergency in the regular, formal sessions.

But, it seemed to me, that reality enshrouded us. They talked, from many points of view, of the impossible, incredible diversity of India—its multitudes, not simply of languages, but of cultures, and significant cultures at that. In my brief visit, I had only begun to perceive or, better, to suspect that complexity. Now I knew that Marathi was spoken in Bombay, Tamil in Madras, Bengali in Calcutta, Hindi in Delhi, and that each of these and the other tongues had its history, its literature, its tradition.

Now the scholars were saying, how do you democratically integrate this fantastic variety into a nation. India, as someone remarked to me, is not a nation; it is a continent, like Europe. If at the time of the French Revolution, one had been trying to bring together the Italians, the Germans and the French and not merely the Parisians, the Marseillaises, the people of Vendée, would France have ever emerged? I exaggerate. India had been brought together under the British raj as Europe had never been under the various emperors. Whatever the precise historical parallels, clearly the unification of this vast and unbelievably varied land was an unprecedented task. Could it be done democratically? This became a particularly acute problem—and I was the seminar participant who formulated this aspect of the reality—when the political unification is attempted under circumstances of governmental responsibility for economic policy. For then, each one of those languages and cultures made, not simply political, but economic and social demands upon the central power. By the "law of combined and uneven development," as Marxists call it, the fishermen on the beach at Gopalpur, with their traditional triangular hats and boats tied together without benefit of nails, asserted themselves in the style of a Steelworker local in Pittsburgh. The United States not only could tolerate that local; it could be forced to a productive redistribution of resources by it. But India?

That of course is Mrs. G.'s—and Mao's and any antidemocrat's— basic argument: that in a developing nation, such differences are inefficient, antimodern, antidevelopmental. Most of the scholars at Gopalpur would not buy that thesis; and those who veered toward it did so, it seemed to me, despairingly, desperately. In my last formal intervention I spoke to them in Aesopian terms, with more than a little emotion. I observed the rule that no one mentioned the Emergency by name. I talked of the grave problems facing a democrat in a developing society and said that it could be that authoritarianism would triumph for a period, perhaps even a long period. But then, I went on, the task of the democrat—and I really meant the democratic socialist—was to fight for as much democracy as possible, to assert the values, even if a gain of only one wish were possible, or if it were a case of holding down the losses. For, if modernization proceeded undemocratically, it might succeed in a massive mobilization of resources—and that could well be a gain, a progress—but it would do so by institutionalizing inequality and creating an undynamic society, which would come to pay for its authoritarianism with inefficiencies that would weigh upon the fate of masses of people very much like, if not exactly in the mode of, the ancient irrationalities that had permitted men and women to starve to death. There would be a higher level of an inhuman society.

I said these things matter-of-factly, dispassionately. Only, I was talking to intellectuals who lived in a country where you could be jailed for your ideas, and who were now working in an atmosphere of the most frustrating, personally dangerous uncertainty. When I formulated my thought, tears welled up in my eyes, for I was asking people to be courageous, and I am not at all sure how tough, how principled, I would be under these circumstances. But I controlled myself when I spoke.

Secondly, the perception of the cultural infrastructure forced me to correct one of my most complex errors. I, like Marx, but without his excuse of living at a time when the mistake was natural, had always thought of India "economistically." That is, I had assumed that if only American capitalism would cease its maximizing of corporate priorities in both aid and trade policy, then the capital we would generously provide—the steel mills, the communications systems—would permit a democratic and nonviolent transition to the modern world. There is obviously some truth to that, but I know now how limited it is. For even if there were absolutely "free" resources available to the Indian planners, the way of life that I saw along the dusty roads would have to change from within. The "spread effects" of technology took several bloody tumultuous centuries to assert themselves in Europe; how could one assume that the process would be any less tortuous in the Third World? I put that in my old, analytic language, only it is now bone of my bone, flesh of my flesh, a sense of the irrepressible life I glimpsed by the light of naked, modern bulbs hanging in the half-commercialized, half-precapitalist shops along the roadways of Orissa.

Then I had learned something else that I have already said: that, contrary to all the rules of logic, the mother bathing her child in the pool of street water in Calcutta could be happy. "Be" happy? "Seem" to be happy? Have a right to be happy at what could be the expense of the child? I am not sure of the gradations. I am sure that, as I passed by, she *was* happy.

And, finally, there is the moral change this had wrought in me. When I began to think of this book on the Third World, I did so because I thought I should. I knew intellectually that we in America were turning our backs on these millions, yes these billions. I decided intellectually that I, ever responsive to the noblesse that obliges, would come to the aid of these, my unfortunate brothers and sisters. How splendid of me! Only now, Lord Bountiful has become chastened and impassioned. A mere sixteen days of trying to be open and perceptive, of compulsive empathy, has led to a spontaneous empathy. I would not dare to try to summarize the sensations; for one thing, the evocation of the images would make me cry here in this cold, snowy New York dawn; for another thing, it is beyond the competence of my pen. Suffice it to say that the huts and the people, the color of mud, and the babies and the shit on the beach and the beggars, whom I learned to hate—

the immense, appalling, appealing, vital-in-spite-of-itself India that I encountered—will haunt me the rest of my days.

But that is not smugly said; my phenomenology does not end with an absolute and serene knowledge like Hegel's. For I also discovered what a corrupted Northerner I am. Once upon a time, say when I was at the *Catholic Worker*, this experience would have sent me, sandals unlatched, into a reckless search for all the huts of India. But my middle-aged truth now is much more conservative and unromantic and unsatisfying. I don't want to go and join them, to live like them, to share their agony. I am afraid—and that is natural. So, what I must do in this book is to try as best I can to persuade people, not to a maximum of heroism, but to that minimum of decency that is all I can muster. Having toured an abyss where hope yet survives, for a mere sixteen days, I will be passionate about that minimum of decency for the rest of my life.

N.Y., 1/21—7:15 A.M.

Chapter Four **The Creation of the World**

The world was created between the sixteenth and nineteenth centuries. As an economic, social and political reality, it is of relatively recent origin; indeed, it is unfinished. I do not speak in this way for mere rhetorical effect. There is a critical analytic point to my metaphor.

The conservatives, Condorcet once remarked, always try to "make nature herself an accomplice in the crime of political inequality." Now that argument has become both international and economic. Are there some countries engaged in the struggle against overeating while others are threatened with famine? That is because the nations have specialized in the production that nature, sometimes lavish and sometimes pinch-penny, made most advantageous for them. Each has simply made the best of the lot assigned to it.

In fact, the world in which we live was created by European capitalism and its overseas progeny. It was not, and is not, the result of the inexorable workings of some inhuman necessity—geographic, geologic, genetic, or what have you—but of economic and social structures.

The chief feature of this man-made world is that it is divided into rich and poor nations. At the beginning, that was done by means of an international system in which the wealthy minority industrialized and the impoverished majority were the hewers of their wood and the bearers of their water. More recently, as we have seen, that essential unfairness has changed its form in order to preserve its content. Now the elite increasingly engages in intellectual and administrative work, the mass in grubby manual tasks as well as agriculture and raw-materials production. At the beginning of this process, it should be noted in honor of Adam Smith, there was, not a conspiracy, but an invisible hand, which vectored the individual greeds of the earth into the organizing principle of a new globe.

I wish it were not necessary to make this point. Since I write in an America in which liberalism is as far Left as serious mass movements go, and where a shallow, superficial conservatism still has a hold on many people, I wish I did not have to transgress the normal ideological limits of the society. That could well alienate a part of the audience—the decent, generous part—that I want to reach. My problem is further complicated by the fact that many of the anticapitalist explanations of the agony of the Third World are simplistic, monochromatic, unicausal. That has given the intricately radical truth a bad name. If I could, then, I would focus on the existential injustices, the gross, unanalyzed statistics, and forget about the larger generalizations.

That would omit the essential. The creation of the world with a North Pole of affluence and a South Pole of wretchedness is the outcome of a systemic process. If that theoretical point is not understood, it is literally impossible to come up with practical solutions for immediate and outrageous problems. I will not, given the strategy of this book, attempt to describe this mechanism in scholarly detail, even though my brief summary statement is based on data fully documented in the notes. I will, however, attempt to present the evidence that shows, contrary to the American innocence, that it is men and women who fabricated these evils rather than an implacable nature that requires them. In this chapter I will outline an interpretive history of how this world was created; in the next I will describe the present structures that are the result of that past.

I

A decisive break in the history of mankind occurred in late-eighteenth-century Europe. That moment was itself prepared by a chain of events that leads back to the sixteenth century. These seemingly remote happenings largely determine whose children die at childbirth in the late twentieth century, and whether people live to be fifty or seventy-five. One looks back into time in order to understand why here and now there are lepers on the streets of Bombay but not on those of New York.

Before turning to the more distant reaches of these events, a few of their current consequences should be noted. That means defining the famous "gap" between the North and the South.

When the nineteenth century began, the difference in per capita income between the rich and the poor countries was 2 to 1. Then, between 1815 and 1914, there was a century of relative peace and unprecedented material progress. In that period, world income grew at the incredible rate of 2.5 to 3 percent a year. But the benefits of that surge were unevenly distributed (and had to be, as we shall see). There are today various measures of the differential and the exact number depends on complex matters of definition. Measured in income terms (which includes the transfers from the hungry to the affluent) the gap may well be of the order of 20 to 1, or ten times what it was at the beginning of the nineteenth century. Quantified in terms of per capita product, the developed countries are roughly twelve times better off than the underdeveloped. For a comparison, one might remember that the difference between the richest and the poorest regions of the European Common Market is 3 to 1, a fact that strikes most people as intolerable.

However, it may seem that there is hope, for in the 1950s, the gap stopped widening if it was defined by rates of growth in GNP. In that first full postwar decade, the South did fairly well and the North, most definitely including the United States, performed rather poorly. So both poles of the world grew by about 4 percent a year, which meant that the abyss between them did not become deeper. The problem with these optimistic numbers is that during these times population went up by 2.5 percent a year in the Third World and by less than 1.5 percent in the advanced capitalist economies.

So, even though the GNP rates stabilized, the per capita income of the hungry suffered a further decline relative to that of the affluent. Even the absolute numbers were cold comfort: Between 1965 and 1975, the per capita income of the 1.2 billion people in the poorest countries grew at an annual rate of $2 a year—which is the projected rate for 1975–1985.

Still, there is hope that the disparities might narrow a bit. In 1965, the poor nations had 65 percent of the world's population and 15.3 percent of its production. One serious projection for the year 2000 puts the population figure at 77.5 percent and the GNP all the way up to 18.3 percent. Only, putting the matter in percentages conceals a chasm. Today, the gap in per capita income between the rich and the poor is $3,500. If that very positive scenario for the year 2000 works out—and Wassily Leontiev's UN Commission thinks it too optimistic—the gulf will be $9,830. The United States now has forty times the per capita income of India; with luck, the differential will be a mere 36 to 1. That is, in the crucial determinants of human existence, the North-South gap will remain a matter of life and death during the next generation.

These tragic disparities persist in good times as well as bad. The early seventies were, until the outbreak of the great recession in the advanced capitalist world and the quadrupling of oil prices, favorable to the poor countries. For a significant number of them, the terms of trade—the prices they received for their exports compared to those they had to pay for their imports—were improving. As a result, exports went up by 25 percent a year, imports by only 20 percent. So, one might think, the impoverished economies were on the march. In fact, the gains were very narrowly confined. In 1971, for instance, 10 underdeveloped countries accounted for 55 percent of all the manufactured exports from the South. At the same time, during these "good years," 60 percent of the Third World economies failed to maintain their agricultural output even though this was the time of the "miracle" seeds of the Green Revolution.

So it was that under favorable circumstances the Gross Domestic Product of countries which contained roughly half of the Third World's people went up by less than 1 percent, and those with around 70 percent of that population by less than 3 percent. Meanwhile, during a slightly longer period, from 1963 to 1973, the rich powers of the Organization for Economic Cooperation and Development (OECD) saw their per capita real income rise by almost 50 percent. They celebrated this tremendous increase in their material well-being by cutting the real value of their foreign aid by 7 percent. When that act of moral indifference is taken in conjunction with the population increase in the poor nations, it meant that the latter had 30 percent less assistance in 1973 than in 1963. The world market at its most benevolent had not been of much help to the hungry, and a soaring prosperity among the affluent had been the occasion for a growth in their public miserliness.

Most depressing of all, there is no sign whatsoever that, under the present conditions, the underdeveloped countries can escape from their position of inferiority.

Take one case in point. Manufacturing is one of the most important indices of economic progress. In 1955, the poor nations had a 6.2 percent share of international manufacturing. In 1973, after years that had seen some real advances and during which multinationals were moving some production to the periphery, the Southern portion had climbed to 6.9 percent. This was true even though the annual increase in manufacturing in those countries had been significantly higher than that of the advanced capitalists. How could that be? Because of the enormous advantage that the wealthy achieved for themselves when they began to create the world four hundred years ago. That institutionalized superiority is so enormous that even when the poor outperform the rich, they stay disastrously far behind them.

We confront, then, a system of injustice, a complex global mechanism that reproduces its essential inequities in good times and in bad and does so purposefully (though not conspiratorially). It is the outcome of four centuries of a history to which I now briefly turn.[1]

II

It is important to clearly state at the outset what will *not* be proved in this analysis. There are three simple-minded propositions that are often, and quite wrongly, attributed to people of my political persuasion. One of the reasons that some are so anxious to impute these notions to us is that if we held them we would be very foolish indeed, which is precisely what these critics want to demonstrate. To avoid this misunderstanding, which is often accompanied by some malice, I propose to begin with some negatives, making precise how I will *not* explain the gap.

To begin with, it is patently not true that underdevelopment is merely the result of "economic" mechanisms. The economic, as I showed in *The Twilight of Capitalism*, never exists in isolation. It is always intertwined with the political and the cultural. And, in the specific cases of the Third World there are obviously instances in which noneconomic factors have great weight. For example, of the 42 independent countries in Africa, only eight have populations of more than 10 million, more than half have fewer than 5 million people, and several are under 1 million. In part, of course, this fragmentation was imposed upon Africa during the European scramble for territory in the nineteenth century, and thus one might relate this phenomenon back to colonialism. But in part it is a result of the tribalism and relatively low level of integration that characterized the continent even before the Europeans began to carve it up. It is a serious obstacle to economic development and its origins predate the very existence of capitalism.

Secondly, there is a related absurdity: that the politics of imperial powers were, and are, to be explained solely and immediately in terms of their pursuit of material self-interest. Thus, a contemporary academic critique of the Marxist theory of imperialism assumes that it is an "economic interpretation" which attempts "to reduce reality to a single causative factor." It is then child's play to show that such an analysis must fail. But even Lenin, whose *Imperialism* is less complex than other major Marxist writings in this area (it was explicitly subtitled "A Popular Outline"), never committed such an obvious stupidity. And when one turns to the truly rich Marxist studies—say Rosa Luxemburg's "Junius" Pamphlet—one finds that the historical, the political, the cultural are all assigned considerable importance. Indeed, in some cases it is clear that the illusions of material self-interest are more significant than the accurate perceptions of it.

Thirdly, as I mentioned in Chapter One, I am not fashioning an alibi that excuses every action by a Third World leader on the grounds that he or she was fated to behave thus because of the evils of imperial capitalism. The Third World is sometimes responsible for making the worst of an intolerable situation. One can, for instance, rightly attack the British raj for having underdeveloped India so as to make it extremely difficult for democracy to take root there. But one must then add that Indira Gandhi was wrong to assault the political freedoms of her nation in 1975–76. There is no generic Western guilt that robs the Indians of free choice.

With these three straw men excluded from my argument, it is now possible to begin a summary, interpretive outline of why the North-South gap exists today. The basic point that undergirds the entire analysis is that it was social structure, not geographic or racial or even cultural endowment, that led to the great European breakthrough of the sixteenth century that started to split the world in two. A corollary is that once the West found itself in possession of this decisive, but modest, advantage, it moved quickly, by force of arms where necessary, to institutionalize it. If there was an initial element of accident in this enormous discontinuity in human history, European capitalism quickly and consciously used all of its power to turn its good luck into an imperial necessity.

In the sixteenth century, Western Europe had a slight lead as against the rest of the civilized world. That, however, was a recent development. In the period before that, say stretching back to the year 1000, it was technologically and culturally inferior to Byzantium, China and India. The scientific revolution was to play a critical role in the rise of capitalist power, yet in 1000, one contemporary historian has suggested, Europe was inferior in this field to ancient Athens and Alexandria. Indeed, the inventions that were to pave the way for the great leap from feudalism to capitalism in the West—the compass, gunpowder and printing—were Chinese. The zero concept and a numbers system of positional notation, which were the preconditions of scientific progress (roman numerals were much too clumsy), were taken from the Arabs, who borrowed them from the Indians.

In the fifteenth century, immediately before the European take-off, contemporary scholars believe that Europe was at roughly the same level as China. What is to be explained, then, is not the innate and persisting superiority of Western Europe, or of Britain, but rather why this corner of the world moved from a position of inferiority in the year 1000 to utter dominance by the nineteenth century. If "nature" had been the basic cause of the Western triumph it would not have had to wait around for several millennia of civilization before it asserted itself. So, a superficial glance at just a few of the facts suffices to suggest that it is history and social structure that were decisive in this transformation. This will help us to understand why inventions that were the work of China's genius could enable Europe to come to lord it over the Chinese.

Those social, structural factors can be divided, broadly, into two. First, there were rigidities in the non-European societies that prevented them from taking advantage of new opportunities. Second, there was in the European system a contrasting openness that allowed it to turn a slight advantage into a position of dominance, which has endured for four hundred years.*

Capitalism is a deviation in terms of the human history that preceded it. The institution of private property did not develop in the other great societies. They therefore tended to be centralized, despotic, rigid; the individual was allowed to use, but not to own, the land. As two scholars recently summarized current research, "these bureaucracies [in China, India and the Near East] aimed at, and succeeded in maintaining, vast peasant societies through long ages and at all population densities in a state of virtual homeostasis." In the West there were communes and then independent city-states that were much more decentralized than the "Asiatic" or "Oriental" despotisms of China and India.† This meant that there was much more room for innovation, change, discovery.

Max Weber, of course, placed a major emphasis on the ideological aspect of this reality, of how Christian, and specifically Protestant, individualism was so congenial to the capitalist spirit. But Weber too made the rise of self-governing cities and the mid-

* On both these counts, I want to signal an intellectual debt. The broad outline of the analysis that I will present derives from Marx's writings, particularly *Das Kapital* and the *Grundrisse*. Since I am reaching out to a broad, general audience, I will not quote Marx at length but will summarize his gist in my own words. This is not to say that I have ignored more recent scholarship. I find Marx's fundamental analysis confirmed by books like Barrington Moore's *Social Origins of Dictatorship and Democracy*, Immanuel Wallerstein's *The Modern World-System*, and Alexander Gershenkron's *Economic Backwardness in Historical Perspective*. Even though some of Marx's empirical citations are now dated or obsolete, I agree with the non-Marxist, Gershenkron, that this part of his work is "magnificient historical generalization." More to the point of this note, it is the source of much in what follows.

† Marx's concept of the "Asiatic" mode is problematic in other respects, as Maxime Rodinson has pointed out, but that does not affect the argument here.

dle classes that lived in them a decisive moment in this development. More recently, the Nobel laureate Simon Kuznets argued that it was the "social invention" of the independent city that provided the context in which the scientific, and then technological, breakthrough could take place.

I do not pretend that the few variables that I cite—private property, decentralization, the middle classes, Protestantism, the city-states—"explain" the epochal transformation of the West by Renaissance, Reformation and Revolution. I summarize a few relevant facts from disparate sources to make a single, rather narrow point: it was the capitalist social revolution—the changes in institutions and attitudes, in class structures and political power relationships—that made the scientific and technological revolution possible. A China could produce potentially revolutionary inventions, but it was not revolutionized by them; a Europe, though perhaps inferior to the Chinese at the point at which it borrowed from them, could exploit those inventions to their full, and explosive, potentiality. What distinguished these two civilizations was not innate ability or climate or genetics, but social structure.[2]

This leads to the second part of my theme: that the sixteenth-century West was able to take the slight advantage offered it and to convert it into global hegemony.

In the sixteenth and seventeenth centuries there were great revolutions in trade, great voyages of discovery, and a consequent increase in merchant capital. As Marx put it, "The sudden expansion of the world market, the multiplications of the circulating commodities, the competition among European nations to get hold of the products of Asia and the treasures of America, the colonial system, all contributed tremendously to the destruction of the feudal fetters on production. . . . The world market itself was the basis of the capitalist mode of production." More recently, Immanuel Wallerstein has developed this point, producing a remarkable synthesis of all the available scholarly material.

It is Wallerstein who formulated the concept of the "slight edge." In this period, he argues, Western Europe was able to take advantage of the expansion of the world of commerce and it invested the resulting profits in a further specialization in the activities that had made money in the first place. What other writers call a process of self-generating growth was taking place. When this development first began, Wallerstein notes, Western Europe might have been the agricultural breadbasket and Eastern Europe the commercial, and then industrial, center. But Western Europe had the "slight edge," a fact which was to be fateful for the next four hundred years (and its impact is not yet spent).

Once the barest outline of this specialization was in place, capitalist Europe began to reinforce it in every possible way. In the early period this was done by slavery, murder and theft.

Montesquieu caught the essence of this process in a savagely ironic observation. "The peoples of Europe," he wrote, "having exterminated the peoples of America, had to enslave the people of Africa to use them to clear all the lands they had acquired in America." And he added that one could not possibly think of the African slaves as human, "for if we suppose them to be men, one would begin to think that we ourselves are not Christians." In our time, Owen Lattimore formulated a similar insight with great brilliance, writing that "Civilization gave birth to barbarism."

It hardly takes a subtle analyst to see that it was armed power, rather than an impersonal nature, that was at work in these events. In Latin America, the Spanish and Portuguese expropriated primitive peoples, often with catastrophic loss of native life. In India, the East India Company acquired an empire as its private property and ruled it with a corporate army. It was, Eric Williams notes, a common saying that "several of the principal streets of Liverpool had been marked out by the chains, and the walls of the houses cemented by the blood, of the African slaves, and one street was nicknamed 'Negro Row.' The red-brick Customs House was blazoned with Negro heads."

This cruelty, it must be emphasized, was not random or individualistic; it functioned to make the new system work. In the eighteenth century, the Liverpool naval yards were enriched building ships for the slave trade, and the manufacture of cotton goods to buy slaves was a foundation of Manchester's prosperity. Slavery, in short, was an important impetus to the emergence of capitalism. Even more to the point of this book, the kind of production in which the various parts of the world specialized had a profound effect on their social structure. The simple, uncomplicated labor of cotton and sugar growing could be done by slaves; the more complex agricultural tasks of Eastern Europe required a kind of compulsory sharecropping and the persistence of feudal relationships; industry demanded more skilled and educated workers, a minimum of coercion and a maximum of consent. To a certain degree, the freedom of British citizens was purchased by the servitude imposed on black Africans.

These things did not, of course, transpire in total independence of natural conditions. The temperate zone was, Karl Marx remarked, the "motherland" of capital. But then Marx quickly added that favorable natural conditions only create possibilities, not inevitabilities, of development. And in another context, Marx went to the heart of the matter: "Perhaps, gentlemen, you think that the production of coffee and sugar are the natural destiny of the West Indies. But up until two hundred years ago, when it was not a question of trade, neither coffee trees nor sugar cane were planted there."

So, the system of European superiority in the world economy was established in the sixteenth and seventeenth centuries. Yet there was one country that was most successful in escaping from this international division of labor. It was, of course, the United States (or, more precisely, the American colonies). At first glance, this provides one more historical reason for this country's innocence: the fact that we came from behind and then utterly surpassed the original capitalist powers might make us think that any other nation can follow in our path if only it has the will. But at second glance, the American accomplishment proves the exact opposite. We achieved our success precisely by acting on the basis of an analysis that is quite similar to the one urged by the Third World in the United Nations today.

To begin with the British followed policies toward America analogous to the policies that America follows in the Third World today. They were officially dedicated to keeping us underdeveloped, discriminating in their tariffs against our manufactures, destroying the cloth industry in 1719, and prohibiting new iron works in 1750. Chatham, one of the more reasonable British leaders, even said that he would not allow a nail to be made in the colonies without the express permission of Parliament. Much of this was, to be sure, bluster, since one third of the British merchant fleet was being built in America by 1774. However, there is no doubt that these British declarations were a factor in promoting revolutionary consciousness in the colonies.

Moreover, one of the shrewdest of the founding fathers developed a theory that has more than a superficial similarity to the Marxist theory of neocolonialism that has been worked out in recent years. In his "Report on Manufactures," Alexander Hamilton wrote in 1791,

The superiority antecedently enjoyed by nations which have preoccupied and perfected a branch of industry, constitutes a more formidable obstacle . . . to the introduction of the same branch into a country in which it did not before exist. To maintain, between the recent establishments of one country, and the long-matured establishments of another country, a competition upon equal terms, both as to quality and price, is, in most cases, impracticable. The disparity, in the one or the other, or in both, must necessarily be so considerable, as to forbid a success rivalship, without the extraordinary aid and protection of government.

One wishes that the latter-day Ricardians in the White House and State Department would ponder that Third-Worldist—and quite accurate—analysis from out of the nation's hallowed past.

But why did the United States succeed in resisting the power of the emergent world market? Why, for instance, did Latin America fail? There were a number of factors at work, some of them having little to do with social structure. Countries with large indigenous populations were more difficult to develop than those that were sparsely settled. That is one reason why Argentina and Mexico are more advanced than other countries in their hemisphere. But then Argentina and Mexico fell far behind the United States—and here the structural factors assert themselves once again—because they were colonies of Spanish feudalism while this country was peopled by capitalist "kith and kin." Once genocide was carried out against the Indians, North America had the enormous advantage of possessing an immigrant population that had gone through the cultural process that culminated in European capitalism. Latin America did not.

So, the United States participated vicariously in the Western European social revolution. And in that revolution, the accumulation of wealth that made it possible to turn a slight edge into an industrial-technological chasm was based, in some measure, upon two hundred years of piracy, robbery and rape. African slaves, American Indians and the masses of the Indian subcontinent made an enormous contribution, exacted from them by force of arms, to the system that was to keep them in economic inferiority until this very moment.

What that accumulation of wealth did was to provide capitalism with a running head start for a gigantic leap into the nineteenth and twentieth centuries. It is to this second phase of the history of the North-South gap that I now turn.

Here is the result of the violence, trade and conquest of the sixteenth and seventeenth centuries:

Per capita GNP, measured in 1965 dollars, at the beginning of modern economic growth. *

COUNTRY	YEARS	PER CAPITA GNP
United Kingdom	1765–85	$227
France	1831–40	242
Belgium	1865	483
Netherlands	1865	492
Germany	1850–59	302
Switzerland	1865	529
Denmark	1865–69	370
United States	1834–43	474

* Source: *Economic Growth of Nations*, by Simon Kuznets, Table 2, p. 24.

Now capitalism was to take this initial advantage, achieved in part through the forced contributions of the globe's poor, and to create a world with it. I am *not* saying that slavery and looting in the sixteenth and seventeenth centuries explain the unprecedented successes of the eighteenth and nineteenth centuries. They were, as Michael Barret-Brown has pointed out, necessary preconditions for that surge; they were not sufficient conditions for it. There had to be new social classes, scientific and technological breakthroughs as well as the particularly brutal exploitation of the poor.

Max Weber did not understand this crucial distinction and that led him to conclude that colonial trade was "of little significance for the development of modern capitalism" since it "rested on the principle of exploitation and not that of securing an income through market operations." That is true enough. But then Weber was also forced to recognize that colonial trade was key to the enormous accumulation of wealth which preceded—and was a precondition of—the capitalist take-off. That created a possibility, one which became actual only when it functioned within the context of an indigenous European social and economic revolution.

But when these various conditions did come together, one of the most dramatic discontinuities in human history took place. As Joan Robinson remarks, "From one point of view, the whole of human history from the Neolithic revolution to the eighteenth century can be treated as one period, and the Industrial Revolution till today as another." The North-South gap is bound up, then, with a shift that divides ten thousand years of history from the past two centuries. That enormous fact should, by itself, dispose of the "natural" explanations of what has happened.

Between the eighth millennium before the Christian era and the late eighteenth century, Carlo Cipolla estimates, roughly 80–85 percent of the total energy available to society came from plants, animals and human labor. Then the scientific revolution provided man with the conceptual tools that enabled him to master new sources of energy. "A cumulative interaction was soon set in motion. The extraordinary growth in the supply of energy stimulated economic growth, which in turn stimulated educational and scientific research leading to new sources of energy." This epoch-making transition occurred first in a most unlikely place: on an island that then contained one percent of the world's population. And one of the reasons why Britain was able to make such enormous strides is to be found in the Third World.[3]

III

As capitalism came into its own with the Industrial Revolution in Britain, it shifted from brute force to the gentler compulsions of trade. Yet the latter were even more effective than the former in holding the world's poor in subjection since it seemed to be simply a matter of equal and just exchanges. In fact, as we know, the rich got the very best of the bargain as the gap between them and the poor expanded from 2 to 1 to at least 12 to 1. Here again, it would be absurd to suggest that the resulting system of international exploitation was the sole, or even the primary cause, of capitalist success. Just as in the case of the cruelties of the original accumulation of capital through slavery and violence, in this later development the suffering of the periphery was a necessary, but not a sufficient, condition for "progress." Moreover, the British were aware of how enormously they benefited from these arrangements —even though they managed to convince themselves, by the theory of comparative advantage, that they were also doing a kind deed for the rest of mankind.

The present relevance of this past is to understand how the world market was, from the very beginning, an instrument of development for the original capitalist powers and of underdevelopment for everyone else. This history, let it be clearly stated, points to the policy conclusion that there must be structural change in that world created by nineteenth-century capitalism if there is to be any real hope for the outcast masses of the late twentieth century.

The first witness on behalf of this proposition, so heretical in terms of the official American ideology of today, is one of the greatest geniuses of the eighteenth century, the patron saint of contemporary conservatism, Adam Smith.

In the "natural order of things," Smith said, society should first achieve an agricultural surplus, which would make cities possible; then develop industry in the cities; and finally find markets for the resultant manufactures in foreign trade. In fact, he noted, history had inverted that logical order and—on this count the last section— the whole process had really begun with trade. But in either case, he understood that international commerce was necessary for the domestic functioning of the system. The surplus produce of British industry paid for 96,000 hogsheads of Virginia and Maryland tobacco, but Britain could consume only 14,000 hogsheads, so it had to sell the rest. At each point in this process—selling its own manufactured products to the colony, reselling the colony's tobacco—it was necessary to have markets in other countries.

A second authority is also a procapitalist genius. David Ricardo disagreed with Smith on a crucial point, but then he developed his own theory of why capital had to internationalize itself. A nation, Ricardo argued as against Smith, could absorb its own surplus. The problem was that the level of profits depended on the rate of real wages, and real wages were determined by the cost of the necessities of life, with food a critical factor. In order to nourish the growing mass of workers in industry, the farmers would have to expand production, but that would mean that the less fertile land would now be cultivated. There was, therefore, a tendency toward a declining yield in agriculture, which meant that its products would get more and more expensive as the society grew. If unchecked, this trend would ultimately drive the rate of profit down by driving the cost of real wages up. Expansion would become impossible; the system would stagnate.

Ricardo was clearly wrong on some very important issues, and yet he persuaded his countrymen to a policy that served them very well. He had assumed that agriculture would be unable to increase its productivity, which was not true; he said that Britain should import cheap food from abroad and pay for it with industrial products, and that worked marvelously well. One of the first victims of this inspired insight was Ireland, which, as Marx was to note, was turned "into mere pasture land which provides the English market with meat and wool at the cheapest possible prices." In effect, then, Ricardo's partially erroneous theory rationalized the first great capitalist division of international labor: the center specialized in industry, the periphery in agriculture and raw materials.

The third great thinker who saw these trends was Marx himself. It was, he argued, in the very nature of capital to be international, for it regarded every barrier to the expansion of production as a limit to be overcome. Indeed, this imperial aspect of capital was, in his view, one of its historical justifications, its "great civilizing influence." All the previous systems were merely local; this one was worldwide, cosmopolitan in the best, as well as the worst, sense of the word. It spread out over the entire globe seeking new useful objects, or new uses for old objects. Indeed—and contemporary scholarship corroborates the bizarre point—the British even lent money to foreigners, so that they could buy British products.

Marx summarized his insights in the *Communist Manifesto,* and his description is so apt, so accurate to this very day, that I will break my self-imposed rule and quote it at length. Indeed, in a brilliant analytic maneuver, Steven Hymer changed the word

"bourgeoisie" in this passage, substituted "multinational corporation" for it, and discovered a statement that holds for the late
twentieth century. Marx wrote:

The need for constantly expanding outlets for its products drives the
bourgeoisie over the entire globe. It must plant itself everywhere, build
everywhere, produce interconnections everywhere. The bourgeoisie has
formed the consumption and production of all lands in a cosmopolitan
way by the exploitation of the world market. To the great sorrow of
the reactionaries, it has pulled the national basis of industry from under
their feet. Ancient national industries are annihilated and are daily
still being annihilated. They are forced by new industries, whose
introduction become a matter of life and death for all civilized countries, by industries which no longer use the raw materials of their own
land but raw materials that come from the most distant places and
whose products are no longer consumed within the nation itself but
at the same time in every part of the world. In place of the old needs,
which were satisfied by products within the nation itself, there are
now new needs which require the products of the most distant lands
and climates for their satisfaction. . . . The cheap prices of their commodities are the heavy artillery with which the bourgeoisie destroys
all the Chinese walls, with which it forces the most stiff-necked and
xenophobic barbarians to capitulate. . . . *In a word, it creates for itself
a world in its own image.* [Emphasis added.]

This passage, like the comment on the "civilizing influence" of
capital as it moved around the world, is filled with a sense of grudg-
ing admiration for the system Marx hated. Indeed, that attitude
was to lead him, and then all his followers for more than half a
century, into a procapitalist error. As he put it in a famous, and in-
correct argument, the introduction of the railway into India by the
British was to be "the forerunner of modern industry" on the subcontinent, an act that would lead to the development of the society.
This error was repeated by Rosa Luxemburg, Lenin and Hilferding. That mistake, that Marxist—and Leninist—overoptimism
about capitalism, will be dealt with in the next chapter.

For now, the main point has been established. There was a remarkable consensus, including Adam Smith, David Ricardo and
Karl Marx, which saw capitalism as inherently expansionist. And
Marx, the most brilliant of the three on this count, saw that this
drive led to the fashioning of an international division of labor, in

which "one part of the globe is transformed into primarily agricultural production for the other part's primarily industrial production." The North-South gap was initially fashioned by means of slavery and conquest; now, in the nineteenth century, it was deepened and institutionalized by means of the world market.

Or was it? After all, it has only been demonstrated that three geniuses *thought* that capitalism needed such expansion. But Smith, Ricardo and Marx had been wrong on other issues and one must therefore ask whether their perception was borne out by the facts. There is, after all, a great deal of contrary evidence. As Sir John Seeley put it in a famous witticism, Britain during the seventeenth and eighteenth centuries "conquered and peopled half the world in a fit of absence of mind." Beginning as far back as 1783, there were in England those who thought of the colonies as a "millstone," and between 1840 and 1870 that country saw a veritable "anti-imperialist" movement. In 1857, Marx himself speculated that India, though it enriched British individuals, may well have cost the nation more than it returned.

To be sure, in the last quarter of the century there were many politicians who proudly proclaimed themselves imperialist and reasoned in classic Leninist fashion for utterly conservative purposes. Here, for example, is the radical Liberal, Joseph Chamberlain: "Is there any man in his senses who believes that the crowded population of these islands could exist for a single day if we were to cast adrift from the great dependencies which now look to us for protection and which are the natural markets for our trade?" Was it really true that Britain thus needed the colonies?

My answer is yes, but in making it I do not for a moment endorse everything the proimperialist politicians, like Joseph Chamberlain, said. Often, as Rosa Luxemburg was careful to point out, such enthusiasts vastly overstated the economic importance of their political and military maneuvers. The dispute between the British and the Germans over Southwest and Southeast Africa was, Luxemburg clearly understood, never very important, and certainly not worth a war. Secondly, if one holds that the markets of some of the Third World countries were exceedingly useful to the development of capitalism up to World War I, that is not to underestimate the even greater significance of trade between the great powers themselves. From the very beginning to this day, that has always been crucial. I am not, in short, saying that the exploitation of the globe's poor was the basis for the growth of capitalism. I only, but most emphatically, assert that it was a necessary link in that process.

One simple set of figures should suffice to document this point. Between the 1790s and 1914, the export percentage of Britain's Gross National Product doubled, from 10 percent to 20 percent. During that same period, exports to Asia, Africa and Latin America went from 23 percent to 42 percent. As a contemporary Keynesian, John Knapp, put it, there had to be export opportunities capable of absorbing the high savings, the technological advance and the increased imports that were an indispensable part of the triumph of capitalism in the nineteenth century. The Third World made a significant contribution to solving that problem for the rich and became relatively poorer in the doing. And that is a major reason why there is a North and South today.

There were other reasons why this imperial expansion was so critical. It provided, as James Mill was to remark, "a vast system of outdoor relief for the Upper Classes." Even more significant was the fact that this expansion offered an escape for the millions who migrated to the Americas, Australia, Africa and Asia, in what may well have been the largest migratory movement in all human history. Consider, for example, what it would mean if contemporary India had other countries to which it could export at least some of its teeming masses. To be sure, many of those people went to the United States, Canada and Australia, i.e. to the "white Dominions," which never became part of the Third World. But many of them went to Latin America, and some to Africa and Asia. Again, it is not the absolute size of the numbers involved that is crucial, but the existence of one more link, one more factor, which made the rise of capitalism all the more easy.

But finally, let me emphasize that the crucial point here is not narrowly economic. One of the flaws in some of the classic theories of imperialism—say, the one that Lenin borrowed from Hilferding —is that they overgeneralized their specifically economic data. (Hilferding and Lenin put "finance capital" in the center of their analysis, which worked well enough in Germany but not at all in Britain.) For me what is basic is not this or that particular mechanism of expansion, but a system that had expansion and competition built into its very concept from the first moment on. It was not simply the capitalist economy that was at work in this history, but the capitalist psychology and ethic and—it must never be forgotten —the attendant capitalist racism. Europeans became, as V. G. Kiernan so well put it, "the lords of human kind." [4]

IV

Thus far, the villain of this analysis has been capitalism. Now, however, another possibility must be entertained: that the workers in the advanced economies have become the willing accomplices of the industrialists. This is a criticism of my point of view, and it comes from the Left, not the Right. It has been heard increasingly in recent years from Third World Marxists and their allies in the affluent North.

The idea is not new. As far back as 1915, the Bolshevik theorist, Nikolai Bukharin, went far beyond Lenin in considering this issue. Given the gigantic profits business was making in the colonies, Bukharin wrote, ". . . there is a possibility for raising the workers' wages at the expense of the exploited colonial savages and conquered peoples."

After all, the welfare state was pioneered by the protectionist Germany of Bismarck. And both Joan Robinson and Gunnar Myrdal have argued that to this very day this reformed version of capitalism is inherently expansionist. "*The welfare state*," Myrdal remarks, "*is nationalistic*, indeed very much more so than a laissez-faire type of state would be." On protectionism he adds, "*On this point, the people are the reactionaries*." Unfortunately, Myrdal supports these assertions with some very questionable sociology— that the Joe McCarthy movement was populist—but even discounting for that, his critique is a serious one and comes from a compassionate thinker who does not indulge in rhetorical extremism.

A much sharper formulation can be found in a paper Arghiri Emmanuel delivered at a Yugoslavian conference in 1976. If socialists were to come to power in the advanced countries, Emmanuel said, and were faithful to their pledge to equalize global living standards, then they "would not only have to expropriate the capitalists of the entire world, but also dispossess large sections of the working-class of the industrialized countries." On another occasion Emmanuel wrote: "It is not the conservatism of the leaders that has reigned in the revolutionary *élan* of the masses [in the advanced countries], as one believed in the Marxist-Leninist camp. It is the slow, but steady, coming to awareness of the masses that they belong to privileged, exploiting nations which constrained their leaders to revise their ideology so as not to lose their clientele."

Thus both Third World Marxists and Western democratic socialists raise the possibility of an imperialist working class in the global North. Is it real?

Yes and no. If I am right, and the Third World has been making involuntary contributions to Western economic success during the past four hundred years, then to the degree that the workers shared somewhat in the resultant growth, they have profited from the exploitation of the colonies. This gain, it must be immediately added, was not automatic. The profits went to the capitalists, and the workers in the metropolitan countries were able to get a share of them only in so far as they prevailed in a bitter economic and political struggle. To the extent that that did happen—and the welfare state is clear evidence that it did—labor was an unwitting, and very junior, partner in the exploitation of the world's poor.

Moreover, it is true that the AFL-CIO did shift toward protectionism in the 1960s and '70s. But the reason for that change requires that one qualify any statement about workers gaining from capitalist expansion. Labor loses in this process, too. Broadly put, it is an enormous advantage of capital in its confrontation with unions that it is the most mobile factor of production, able to flee to low-wage areas within the nation or abroad. This means that even when a company stays put, it is able to exact a price from its workers for that decision.

The Texas Instrument company provides a recent example of how this mobility factor can even be used against Third World workers. Texas Instruments had successfully resisted union organization in the United States, which meant that it was able to leave this country without any trouble from its own labor force. It went to Curacao in the Caribbean. There was a bitter struggle, including a strike supported by the International Metalworkers Federation, and the union not only gained recognition but also won a court suit against illegal firings. At that point, Texas Instruments moved on to Haiti. This kind of search for low-wage, nonunion labor has, of course, has a profound impact on workers in the United States.

As one of George Meany's key economic advisors pointed out, in 1971, 18 percent of steel sales, 24 percent of autos, 35 percent of television sets, 60 percent of phonographs, 86 percent of radios, almost all tape recorders, 60 percent of sewing machines and calculating machines, 80 percent of electronic microscopes and 33 percent of shoes were brought into this country from around the world. This obviously had a devastating impact on major unions, particularly those in consumer electronics (the International Union of Electrical Workers) and in apparel (the Amalgamated Clothing Workers and the International Ladies Garment Workers Union). In the Steelworkers, the third-largest union in the United States, one of the reasons advanced by the leadership for signing a no-strike agreement with management was the fear that a walkout would further increase the foreign share of the American steel market. On the other hand, 400,000 European workers, some of them in nationalized plants, suffered major losses because of American aerospace competition.

Secondly, it is important to note that the trend toward labor protectionism in the United States was a defensive maneuver, not an attempt to get higher living standards at the expense of Third World suffering. In particular, it was a function of the abysmally poor performance of the American economy, which saw chronic, high unemployment from 1969 on. Under those conditions, there is guaranteed to be a union push to solve the jobless problem by keeping work within the nation. But again, that is a way of maintaining living standards already won, not of improving them.

For example, the January 1977 *Federationist,* the official journal of the AFL-CIO, took up the question of "Labor's Stake in the World Economy." One article noted that Third World manufactured exports to the United States had risen from $2.5 billion to $6.6 billion between 1969 and 1975, thus taking jobs away from American workers "during the worst economic downturn in our recent history . . ." Another feared that the industrialization of the periphery would create a labor force in the United States split into extremes of the highly trained and the completely unskilled, with the middle, i.e., the majority of the present American working class, squeezed out. Indeed, the tone of the entire issue of the *Federationist* was defensive, worried, much more protectionist than it would have been in the Sixties when joblessness was on the decline.

That point leads to the most critical consideration in this area. In Emmanuel's image, a victorious socialist movement in an advanced country that wanted to redeem its pledge to the Third World would have to attack the privileges of its own working class if it were going to "equalize" incomes around the world. The first problem with that image is its apocalyptic character. Of course, it is impossible to instantly dismantle a system that has been built up over four hundred years. Equalization will be the work of a historic period, not an act of a single government on the morrow of a victory. And then there is a crucial question: what living standard is being equalized? The American? But it contains an enormous amount of waste that is designed, precisely, to maintain capitalism. If one hypothesizes a historic trend toward democratic socialism, that standard would become less costly as it simultaneously becomes more rational.

And that points to the heart of the matter. Capitalism, as this and the next chapter show, requires international inequality as a precondition for its contradictory existence. A society of democratically planned full employment and production for use—socialism—would not. It is at least possible—not guaranteed by some benign historic inevitability, but possible—that socialist governments in the advanced economies could participate in a globally planned increase in real, and often un-American, living standards. At the Congress of the Socialist International in Geneva in 1976, the leaders of the European social democratic and labor parties resolved to do precisely that. It is, of course, easy to pass such a resolution and extremely difficult to implement it. My point is that the practical politicians of the European Left, who are not given to flights of ideological fantasy or utopianism, thought both that they should, and that they could, do these things.

For instance, in the winter of 1977 there was pressure within the Common Market, from labor as well as from capital, to get protectionist measures against Third World textile imports, which, it was said, had taken away 430,000 European jobs. But that move was clearly and directly related to the abysmal performance of those countries in the years since an international pact was signed permitting that textile trade in 1973. If one assumes that the boom-and-bust cycles which are inherent in capitalism are a "natural" necessity, then it may well be that workers will participate in "beggar thy neighbor" policies along with business. But if one thinks, as I do, that planning and laws guaranteeing displaced workers jobs or incomes can overcome these necessities, then the victory of the working class in the advanced countries would make it possible for it to behave humanely on a global scale.

The relationship of the Western workers to the process I have described in this chapter is thus somewhat ambiguous. They have benefited in some cases along with "their" capitalists, but to a much more modest degree than some of the formulations suggest. Secondly, they, too, have suffered from the expansion of capital. And thirdly, they do not have any inherent commitment to global wrongdoing, and a socialist politics could move forward to the creation of a better world if—but only if—it were willing to transform basic capitalist structures.[5]

V

Am I, then, saying that the capitalist North is imperialist? As a matter of American political rhetoric, no. As a matter of serious theoretical analysis, yes.

The term, imperialism, is a hopeless muddle as far as commonplace speech goes. Many people confuse it with colonialism—that is, with actual political-military domination of one country by another. Understood in that way, there is practically no capitalist imperialism in the world today. (But there is a good argument that the Soviets have something like an old-fashioned colonial relationship with Eastern Europe.) But, then, even those who are more sophisticated and conceive of imperialism as a system that can operate through markets and investments rather than through gunboats and viceroys do not necessarily get the matter right. A good many of them—including the overwhelming majority of those influenced by Marxism around the world—assume that Lenin's popular booklet is the last word on the subject. But, as I have already indicated, that analysis is outmoded on a number of basic counts and, in any case, was inferior to the work of Luxemburg, Hilferding and Bukharin in its own day.*

To complicate this last difficulty, many of the simplifiers and shouters in the anti-Vietnam-war movement of the sixties and early seventies—a movement that was transcendently right in its opposition to America's intervention in that unconscionable war—used the term as ritualistic cant. Some of them even embraced the caricature of Lenin on imperialism put forward by his more ignorant disciples and sophisticated enemies. They argued that there was oil off the Indochinese coast and that this was the real reason for the American presence, assuming a mechanistic, one-to-one relationship between foreign policy and corporate economic interest. Moreover, if the United States was, as the ultra-Left rhetoricians said, absolutely foredoomed to do evil in the world until there was a socialist revolution, and if that revolution was not, and is not, exactly imminent, then the practical implications of this seemingly radical theory are either quietism or a despairing terrorism.

So in terms of everyday political discourse, I would not use the word *imperialism* to describe America, since it is almost certain to be misunderstood. But when it is a case of presenting a worked-out analysis to an audience concerned enough to read a book, it is important to stress that the term, if properly defined, does indeed apply to this country. America is the key nation in a planetary economic system that, in good times and bad, reproduces the relations of domination and inferiority that are so dramatically visible in the North-South gap. The foundations of this system were laid by protocapitalist adventurers, slave traders and pillagers as well as by entrepreneurs and scientific geniuses between the sixteenth and eighteenth centuries. Then in a development that was less dramatic and more important than that often bloody process of capital accumulation, the capitalist economies deepened and institutionalized their original advantage by means of the world market of the nineteenth century. The content of that

* For instance, in a scholarly debate among economic historians—the "Robinson and Gallagher controversy"—which has been going on since 1953, all sides seem to be unaware of the fact that the "anti-Marxist" theory in the dispute closely conforms to Rosa Luxemburg's Marxist theory of imperialism.

structure persists to this day, even though there have been many changes in form.

I think that such a history—and present structure—are fairly called imperialist if, but only if, all the proper qualifications are made. Even if there are the practical difficulties with that term that I have already noted, I would hope that serious political leaders in this country would begin to talk about the reality that it describes. The choice of language is not critical as long as the words communicate the fact that this country is the beneficiary of a systemic, unjust, self-perpetuating advantage.

The fact, then, is as Hannah Arendt, a determined critic of Marxism, stated it:

Imperialism was born when the ruling class in capitalist production came up against national limits to its economic expansion. The bourgeoisie turned to politics out of economic necessity; for if it did not want to give up the capitalist system, whose inherent law is constant economic growth, it had to impose this law upon its home governments and to proclaim expansion to be the ultimate political goal of foreign policy.

But there is another, almost startling admission on this count. It came from Henry Kissinger when he was still the Secretary of State, and it admitted the basic thesis of the history outlined in this chapter—with one huge exception. Kissinger told a New York audience in 1976,

In the nineteenth century the Industrial Revolution gave birth to improved communications, technological innovations and new forms of business organization which immeasurably expanded man's capacity to exploit the frontiers and territories of the entire globe. *In less than one generation one fifth of the land area of the planet and one tenth of its inhabitants were gathered into the domain of imperial powers in an unrestrained scramble for colonies. The costs—in affront to human dignity, in material waste and deprivation, and in military conflict and political turbulence—haunt us still.* [Emphasis added.]

That past, Kissinger also said, had been marked by "unrestrained commercial rivalry, mounting political turmoil, and eventually military conflict." [6]

Kissinger had not become a Leninist. Instead, he was following a classic conservative strategy: Admit last generation's evil in order to build confidence in this generation's reformed status quo. The apologists of present power will sometimes even exaggerate how bad things used to be during the reign of the apologists of past power, in order to point out how fine they are now, a tactic that the apologists of the future will no doubt employ in their turn. But the point of this book, and the specific thrust of the next chapter, is to say that the history that has just been described is very much alive right now.

Chapter Five "The Development of Underdevelopment"

The forms of Northern domination over the South have changed from time to time, but the basic content has persisted throughout four hundred years. This chapter views that long process from a specifically contemporary point of view, outlining the structure of global injustice as it exists in the late twentieth century. That will require some historical references, of course, but the focus will be upon the present, not the past.

In part, I proceed in this way because there are new theories responding to new data. Up to World War II, it was still possible to believe—as both Marxists and neoclassical economists did— that capitalist expansion would develop the Third World. It might do so in an outrageous, exploitative way, but still the result would be development. Since World War II, it has become clear to a number of serious thinkers that this is not the case. Most of them have been Marxists, but there are representatives of the established wisdom, like John Hicks and Hyla Myint, who agree with them on some crucial questions. Indeed, a book written to debunk the Marxists, *The Question of Imperialism,* by Benjamin A. Cohen, corroborates their recent work on every important point (it simplistically caricatures the older Marxist arguments, but that is another matter).

There is, then, a post-World War II understanding of what André Gunder Frank calls "the development of underdevelopment." Here, for example, is Samir Amin's version of this theme:

As economic growth progresses, each of the characteristics by which the structure of the periphery is defined is not attenuated, but on the contrary is accentuated. So at the center, growth *is* development—that is, it integrates; at the periphery, growth *is not* development, because it disarticulates. In a very real sense, at the periphery, growth based on integration in the world market is the development of underdevelopment.

Before exploring these ideas, an important qualification has to be made. This theory is extremely brilliant in its negatives, explaining why the Third World does not develop. It is, unfortunately, much more modest in the depth and sureness of its positive proposals. I present these concepts, then, not as the final and ultimate truth, but as a significant way station. That does not mean that I am agnostic about what should be done. There is a theoretical divide about as wide as the chasm that separates the rich countries from the poor, and I do not have the least doubt on which side of it I stand. But it is precisely because of my confidence on this score that I can afford to be candid about what I assume to be the temporary weaknesses of the position I defend. We know about what is wrong better than how to make it right.

I

Let me begin this outline of the institutions of international inequity with a few definitions. That is not a matter of formalities, but it touches upon a fundamental, underlying concept: *that underdevelopment is not a "thing."*

What is critical to underdevelopment is not some physical fact but a world economic structure that perpetuates backwardness. For instance, it is often said that the poor countries suffer because they are agricultural and raw-material, rather than industrial, producers. But, then, wheat is a "primary" commodity and one of the most important American exports. In the United States, that business is dominated by five firms, which control 85 percent of the grain shipments abroad. Two of them, Cargill and Continental, each have 25 percent of the market, and if Cargill weren't a privately held company, it would be the twenty-seventh-largest corporation among *Fortune's* five hundred industrials, outranking Bethlehem Steel and Lockheed. Both Continental and Cargill are currently (1977) involved in a scandal that charges that they did, among other things, "embezzle, steal, take away and conceal by fraud with intent to convert to their own use" grain bought by India.

It should not have come as a surprise, then, that Jimmy Carter's Secretary of Agriculture, Bob Bergland, proposed what might be called the Organization of Wheat Exporting Countries in 1977. Modeling himself on OPEC, Bergland proposed that the United States and Canada, which control 75 percent of the commercial wheat exports, should join together to set the world price. The purpose of this move, as Bergland described it, was to "shave off the peaks and valleys" of fluctuating wheat prices, i.e. to do for the First World commodity precisely what the Third World wants to do for their commodities. When challenged on the grounds that this policy would violate basic American principles, Bergland correctly replied that the idea of an international free market is a "dream world." He did not, of course, add that the United States has used all of its power for a generation to force the poor of the globe to observe the rules of that dream.

In short, wheat functions within the American economy just like any other oligopoly product and promotes general economic growth as much as a sophisticated manufactured item. So, to take another example, what differentiates American from Egyptian cotton is not the boll but the economic structure within which it is grown.

The Third World, another argument says, is composed of countries dominated by foreign capital; the advanced economies are not. Only India has a relatively low percentage of foreign investment, and is abysmally poor, while Canada leads the world as a "host" to moneys from abroad and is affluent. The United States, according to one 1973 report, owns 45 percent of Canada's manufacture, 56 percent of its mining and smelting and 60 percent of its oil and natural gas. That, I think, is intolerable on many grounds but it does not make Canada impoverished any more than India's relative freedom from foreign investment makes it wealthy. It is not the presence or absence of foreign investment that is decisive, but the way in which the society is organized. The same amount of money, even an identical plant, can have a completely different effect in two different national systems. Again, it is the system that is crucial.

Industrialization, some believe, is the sign of a developed economy. But then Hong Kong is more industrialized than the United States, since it devotes 41.4 percent of its labor force and 38 percent of its output to manufacture, while the corresponding figures for this country are 26.5 percent and 28 percent. Only, Hong Kong specializes in the low-wage production of products that are no longer profitable for the better-paid labor force and high technology of the United States. So it is not industrialization per se, but the type of industrialization and the nature of the economy in which it occurs, that are critical.

Finally, it is well known that it is the superior productivity of the factories in the metropolitan centers that guarantees their advantage as against the more backward technology of the periphery. After all, not only Marx, but also Adam Smith and David Ricardo insisted on the point—and in any case it makes good sense. Indeed, it was once true; only, it does not hold now. Writing on the basis of 1966 figures, Samir Amin estimated that of $35 billion in underdeveloped-country exports, $26 billion, or just under 75 percent, came from ultra-modern sectors. A brand-new, highly innovative plant will have a cumulative and integrated expansionary effect in the United States; in India, or even in Brazil, it will create an enclave of modernity, and the "spread effects" will be limited.

Thus it was that a 1972 World Bank study found that the productivity of labor and capital in some of the poor countries is *higher* than in the advanced economies. This is one more stunning refutation of the thesis that the structure of the world economy is determined by "natural" disadvantages. When it is profitable to do so, multinationals demonstrate that the people of the South can run the best machines of the North.

So, underdevelopment cannot be defined in terms of "things"— of agriculture or industry or foreign capital or productivity. It is an economic structure that gives these "things" a perverse quality, which they do not possess in an advanced society. Therefore, there is a limited value to an inventory of the characteristics of the South. It is true that most of these societies tend to experience urbanization without industrialization and therefore produce huge slums on the edges of their cities; that the most export-oriented among them tend to be specialized in one or two commodities and so are extremely vulnerable to fluctuations in just a few markets; that income and wealth are even more badly distributed in poor nations than in rich; and so on. One can compile almost endless lists of aspects of underdevelopment—lists that are all but worthless if the dynamic in which they function is ignored.

For example, Simon Kuznets, a man of enormous and genuine accomplishment in his field, summarizes the marks of underdevelopment, but omits to even mention the international domination of the South, which trades mainly with the rich, who trade mainly among themselves. This error is typical of academic social science, even when practiced by a genius like Kuznets. One classifies, but without illuminating the concepts that make the definitions possible; one identifies hidden empirical uniformities, sometimes showing great ingenuity in the process, but they are then assumed to be their own explanation rather than that which is to be explained. As Hegel said of this procedure long ago, it presents the table of contents and dispenses with the book. Thus, I will not concentrate on sorting out the characteristics that afflict the South but will proceed toward the analysis of the structures which give the characteristics their meaning.[1]

II

There is a historical thesis that applies most particularly to Africa, but is also revelant to the rest of the Third World: *The structure of underdevelopment today results from a growth process that was induced from the outside rather than generated from within.*

There is still a hot academic debate over exactly how and why capitalism developed *within* feudalism, eventually replacing that system. But there is no doubt that it was, in the main, an internal process. That transition was hardly a harmonious, peaceful affair. It was carried out at the cost of great human suffering, was punctuated by rising civil wars and restorations, and was culminated in huge, dirty, disease-ridden cities. Some of its equilibrium mechanisms were grisly: cholera helped maintain a rough balance between available humans and job openings. And yet, although the transformation was not planned, it had an inner logic that came from the emergent system itself. To put a complicated and crucial idea in compressed form, the social forces that dispossessed peasants were also creating a need for a working class that was recruited from the ranks of those driven from the land.

John Hicks, an eminent mainstream economist, points out that innovation was often labor-saving during the Industrial Revolution. That created unemployment. But it also gave rise to profits, which would finance expansion and increase the demand for labor. But the situation was quite different in the international economy, even during the heyday of free trade.

For the labor that is thrown out may be in one country and the expansion in demand for labor which is the effect of the accumulation of capital that results may be in another. The English weavers, who were replaced by textile machinery, could (in the end and after much travail) find re-employment in England; but what of the Indian weavers who were displaced by the same improvement?

Let's generalize this point. Growth in the periphery was stimulated by the penetration of alien capital into a stagnant economy. Only part of the society was drawn into the web of monetary relations—the part that was brought to life to serve some of the specific needs of the metropolitan power. If the peasant in this sector did acquire some buying power in the process, he did not spend it on the home market, which did not exist. He had to import. Within European or American capitalism, the exchange between the city and the countryside had a multiplier effect throughout the entire society; on the periphery, the city and the countryside were two different nations.

Moreover, in Europe, capitalism marked the triumph of the industrialist over the landlord, of profits (which are the reward for energetic entrepreneurs) over rents, the return to passive, parasitic landlords (of whom Ricardo contemptuously said, they grow rich in their sleep). But on the periphery, local wealth, if it existed, tended to be land, and it was the rent collectors who benefited from the partial commercialization of agriculture. They spent their gains, not on investing in national capitalism, but in importing luxury goods from the advanced economy. However, it should be noted that this selfish, wasteful decision was quite rational in such a society.

Given the limited domestic market on the periphery, there was no basis for a vigorous internal industrialization. So why invest? And when investment did take place, it was complementary to that of foreign capital, not competitive with it. When this process began, the real wages at the center and at the periphery were roughly equal—that is, they were subsistence wages. But, then, as the outsiders penetrated more deeply into the economy, ruining the artisanate with cheap manufactured goods, but not, as in Europe, providing new employments for those thus displaced, there was a tremendous "oversupply" of labor. This, it should be noted, is not a demographic fact of nature, but an artificial construct of the way in which development was introduced from without. As a result, the wage gap between center and periphery began to widen, and that, in turn, made an internally sustained development even more of an impossibility.

One way of dealing with this complex process is to reduce it to one of those abstractions that classify in the guise of explaining. The underdeveloped society, we are told, is "dualistic." That can be put in a number of ways. Economists focus upon the great differences in productivity between the sectors; sociologists describe the "traditional" and "modern" spheres and speculate on how the rigidities of the former inhibit the emergence of the latter. Sometimes, these definitions are actually put into the context of a dynamic theory, one that sees dualism as a necessary stage on the road to full development.

But what the dualism notion sorely misses is any concept of the whole. From the point of view of foreign capital, the traditional and modern sectors of the underdeveloped economy are marvelously integrated. The subsistence farming, extended family practices and the constant back-and-forth movement between the traditional spheres are precisely what make it possible to have such low wages in the modern sphere. Moreover, a point that both Marx and Lenin failed to understand, the metropolitan nation does not want an industrialized competitor on the periphery. The "dualism" within the underdeveloped society is thus an integrating element for the world market. It helps to keep everyone in his "proper place."

One way of summarizing the present impact of these historical trends is to say: *Underdeveloped societies are not internally coherent.*

Hyla Myint defined this insight from a mainstream economic perspective; his point of view is, on this count, the same as the neo-Marxists. The precapitalist traditional societies were poor, stagnant and backward, but they did not suffer from economic discontent and frustration, because "wants and activities were on the whole adapted to each other, and the people were in equilibrium with their environment." But once they were "opened up," that coherence was destroyed. A nutrition expert gives an example. The Mayans in Guatemala lived on corn and beans, supplemented by fruits, vegetables and meat from wild animals. They were even careful to allow tilled patches of forest to lie fallow so that they could reconstitute themselves. Then the Spaniards came. They cleared the ground for coffee and beef and thereby destroyed the possibility of an adequate diet; their progress brought malnutrition.

Samir Amin makes the same point with regard to India: "Pre-colonial India was a society (or societies) which was coherent, characterized by a correspondence between its various structures (economic and others), and which, for this reason, could be analyzed and understood in itself. Modern India is incomprehensible outside of its eternal relations." Obviously all nations, even the most powerful, are part of an interconnected world system. American Secretaries of State never weary of emphasizing that fact when they want to urge moderation on the Third World. They do not add that the economic structures of some nations—the advanced capitalist powers, for the most part—are determined by their own history and therefore are structurally interrelated; while the economic structures of other nations—the poor—were determined by alien history and lack an internal coherence of their own.

Here is Samir Amin's description of the contemporary result of all this:

the "developed" economy constitutes an integrated whole, character-ized by a flow of internal exchanges which are quite dense, while the flow of external exchanges of the atoms which compose the whole are, in the main, marginal compared to the internal exchanges. By contrast, the "underdeveloped" economy is composed of atoms which are, relatively speaking, juxtaposed, not integrated, and the density of the external exchange of these atoms is relatively greater than that of the internal exchanges.

Therefore, Amin concludes, you cannot really speak of "national" economies in the poor world. There is a national economic space, but, economically speaking, not a nation.

So it is that these structures give rise to a vicious circle, a coherent incoherence. As Ragnar Nurske described the process, on the supply side there is a low rate of capital saving because there are low incomes because there is low productivity (throughout the entire economy but not in the modern export sector) because there is not enough capital. And on the demand side, there is no inducement to invest, because of the low buying power in the society as a result of the low productivity that derives from the lack of capital, which results from the fact that there is no inducement to invest.

This first theory, then, emphasizes the historical genesis of underdevelopment as a crucial factor in giving it the structure it has today. Because growth is induced from the outside, and not from within, the economy becomes subordinate to the foreign capital that called it into a new life. It therefore lacks the reciprocal interactions that are necessary if there is to be self-sustained growth. This system is disintegrative from the point of view of those who live in it, and integrative from the perspective of those who dominate the world. Next, we shall see how the resultant alien priorities are often internalized by those whom they afflict. This is not necessarily because these people have "sold out"; it is also because the foreign priorities, and only they, make sense in a framework that was designed to accommodate and perpetuate them. In short, it becomes rational to be irrational—for the leadership of a poor country to voluntarily preserve the conditions of its own economic inferiority.[2]

III

This thesis was developed primarily in response to Latin-American history, although it applies to countries throughout the world: *the upper classes in the impoverished lands often subordinate them-*

selves, politically and culturally, to the rulers of the affluent countries.

Between the 1820s and the 1850s, some of the newly independent Latin-American countries seemed to be heading toward a classic capitalist takeoff.* There were domestic industries, national-flag shipping, some of the old mines were opened up under local ownership, and so on. But that trend was frustrated and one of the reasons had to do with lineup of social class forces within the countries involved. This factor is at work to this very day.

One way of putting the historical point is to say that in much of Latin America, the South won the equivalent of our Civil War. Three basic classes confronted one another. The agricultural, mining and commercial interests wanted to keep an export-oriented structure, for the obvious reason that it would bring them profit. This, in North American terms, was the Confederate, or Free Trade, party. Then there were the industrializers who, like the Union forces in the United States, stood for protectionism. And finally, there were the British, who in this case, as in our Civil War, supported the Southerners. The British Foreign Secretary Canning put the matter with cynical candor in 1824. "Spanish America," he said, "is free; and if we do not mismanage our affairs sadly, she is English." That is, Canning was shrewd enough to understand the truth that became so apparent after the post-World War II decolonizations: that national and economic independence are by no means synonymous, that political freedom can be a mask for material subjection.

The South won in Latin America. As Frank describes part of that event,

The metropolitan powers aided their Latin-American junior trade partners with arms, naval blockades and, where necessary, direct military intervention and instigation of new wars, such as that against Paraguay, which lost six out of seven members of its male population in the defense of its nationally financed railroad and genuinely independent, autonomously generated development effort.

* In this section, I rely heavily on André Gunder Frank's *Capitalism and Underdevelopment in Latin America.* That study is controversial in respect to some issues—how capitalism and feudalism are described, for instance—but these are not relevant to my theme here. Moreover, I find Frank's basic thesis on the Latin ruling class corroborated by authorities like Raymond Vernon, Michael Barret-Brown and Karl Deutsch.

Even so, a country like Argentina, Karl Deutsch notes, had a high standard of living in 1900. But once again, the merchants and landlords made an alliance with the imperial interests in the advanced economies and frustrated their own economic independence.

This pattern persists to this day, but now it has a cultural, as well as an economic, dimension. As Celso Furtado, a brilliant Latin analyst of underdevelopment, has emphasized, in these countries the living standards of the upper classes are based on those of the affluent in the richest economies. They satisfy their desires in one of two ways, both of them profoundly antidevelopmental. Either they import luxury goods, which is an enormous drain on hard currency and channels needed resources into domestic waste and foreign profit, or, when the tactic of "import substitution" is adopted as a way of achieving internal growth, the upper class's tastes still decide what is going to be produced. Now, instead of importing their luxuries, they see to it that they are manufactured locally. The problem is that the capital intensity of such undertakings—the technological investment per worker—is thereby determined, not by the needs of the poor society, but by the reflected priorities of the rich in the advanced countries.

Furtado's insight was elaborated to deal with the Latin-American evidence. Yet the process that he identified is at work in India, as one of the economists at the conference at Gopalpur told me. And it is an important fact of life throughout the Third World that the rich are richer there than in the affluent economies. In Kuznets' estimate, the top 5 percent in the underdeveloped nations get between 30 percent and 40 percent of before-tax cash income. This is not merely a sign of maldistributed wealth; it is also a mechanism for imposing the desires of that parasitic class upon the society in a way that works against development.

Latin America, then, helped to lock itself into a relationship of dependency upon the major powers. Through the connivance of the conservative section of its own upper class with an imperial bourgeoisie in the advanced countries, it "voluntarily" accepted an emphasis upon an export production that offered gains for some but involved only the most minimal changes in production methods. The advanced countries got the dynamic sectors; Latin America had plantations, mines and industrial enclaves. And in more recent times, the Latin ruling classes have reinforced this pattern by a cultural mimicry that had further antidevelopmental effects.[3]

These structures laid the basis for an important and dramatic phenomenon of the post-World War II years: *the flow of money from the poor to the rich.*

IV

The way in which the terms of trade have transferred wealth from the impoverished to the affluent during the post-World War II years was the great discovery of the United Nations Conference on Trade and Development (UNCTAD). The research was done by scholars like Raoul Prebish, UNCTAD's first Secretary General, and Celso Furtado. It then became a central political theme of Third World diplomats and it is the theoretical inspiration for one of their crucial demands, a system that would smooth out the wild fluctuations in commodity prices. This thesis contains a most important truth, but it is sometimes overgeneralized.

According to the International Monetary Fund and the UN's Economic Commission on Latin America, between 1951 and 1966, taking 1950 prices as a base year and omitting Cuba from the calculation, the Latin-American countries lost $26.3 billion through a deterioration in the terms of trade. That means that the prices received for their exports fell, and those paid for imports rose, with a resultant gap of $26.3 billion. This phenomenon, it should be noted, is recognized by both radical and mainstream theorists, and one anti-Marxist writer even argues that the traditionalists identified it first, with the Left only belatedly picking up, and exaggerating, their finding.

These data must be used carefully, which is not always the case. On the one hand, neo-Leninists have sometimes used this thesis casually, without even noting that it contradicts the central assertion in Lenin's analysis, that the developed capitalisms must export capital, not, as in this case, import it. On the other hand, UNCTAD writers sometimes argue as if this is *the* mechanism promoting underdevelopment. This overlooks the fact that, during long periods in the nineteenth and twentieth centuries, the terms of trade were favorable to the poor countries and that, as Ernest Mandel has pointed out, the corporations importing raw materials in the metropolitan countries worked hard to see that this would be so. The point is that even then they did not escape from their inferiority, but only reinforced it.

And then, if one makes the terms of trade the prime, or sole, villain, that implies that if only "fair" prices are paid for Southern exports, then the problem of world poverty will be solved. In fact, as I documented earlier, the relative poverty of the poor countries was not significantly affected by the good years in the early seventies. Indeed, that will become even more dramatically apparent when we look at financial flows in a moment.

But we do have solid figures which show that, since 1953, the terms of trade have usually been turned against the starving and in favor of the affluent. Moreover, it is at least possible that the post-World War II period marks a structural change in the world economy. The system is now dominated by gigantic multinational corporations with an enormous ability to control prices, jump over the tariff walls of the impoverished in order to rob them of their "comparative advantage" and discover synthetic substitutions for primary commodities which weaken the latter's market position. At the least, even if one denies that such a permanent shift has taken place, it is clear that the international economy has been transferring resources from the desperate to the privileged during the better part of the last generation. And one instrument of that outrage is found in the terms of trade.

A second, and related point, is that foreigners actually control a significant share of the economic activity in the poor lands. This has many consequences, some of which will surface in a discussion of Brazil later on in this chapter. However, the aspect of this reality that is particularly relevant here has to do with the export of profits from the periphery to the center. For instance, between 1950 and 1965, the United States' direct investment in Latin America amounted to $3.8 billion, and income going back to this country added up to $11.3 billion. That was a clear gain of $7.5 billion for the United States over a fifteen-year period.

Repatriated profits are, however, only the most obvious part of this perverse flow of wealth. The Third World nations have to pay, in licensing fees and other ways, for the technology that they get from the rich. The UN currently estimates that charge at between three and five billion dollars a year. If the "demonstration effect"— that cultural mimicry of affluent waste and luxury—is at work, that charge may include hard currency paid out for the "proprietary knowledge" of how to make Colonel Sanders Kentucky Fried Chicken. (I have in mind a Sanders' outlet on Kenyatta Boulevard in Nairobi.)

Finally, a vicious circle is set in motion. Because of the losses suffered through the unfavorable terms of trade and the outflow of profit and fees to the advanced economies, the Third World finds itself short of cash. Note that this is not that they have failed to produce substantial wealth. They have. Only, the structure of the world market has, by perfectly legal means, taken billions of that wealth away from them. So they have to borrow. This became a particularly acute problem in the seventies, when the quadrupled price of oil hit the balance-of-payments situation of the nonpetroleum poor countries harder than anyone else. In 1973, their deficit was $12 billion; in 1975, $45 billion; and it is expected to stay in that latter range for the foreseeable future.

Wassily Leontiev's UN Commission provides a summary and stunning statistic. In 1970, the underdeveloped countries had a net capital inflow of $2.6 billion, but paid out $7.9 billion on foreign investments. In short, they lost $5.3 billion.

So, the statement made by Gabriel Valdés at the White House in 1969 still holds:

It is generally believed that our continent is receiving real aid in financial matters. The figures demonstrate the contrary. We can affirm that Latin America is contributing to financing the development of the United States and the other industrial nations. Private investments have signified, and signify today, for all of Latin America that the funds which are taken out of our continent are many times greater than those which are invested in it. Our potential capital is impoverished. The benefits of the invested capital grow and multiply enormously, not in our countries but abroad. The so-called aid, with all the conditions we know so well, means trade and more development for the developed economies, but certainly has not succeeded in compensating us for the sums which leave Latin America in paying foreign debt and as a result of the profits which private direct investment generates. In a word, we are becoming conscious that Latin America gives more than it receives.[4]

V

There is an exceedingly complex theory that offers another important insight into underdevelopment. It is based on a huge, easily accessible, fact: that wages in the Third World are but a fraction of those in the advanced economies, yet about two thirds of the exports from the poor countries are produced under conditions of extremely high productivity. *These low-wage and high-productivity sectors are another mechanism for the transfer of wealth from the hungry to the affluent.*

Given the design of this book, there is no point in even beginning to explore all the intricacies of this analysis.* However, the essential can be put rather simply and it is most worth stating.

In the classical theory of foreign trade, it was understood—by Ricardo as well as by Marx—that a certain unequal exchange was taking place. Crudely put, but I think accurately, a country with very high productivity received a bonus from a country with low productivity, for the latter had to work much harder, to surrender more hours of labor time, in an exchange with the former. Like the inventor who enjoyed a temporary monopoly over an innovation and could sell his product more cheaply than his competitors and yet at a higher mark-up, the advanced economy benefited from its technological edge. That concept is more than a century and a half old and even the mainstream economists use it—adding only that everyone, including the poor, low-productivity nation, benefits from this unfair exchange.

There is, a neo-Marxist theory holds, a new form of exploitation that differs from this classic case. When United Fruit goes into Central America, Unilever into Malaysia, Firestone into Africa, they operate with the most modern methods. And yet the wages in such countries average from 4 percent to 15 percent of those in the United States. What has to be explained, as Emmanuel put it,

* The stimulus for the discussion, which has taken place mainly in France, came from a book, *L'Échange inégal,* by a most heterodox Marxist, A. Emmanuel. It has been exhaustively criticized (and sometimes supported) by writers like Charles Bettelheim, Christan Palloix and Samir Amin. It has certain resemblances to non-Marxist analyses, most notably that of Raoul Prebish.

is not the difference between the wage of an American metalworker who uses a million-dollar press and the wage of a Brazilian plantation worker who wields a machete. It is easy enough to find reasons, both good and bad, for that gap. But why it is that a mason who builds a suburban New York bungalow gets thirty times as much as a Lebanese who builds the same house in the same way?

I will only note that there are important parts of Emmanuel's answer that I think are wrong—an overly facile analogizing of Marx's theory of "prices of production" within a national economy to the world economy; a tendency to see high wages in the North as the prime cause of low wages in the South and therefore to pit the workers in those areas against one another; and so on.* But the question is brilliant, and so is part of his response (as well as the explication of it by Samir Amin). The critical point is that the high-productivity sectors of the Third World exist within societies dominated by subsistence economy. Therefore, labor is always cheap.

Up until the 1880s, wages in the emergent capitalist powers of Europe fluctuated around the subsistence level, too. The classical economist Jevons computed that the real wages in ancient Greece were roughly comparable to what an unskilled worker received in the nineteenth century. But then laissez faire came to an effective end, monopoly took over, price competition became less important, and capitalism took giant strides toward the periphery. Under these circumstances, the workers were able to organize and increase their wages. Meanwhile, the pay in the poor countries, as Hyla Myint put it, "fossilized." The result was not simply a personal injustice to people who, in the foreign-owned or -controlled sectors, were very productive, but one more profound inhibition to economic development.

The point has been dramatically annotated by Amin. The 1966

---

* In the fierce debate among Marxists over this theory, I find the sociology and economic history much more valuable than the attempt to fit the issue into the classic Marxist formulas of the labor theory of value. When, for instance, Ernest Mandel turns to such equations, he seems to me to take a roundabout way to conclude that economies with high investments of capital per worker use less labor per unit of output than those with low levels of capital, a fact which hardly requires illumination from *Das Kapital*. But when Mandel, and the rest of the unequal-exchange discussants, focus on the function of cheap labor on the periphery, they are on to a crucial variable.

exports of the Third World were worth $35 billion on the market. If the workers in those economies had been paid at the rates prevailing in advanced countries, the value would have been $57 billion. As a result, there were those who were thus enabled to sell these cheap goods at high prices—for the most part, the multinational corporations, which run the modern industries in poor countries. They received from underpaid workers a subsidy worth $22 billion in a single year. This transfer, Amin very rightly emphasizes, is "marginal" for the metropolitan powers at the center. It is *not* the cause of their prosperity, which is what Emmanuel implies. But that same transfer is of disastrous consequence for the poor.

Let me translate these abstractions into a homely example. An American employer, say a dress manufacturer or a producer of consumer electronics, ships work to Mexico or Taiwan or Hong Kong. The wage bill drops enormously; but the price of the product, when it is reimported into the United States, does not. It is sold at levels appropriate to an automobile-buying, steak-eating economy; it is manufactured by the consumers of tortillas and rice. If, however, that "host" country wants to import American goods, whether they be luxuries for the ruling classes or machines for industrialization, it must pay auto-and-steak prices for them.

In a capitalist power during the period of industrialization, low wages were a perverse blessing. They were the source of the high profits, which were invested in development, which eventually created both a militant working class and a level of production capable of satisfying at least some of its demands. But in the Third World enclaves of modernity, one gets sudden injections of high technology into otherwise backward, subsistence societies. Part of the profits are siphoned off by the multinationals, by means of high prices and low wages. And even if the government gets a portion of that subsidy, the conditions for reinvesting it are not at all favorable, since there is no proportionality between productivity and the effective ability of the society to consume, between the modern enclave and the traditional society. Here again, it is the structure that is decisive: low wages had a positive effect in the North, but they institutionalize underdevelopment in the South.[5]

Finally, that surplus population that inhibits development in the poor countries has a by-product that contributes to the affluence of the rich nations. The superfluous workers from the Third World are forced to migrate temporarily from the periphery to the center. In West Germany, they are called *Gastarbeiter* ("guest workers"), a euphemism if ever there was one. In 1971, there were 3 million of them in that country, mainly recruited from the impoverished Southern fringe of Europe (Spain, Portugal, Greece, Yugoslavia—Austrian, Dutch and French workers were not juridically treated in this category). Typically, they worked cleaning streets, digging graves, collecting garbage and, the women among them, as chars. They are extremely useful as a labor reserve, since they can be sent home in fairly short order when there is an economic downturn, and this saves the society the welfare cost of normal domestic unemployment. About 300,000 of them left Germany during the recession of 1967.

In France, they are the *sous-prolétariat* ("subproletariat") and count North Africans among their number as well as Spaniards and Portuguese. They live in *bidonvilles* and are doubly exploited, as workers and as members of a despised group. In Britain, many of these people come from the former Commonwealth countries, including Indians expelled from African countries, like Uganda, as the victims of national and race prejudice.

In the United States, they are called "illegals," and no one knows how many of them there are, for obvious reasons. It is clear, however, that the official statistics on the population of a city like New York are substantially falsified, because the census does not enumerate them. Congressman Herman Badillo, the representative from the Puerto Rican districts of that City, told me once that everyone in the *Barrio* can recognize the illegals (who are not Puerto Ricans, with a legal right of entry, but Haitians, Dominicans, and natives of most of the countries of Latin America) because they are the ones who do jobs on the run, for less than the official minimum. On the West Coast they are usually Mexicans and sometimes Chinese.

The phenomenon of "surplus" population in the Third World, then, does not merely mean that the First World contracts its dirty work out to the periphery. That is often the case, of course. But in addition, we import these people into the wealthy societies, and thus re-create the international caste system within the very heart of those economies that like to refer to themselves as "advanced."

VI

Finally, Brazil presents a particularly compelling example of these trends in action. It is the largest and potentially richest of all the underdeveloped nations. If even it exhibits the mechanisms I have just described, then the overwhelming majority of the poor countries, which do not have such favorable auspices, are certainly subject to them.

For *The Wall Street Journal,* the difference between Brazil and Peru (before the latter abandoned its military radicalism and succumbed to the power of the international bankers) is that "Brazil has opted to tie its economic future to the market economy instead of pursuing the grail of state socialism." To be sure, the *Journal* adds, this dictatorship has "serious political and social shortcomings" (a euphemism for repression and torture—which calls to mind the Soviet description of a quarter of a century of totalitarian terror as the "cult of the personality"). But Brazil is basically on the right track. Its "prescription for economic equality is not to equalize misery, as so many of the socialist governments do, but to increase production for the eventual benefit of everyone."

That is dreamy, dogmatic nonsense. Consider just a few of the facts.

In 1976, *The New York Times* reported that Brazil's $2 billion debt now required 40 percent of export income for servicing. One reason, the *Times* said, was that during the boom period—the "miracle" of 10 percent annual growth that ended with the oil crisis of late 1973—there was such an inflow of imports that the external-debt charges mounted rapidly. Consumer and industrial goods were brought in at a reckless pace in a way that provided excellent documentation for Celso Furtado's description of how Latin elites behave.

For instance, Brazil increased the production of cars until it became the world's ninth-ranking automotive industry, with almost a million vehicles a year being produced in the seventies. But while the number of autos and television sets was climbing at an annual rate of 14 percent, meat and homes with electricity went up by a mere 3 percent a year. The present finance minister put the issue candidly:

A transfer of income from the richest 20 percent to the poorest 80 percent probably would increase the demand for food, but diminish the demand for automobiles. The result of a sudden redistribution would be merely to generate inflation in the food-producing sector and excess capacity in the car industry.

At the same time, foreign domination was proceeding apace, so much so that the nationalistic right wing was as disturbed as the left. Foreign multinationals controlled 100 percent of auto production, 94 percent of pharmaceuticals, 91 percent of tobacco, 82 percent of rubber. A pro-government politician, José Machado, argued that therefore the state must take over the import of agricultural products and all raw materials for the pharmaceutical industry, and should nationalize the biggest utility and establish a state monopoly over newly discovered iron-ore deposits now being jointly exploited by the government and U.S. Steel. But then, Machado's proposals were not a mere burst of angry rhetoric. By some estimates, government manufacture already accounts for one half of total investment as compared to 15 percent at the end of World War II. Government mills produce 60 percent of the raw steel and monopolize the production of flat-steel products, rails, and heavy steel shapes. The debate in Brazil, the *Times* reported, is not about free enterprise but over the amount of government enterprise under state capitalism.

"What irony!" a retired Brazilian admiral complained. "We are establishing Communism under the flag of anti-Communism."

Meanwhile, as foreign debt rose and government intervention into the economy deepened, real wages declined steadily. In theory, the worker's pay was "indexed"—that is, regularly adjusted upward to compensate for inflation. But in the first period of this policy, which ended in 1967, the real minimum wage declined by 16 percent. And between 1967 and 1972, wages advanced at a rate that was only two thirds that of productivity increases. Between 1960 and 1970, according to one scholarly estimate, the share of the wealthiest 3.5 percent in the national income rose from one fourth to one third; that of the bottom 43 percent declined from

11 percent to 8 percent. This heightened exploitation of the working class was one of the chief sources of the "miracle." It was also a phenomenon that disturbed businessmen in the United States who favor American, not Brazilian, exploitation of Brazilian workers. Another *New York Times* dispatch focused on a classic case in point. A Brazilian shoe manufacturer got a subsidy from the government to start a business, and he succeeded. One reason was that he paid 50 cents an hour, as against a $3.50 wage in the United States. In considerable measure his ability to hire people so cheaply was a function of a repressive regime, which outlawed strikes and genuine labor organizations. So, a Brazilian was going to take advantage of the unequal exchange that is so profitable for American multinationals. The latter responded with protectionist pressure on their government. Jonathan Kendell of *The New York Times* commented:

The phenomenal growth of Brazilian shoe exports goes to the heart of one of the most troubling economic questions in the world—that is, how can an underdeveloped nation observe the present rules of international trade and still forge new exports capable of penetrating the markets of the industrialized countries and earning the vast quantity of foreign exchange needed to fuel further economic growth?

So, the "miracle" was up against severe difficulties in the industrial sector, even with the fascistic exploitation of the workers. But the rural areas, where the bulk of the people live, are more seriously menaced by structural problems. As one Brazilian economist, a former banker, described the situation in 1976, "The immediate objectives of attending to the needs of our foreign markets have made us forget the principal problem. That is, agriculture for the domestic market remains inefficient and expensive and has few prospects of overcoming this rut." To translate this generality into numbers, the OECD reports that 60 percent of the people in Brazil exist at levels under the FAO caloric minimum for health. It also noted that the minority with incomes more than double those of the 60 percent eat like citizens of the most affluent countries. Here again, the upper class lives in the First World, the masses in the Third World.

Indeed, in 1976 there were riots in Brazil, as people fought to get scarce black beans—even though agricultural production had increased. The government had concentrated on cash crops for the world market, and bean production in 1976 had declined by 17 percent, in part because of bad weather, but also because the bean growers got only 1 percent of the subsidy that went to the export farmers. As a result, food prices went up, infant mortality soared because of inferior prenatal diets, and 40 percent of the population, in the most "successful" of the developing countries, suffered from malnutrition.

At the same time, the Amazon is being deforested as part of a development scheme. The government is giving massive subsidies to multinational corporations like Anderson Clayton, Goodyear, Volkswagen, Nestlé, Liquigas, Borden, Mitshubishi and Universal Tank Ship, to turn the area into a major supplier of beef for Europe, the United States and Japan. On the basis of past experience, the complete success of this undertaking, involving a major increase in the meat output of Brazil, will probably be accompanied by more hunger among the Brazilian people.

In other words, subordination to the priorities of the advanced powers in agriculture brought an increase in hunger and malnutrition. By the end of 1976, these various troubles had brought a formal end to the "miracle." President Ernesto Geisel announced a regime of austerity and projected a decline in real growth from 8 percent to 4 percent, in part because of the 2.3-billion-dollar trade deficit.[6] So, more than a decade of widely heralded progress did not change Brazil's structural inferiority. It remains dominated by foreign corporations, its policies determined by foreign creditors, and its agricultural planning has been a disaster for the rural millions. A terrorized and exploited working class is the source of enormous gain, but businessmen in the United States want those 50-cents-an-hour factory hands subordinated to North American purposes and profits. Our multinationals want that underpaid labor so much that they work to keep the Brazilians from appropriating it themselves.

The case of Brazil, then, corroborates the basic analysis of this chapter. If proper account is taken of the historical differences between the poor nations and the various levels of misery within the Third and Fourth Worlds, there is a common mechanism that keeps these countries in a structurally subordinate position in the global economy. They were denied the experience of self-generating growth; they were called into modern economic life by aliens; and for that reason their internal and external relationships are shaped so as to inhibit development.

Even a nation as richly endowed as Brazil can experience more than a decade of burgeoning national production and yet remain humiliatingly subject to political power in Washington and economic power throughout the advanced capitalist system. The poor countries, then, and even the most "middle-class" among them, like Brazil, are condemned within the present structure of the world market to a labor of Sisyphus. They progress into their own inferiority, they grow into further dependency.

Chapter Six **A Fearful Horoscope**

Social and economic structures preside over the birth and destiny of babies as well as over the rate of growth of GNP. In the late twentieth century, there could be, not too much life, but too much life for the vicious horoscope that scientific and antisuperstitious people have unwittingly fabricated for themselves.

The Organization for Economic Cooperation and Development (OECD) summarizes the evidence soberly. If, it says, the population of the globe is going to stabilize in the middle of the twenty-first century at eight billion people—if, that is, there is going to be no more than a doubling of the race in the next seventy-five years—then fertility must move from high to low, from more than four children per family to slightly less than two, *in the next fifteen years*. Demographic projections are, of course, notoriously inexact, but even if one works on the relatively optimistic assumptions of Wassily Leontiev's world-economy model, the next twenty-five years will see an "enormous" pressure of population upon food. Indeed, Leontiev argues—quite rightly, I think—that there is no necessity for mass starvation on the basis of the available data. But just as unquestionably, that possibility exists.

So, in this chapter, I have consciously tried not to overstate the case. The facts have a potential for horror that needs no exaggeration. I will treat them within the analytic framework of the last two chapters—the structural account of how underdevelopment "develops"—in order to understand the overproduction of human beings and the underproduction of food in the Third World. I propose, then, to treat of hunger and overpopulation, not as calamities of nature, but as historic and social products.

Darwin described the selection of the species on the basis of the vicious rationality of an irrational nature. What now needs to be understood is how humans are consciously, but without purpose, selecting the species on the basis of the vicious irrationality of an increasingly rational, technological society.

I

The advanced capitalist economies, as we have seen, went through a coherent, self-generated process of growth. The poor countries did not, and their structures are the result of, and the perpetuators of, that fact. This same mechanism can be observed in the generation of babies. The North has discovered a comfortable equilibrium between life and resources; the South lives within a perilous disequilibrium.

There have been at least three population "laws" of human society, each of them geared to a level of energy production. The first, as Carlo Cipolla described it in his classic study *The Economic History of World Population*, has to be inferred, since the details are lost in the reaches of prehistoric time. It was a society of extremely low density—less than two persons per square mile—because that was all the life that could be sustained by the meager catch and gleaning of hunters and food gatherers. There was, we now think, a relatively high birth rate, which was offset by the high death rate that derived primarily from infanticide, war and headhunting. Epidemics were not too common, since the people were dispersed over wide areas and disease therefore had a limited range.

With the Neolithic Revolution there was that basic discontinuity in human history noted in Chapter Four. With agriculture and the domestication of animals, the energy available to the human race made a quantum leap. And though the precise data are, for obvious reasons, difficult to come by, we do have a fairly substantial idea for the population "law" in this kind of society. The normal birth rate was relatively high, between 35 and 55 per thousand. Normal death rates were also high, between 30 and 40 per thousand, but they were below the birth rates. So the tendency of agricultural society was an annual population increase of between .5 percent and 1 percent. If this had, in fact, taken place, "the world population would form today a sphere of living flesh many thousand light years in diameter, and expanding with a radical velocity that, neglecting relativity, would be many times faster than light."

That obviously did not, and could not, happen. The trend was countered by periodic peaks of incredibly high death rates—150, 300, even 500 per thousand. Wars made their contribution to this carnage, but famines and epidemics were also major factors. So, it was a common experience that a third, or a half, of a given population would suddenly disappear. With the Industrial Revolution, the second great discontinuity, this pattern of ten thousand years' duration changed. The death rate went down, due to science, hygiene and increased food output, dipping below 15 per thousand. But then, after a while—much more quickly in France than in England and Wales, which shows that these trend lines are hardly exact—a low "industrial" birth rate developed and created a new equilibrium. Even so, the Industrial Revolution radically increased the European portion of the world's population. The "white," or "Caucasian," people rose from 22 percent of the global total in 1800 to 35 percent in 1930.

There were a variety of reasons why the West could handle this vast increase, all of them economic and social. First there was that enormous migration from Europe, particularly to the Americas, North and South, and to Australia. Secondly, there was an agricultural revolution, which predated, and prepared the way for, the Industrial Revolution. Starting in the seventeenth century, gathering momentum in the eighteenth, it saw new foods and technologies, and above all, the end of feudalism in the land. The same social upheaval that peopled the new, industrial cities also made it possible to feed them. And finally, disease was a grim, equilibrating mechanism, with cholera providing a recurrent relief from a "surplus" of humans. In each case, there was a coherence, a reciprocity, as society created a population "law" that was functional for it.

On practically every one of these counts, the Third World experience was the opposite of that of the advanced capitalist societies. Because growth was set off by external stimulus, much of the traditional economy stayed as it had always been. There was no agricultural revolution that made an industrial revolution possible. The enclaves of modernity introduced by the West, and the attendant science and medicine, did, however, reduce the "agricultural" death rate—only, it did not disturb the "agricultural" birth rate. In Ceylon, an extreme example, the use of DDT against the malarial mosquito lowered the death rate from 22 to 12 per thousand in a matter of seven years—a drop that took seventy years in England and Wales. During a similar seven-year period, Mauritius underwent a decline in the death rate that took a century in England and Wales. Only, now there were no colonies to cushion the demographic explosion.

The result of this induced, incoherent development—which is to say, of underdevelopment—was a new vicious circle. Economic success had reduced the birth rate in the advanced capitalisms. The practical argument for large families in agricultural societies—the need for more hands—disappeared and, with the expected lag, people responded by having fewer children. With the rise of the welfare state, which began in the 1880s in Germany, the "social security" rationale for large families—one wants sons and daughters to take care of their mothers and fathers in old age—became less compelling. And education, urbanization, the shift in woman's role and identity, the growth of professional middle classes, all contributed to the spread of a family limitation movement, which eventually permeated all social classes.

None of these "birth control" economic and social trends are at work in the Third World. The economies are still mainly rural; welfarism is severely limited by pervasive poverty; the urban and educated stratum is relatively small. The systematic underdevelopment of the nation, therefore, leaves the "agricultural" birth rate intact at the same time as it creates an "industrial" death rate. This means that the country must now save and invest simply to avoid becoming even poorer. If one assumes, for instance, a cap-

ital–output ration of 3—that is, that three units of capital are
required to yield one unit of income—then a population growth of
2 percent per year means that 6 percent of income has to be invested merely to compensate for this increase; a 3 percent rise in
population takes 9 percent of income just to stay even.

A nation, then, has a large population because it is poor; and
it is poor because it has a large population. That is a familiar
truth. But what must be emphasized is that it derives from the historic process whereby the West "underdeveloped"—and "under-
develops" to this day—the Third World. The related, and potentially tragic, problems of hunger and population are not primarily
the result of biological or Malthusian inevitabilities, in which the
number of people necessarily increases faster than the food available to them. Rather, they are the result of the interlocking structures of development and underdevelopment, a "law" that is the
product of social and economic organization, not of nature.

II

In the case of food and people, as in all other determinants of
global life, the structures and policies of the rich and the poor
reinforce and reproduce the original historic wrong.

Prior to World War II, malnutrition was rampant in Asia, Africa
and Latin America, yet the Third World—indeed, the entire planet
with the exception of Western Europe—was a net exporter of
cereals. In the intervening years, it is indeed true that world food
output more than kept pace with population and that diets, taken
in the aggregate, improved. These are the facts that the optimists
always keep in mind. But at the same time, most nations, including
all of the poor ones, turned into food importers. Why?

The answer has already been given for the case of Brazil in
the last chapter. As the growing economies specialized in export
agriculture, farm production went up, but the resources available
for domestic consumption went down. Industrial and cash crops
took over from food production, with disastrous results. That pattern, it should now be understood, is universal. It is one more
manifestation of the dependency of all the poor nations on the
rich, and of the perverse priorities built into the world market

(and concealed by the idyllic harmonies found in the ruling theory of "comparative advantage").

Take the case of Peru. It played an aggressive role in extending national control of the seas to 200 miles, and as a result its anchovy fishmeal industry became the largest in the world. The high-protein flour that it produces is not, however, consumed by hungry Peruvians. It is shipped to Europe and the United States, where it is fed to livestock. This process, in which the affluent eat fish protein in the form of meat—that is, where the protein is cycled through the livestock to the consumer—is enormously wasteful, as will be detailed in a moment. For now, the pertinent point is that the logic of the world market makes it "sensible" for a country to let its people hunger, while it fattens up foreigners. In Central America and the Caribbean, there are similar patterns. At least half of the agricultural land—the best half—grows export crops while 70 percent of the children are undernourished. In the Sahel, the site of a disastrous drought, the exports of cotton and peanuts increased even as that calamity approached.

In Haiti, one of the poorest countries in the world, these trends are shockingly apparent. The mountain slopes are ravaged by hungry peasants, while the rich valleys are devoted to low-nutrition and feed crops—sugar, coffee, cocoa, alfalfa for cattle—for export. Recently, the Institute for Food and Development Policy reports, United States firms have been flying Texas cattle into the island, fattening them up there, and then re-exporting them to American-franchised hamburger restaurants.

So the poor countries make a major contribution to the diet of the rich. And the rich want to keep it that way.

Food, it must be remembered, is one of the major profit makers in the American economy, and it is treated by the government as a money-making commodity, not as a means of dealing with hunger. The wheat market, in particular, is an oligopoly dominated by the United States and Canada. Eighty-five percent of the wheat exports originate in advanced countries; 40 percent of them are purchased by the Third World. In 1972 America earned $7 billion in commercial farm exports. By 1974, that figure had reached $20 billion. The poor countries had laid out $1.6 billion for American food in 1972 —and $6.6 billion in 1974. So it was that the increase in the earnings of farmers from the United States as a result of Third World sales was double the total amount of nonmilitary assistance to those same countries. During this period, Americans were up in arms about the quadrupling of oil prices as a result of the OPEC cartel. They did not notice their own food cartel.

In the early seventies, however, it may seem that natural calamities, not American policy, played the decisive role with regard to food. That, however, is to miss the fact that Washington had, for political and profit-making reasons, created a situation that all but predetermined that it would act wrongly when the crop failures came between 1972 and 1974. What could not be predicted was that it would also act stupidly. The Soviet Union got a bargain in the American grain that it imported during that period as a result of subsidized agricultural waste in the United States. In the four years prior to the outbreak of the crisis, both this country and Canada were fearful of a grain surplus. They were both against accumulating "excess stocks" as they had done in the fifties and early sixties. That was politically dangerous, alienating the farm vote, running up high charges for storing the food that could not be dumped through the Food for Peace program. Moreover, American agriculture was under the administrative control of a free-market fanatic, Earl Butz. So there were fierce competition, price cutting, export subsidies, and the minimum-price agreement broke down.

As a result, the United States cut down on its grain acreage between 1967 and 1972. Wheat went from 59 to 48 million acres, coarse grains from 103 million to 96 million. If the 1967 average had been maintained, there would have been more than 100 million additional tons of grain available when the crisis surfaced. Of course, it cost an enormous amount of money not to produce that food. Between 1967 and 1973, Washington paid out $15.5 billion for idling that acreage and thereby saw to it that some eight million bushels of wheat were wasted. Under such circumstances, it is foolish to talk about an objective, or Malthusian, crisis of the food system. The problem is political and economic, not agricultural.

When the Soviets came into the market, Washington still thought that the problem was surplus food, even though the Canadians had warned them that this was not the case. So, Moscow got its grain at subsidized prices, and the American taxpayer helped to improve conditions in a Communist society. But Russia's good fortune was, predictably, a catastrophe for the poor of the globe. When they purchased grain in 1973, they had to pay the high prices that the massive Soviet imports had generated.

Agriculture in the United States is, in short, not merely a product of the soil, but an artifact of policy as well and a policy that normally operates to the detriment of the Third World. This does not mean that Washington brandishes a food "weapon" on the model of the OPEC embargo of 1973. Such a dramatic tactic requires that there be no alternate source of the commodity withheld from the market, that the nation(s) following the policy have the wealth to go on strike for a long time and that there be clear and realizable political aims. But if America cannot engage in that sudden and dramatic tactic, it can use its enormous food power to push its own political and profit purposes.

Indeed, one historian, William Appleman Williams, has argued that the drive for agricultural, rather than industrial, markets was the basic force behind American imperialism from the late nineteenth century on. I think Williams overstates his case and that industry was decisive for the United States, not the farmers. Still, he has assembled evidence which demonstrates that we have used our fields as a powerful international pawn for more than one hundred years. In 1974, it was quite logical—even traditional— that the Secretary of the Treasury regarded food exports as a way of building up the balance of payments which had deteriorated because of the oil cartel. Earl Butz talked "free trade"; only, in recent years he embargoed soybeans, stopped fertilizer shipments for half a year and suspended the market during negotiations with Poland and Russia.

In all of this, the Third World's hunger is at the political and economic mercy of the big powers, particularly of the dominant agricultural economy, the United States. During 1972–74, for instance, the American shipments of food to the globe's poor went down (there was no surplus to be "dumped"), aid decreased, the price of fertilizer soared (in part because of the oil price hikes of OPEC, but in part because big corporations had underproduced in this area for their own purposes), and food prices went up. Each one of these factors had a devastating impact upon people clinging to the very edge of existence; each one of them was determined by the priorities of agribusiness and the governments that worked with it.

Moreover, the diet of the rich also worked against the poor. The affluent are meat eaters, and this is the most wasteful way to consume grain. It takes 3 to 10 pounds of grain to produce a pound of meat, and beef needs ten times the land that corn does. Yet, even though there is some medical evidence suggesting that a heavy emphasis on meat is not healthy, it is clear that increasing incomes bring more "indirect" (meat) consumption of grains. This is one of the reasons why there are experts who foresee a shortfall of grain in the underdeveloped world of between 85 and 140 million tons by the 1980s. It is also why rising world production in the sixties was accompanied by an increase in the inequalities of protein, calorie and grain use as between the rich and the poor.[1]

So, the internal structure of the Third World economies and the policies and luxuries of the advanced world perpetuate the food inequities of the world. This is why the poor countries have become more dependent upon the North in the life-or-death area of food since the end of World War II. The advanced economies have shattered their old coherence, in which babies and resources were in some kind of balance, imposed soaring population rates upon them and, by the very same mechanism, deprived them of the possibility of coping with the new situation.

III

The result of these past and present trends was summed up at the United Nations World Food Conference in Rome at the end of 1974. There are, a speaker said, 460 million people who suffer from "a severe degree of protein energy malnutrition. . . . In some countries, more than half of the deaths of children under five years of age were directly or indirectly attributable to malnutrition." Statistics which support this statement have been accepted by critics of the UN's Food and Agricultural Organization (FAO)—that is, by those who believe that in the past the FAO overstated the case. Since both parties in the dispute accept the figure of between 450 and 500 million severely malnourished people, we can take that as a sober assessment of an incipient tragedy.

In terms of numbers, the greatest concentration of the hungry is to be found in Asia. (It should be noted, incidentally, that the UN figures just quoted omit the Communist countries in Asia and are therefore an understatement of the problem.) In that area, 30 percent of the people, or 301 million human beings, are hungry. In Latin America the corresponding figures are 13 percent and 36 million; in the Near East and Africa, 18 percent and 25 percent, 30 and 67 million people. However, one must be careful about generalizing. There are 26 countries with lower per capita protein consumption than India, including Haiti, Colombia and North Vietnam; the lowest rate is found in Zaïre, not in Bangladesh. In all countries, children are the prime victims of this cruel reality. In Indonesia, for example, a one-year-old child has less of a chance of surviving than a sixty-one-year-old.

Nevertheless, some people are optimistic. As Fred Sanderson commented in a volume sponsored by the American Association for the Advancement of Science, in the post-World War II period, "the growth of population has exceeded the most pessimistic expectations. Yet world grain production (which accounts for the bulk of the original food energy produced) kept sufficiently ahead of population growth to permit an annual improvement in per capita consumption of about 1%." And another expert writing in the same volume commented that "the 3.8 billion people alive in 1973 ate 21 percent more food per person than was consumed by the 2.7 billion living in 1954."

This hopefulness is both understandable and misguided. It is understandable as a reaction against the overstatements of the tragedy that drives people into an awed, helpless passivity instead of motivating them to action. It is also a response to the neo-Malthusians, who see population as the problem and utterly fail to perceive its social and economic dimensions. For instance, Paul Ehrlich and Richard Harriman go so far as to advocate a plan in which the underdeveloped nations would permanently accept their status as nonindustrial powers. For them, family limitation is the crucial weapon; social security is mentioned only as an aside. But the Indian experience demonstrates how conservative, precapitalist social structures resist government campaigns for family limitation.

I am, then, in sympathy with the realistic anti-Malthusians. But I think that these analysts allow the gross figures, the averages and the slopes on the graphs to distract their attention from a real possibility: that a famine will strike in South Asia, or, as happened in the Sahel, in Africa. The gross quantities and the long run are compatible with a short-term catastrophe. If food supply is not organized internationally and if the economic and social conditions for population control in the Third World are not forthcoming, such a horror is all but a certainty even though it will also be a statistical anomaly.

What are the prospects for avoiding such a disaster? They are ambiguous and certainly not reassuring.

The Green Revolution is by now a familiar example of how the West was carried away by what Gunnar Myrdal calls "technological euphoria." In July 1968, Lester Brown, then an advisor to the Secretary of Agriculture, wrote in *Foreign Affairs* that the new varieties of high-yielding seeds promised to be "the most significant world economic development since the economic rebirth" of Europe after World War II. In India and throughout the global South, Brown said, the food situation had changed "almost beyond belief." But it was not long before Brown, and almost everyone else, realized that this optimism was unfounded. (In recent years, Brown himself has been criticized for being too pessimistic!)

Myrdal was one of the first to grasp the essence of the problem. Better seeds, he said, are no substitute for reform. Given the fact that the Green Revolution seeds require considerable inputs of water, fertilizers and other factors, which are also energy-intensive only a small group of the relatively well-to-do farmers will be able to benefit. The landless peasants, or the families scratching a subsistence living out of a tiny plot, will be unaffected. So, one consequence of this revolutionary development will be an increase in inequality. Similarly, Myrdal continued, the credit cooperatives and community development plans, which are held in high esteem by the American Congress, will be, and are, vitiated by patterns of absentee ownership, sharecropping and the like.

The Green Revolution seeds, then, are not "high yielding" in and of themselves but only high yielding if fertilizer is available, irrigation improved, storage facilities protected from rats, and so on. Moreover, innovation has not yet extended to the most important seed of all, rice. Finally, there is this comment of Henry Walters: ". . . despite poverty and the low levels of productivity in many developing countries, the adoption of production-increasing techniques often does not seem profitable because there is a limited market or the prices that farmers receive are too low to justify their use."

This critique of the Green Revolution is fairly well known, and widely accepted, among concerned and informed people. But the same constituency has not grasped the corollary: that the most productive agriculture, that of the United States above all, depends upon industrialization. So the vicious circle in the Third World takes on another dimension. A country must undergo an agricultural revolution if it is to industrialize or else it will not be able to feed the urban masses working in the new factories; but industrialization is a precondition for an agricultural revolution on the American model. That model is not, of course, the only one, as E. F. Schumacher has suggested with great imagination. It is, however, the only one that is working effectively here and now, and the reasons for its success are worth considering.

When many people read of the enormously high productivity of the American farm, they assume that this is explained by Yankee ingenuity, or something like it. To be sure, American food production has been blessed by a number of factors: good climate, rich soil, farmers prepared to take advantage of the innovations that were disseminated by the U.S. Department of Agriculture and, more recently, by the corporate food distributors.* But it is not so widely understood that the system is incredibly energy-intensive. Oil and fertilizer are two obvious examples, but there are many others. The American transportation system—with more than fifty billion dollars' worth of federally subsidized superhighways—is an essential element of the productivity in the fields; so are refrigeration for frozen foods and supermarkets. In 1910, American agriculture consumed less energy, measured in calories, than it produced in the form of food calories. By 1970, the food system required almost nine times as much energy as it produced in food.

So, John S. and Carol E. Steinhart pose the problem in this way: "We know that our food system works. . . . But we cannot know what will happen if we take a piece of that system and transplant it to a poor country without our industrial base of supply, transport

* There is an ambiguity in this last case that should at least be noted. Modern science has created a tasteless tomato, which is marvelously suited to picking, packaging and shipping. The instance is not isolated.

systems, processing and appliances for home storage and preparation and, most important of all, a level of industrialization that permits higher costs for food." In short, even if the United States were, by some unprecedented act of generosity, to decide to outfit a poor country with the technology for an "American" agricultural system, that transfer could not be made.

There is not—there cannot be—a technological resolution of the potential horrors described in this chapter. Either there will be a restructuring of the international market system or else the present mechanisms will go on perpetuating four hundred years of injustice. And what must be stressed is that the massive determinants analyzed in this book are, like the stars of the astrologers, the key to the intimate fate of the unborn. They operate in terms of babies as well as of Gross National Products.

There is, however, no need for a grim act of faith in this terrible horoscope. These stars can be changed. But before turning to the work of outlining the beginning of a positive program, these abstractions should be given more flesh in two chapters describing further encounters with the Third World.[2]

Chapter Seven **Encounters: Africa**

[These excerpts from a journal that I kept on a trip to Kenya and Tanzania in the summer of 1976 are somewhat more edited than the Chapter Three account of my stay in India. For the most part, however, the notes are as I wrote them at the time. The main change has been to exclude some material from the original.]

ORLY, PARIS, 7/24

My mood is different from what it was when I left New York for India. I had been to India before, so it was not a visual mystery to me, and when I arrived at Delhi last January, I was greeted by a familiar scent in the morning air. But even the first time I went there, I had some idea of what to expect. In some ways, India was the "star" of the colonial revolutionary movement for anyone of my generation. The Congress Party had been led by the unforgettable Gandhi, and he had been succeeded by a lesser, but compelling, world figure, Nehru. It was impossible not to have seen pictures of the great masses in the streets when independence came or when Gandhi died. Even the Indian countryside had been immortalized in haunting photography in *Life* magazine. Ironically, the very

165

extremity of India's problems—the famines, the hundreds of millions of people, the violence that wracked the nation—forced an awareness of that country into the average, ignorant Western mind.

Africa is different. Decolonialization came later. The first figure that Americans became aware of was Nkrumah, and his Pan-African hopes were soon blasted. Then there were the confusing events which focused on Zaïre—the former Belgian Congo—in the early sixties. I had some fleeting political contact with those events and knew of the particularly abominable role of Belgian colonialism, which began as a personal, royal preserve in that land in the nineteenth century. I remember being shocked that the Belgians had allowed only a handful of black Africans to get a college education. But still, I had no sense of Africa comparable even to my meager knowledge of India. And when decolonialization proceeded apace, I found it hard to keep up with the new names on the map. I was a perfect example of the well-intentioned ethnocentrism of the Western intellectual in the first years of the post colonial age.

There were a few exceptions to my own innocence. In the fifties I had picketed on behalf of Kenyan independence and had met Tom Mboya, the leader who was tragically murdered after freedom was won. And I had followed the North Africa struggle for national emancipation, supporting the Algerians, Moroccans and Tunisians. In 1959, I had voted in behalf of American young socialists in favor of Algerian independence and against the policy of Guy Mollet's French socialists at a meeting of the Executive Committee of the International Union of Socialist Youth in West Berlin.

But all these things do not change the main, unfortunate fact. I do not have the slightest idea of what I will see tomorrow when I arrive in Nairobi. I am as culturally dumb as the European tourist who comes to the United States thinking he will find cowboys and Indians.

NAIROBI, 7/25

We arrived after an uneventful flight from Frankfurt. Outside was Africa and even though the books had warned me that the highlands around Nairobi have nothing in common with Hollywood images of steaming jungles, I was unprepared for the utterly undramatic landscape of flat plains and distant hills. On the drive into the city, there was no sense of teeming humanity and poverty which assault the eyes in Delhi or Bombay or Calcutta. The people walking along the road are few in number—it is Sunday—and all in Western dress. The nearest thing to a picturesque scene was a cart being pushed by two barefoot young men. They were the only people without shoes I was to see all day.

What I did notice, though, was the corporate presence here. There was a sign proclaiming that General Motors had confidence in Kenya, and there were installations for Firestone, Toyota and other multinationals. The Intercontinental, where I am staying, is a totally modern place, operated by a company that has seven or eight such hotels around Africa and many more scattered around the world. In the lobby, one of those visual displays built into a kind of television set is projecting a movie about how you can come to Africa at special group rates, play golf, enjoy water sports on the African Riviera, see wild game, visit one of the Seven Wonders of the Ancient World, et cetera. Apparently I am not only studying multinationals. I am staying at one.

I stroll through the city. The downtown area is dominated by modern skyscrapers (if ten or eleven stories merit the name) and one is again struck by the ubiquitous corporate emblems. There are no beggars, though I do get five or six offers to shine my shoddy, down-at-the-heels shoes. I pass by a Colonel Sanders Kentucky Fried Chicken restaurant on Jomo Kenyatta Boulevard. A line from a radical book leaps into my mind. Isn't it preposterous that an underdeveloped country has to pay a fee to an advanced corporation to get the "proprietary knowledge" of, in this case, how to fry chicken? The answer is that such a transaction makes a great deal of sense in an integrated, rationally irrational world economy.

At the hotel pool after I get back from my stroll, the people are about 25 percent black, 75 percent white. The colonialist skin privilege per se has been abolished; there are black Africans here. The neocolonialist dollar privilege is in force; you still have to buy your way into the places that now admit everyone. Here again, there is that basic ambiguity of justice versus incremental change. Kenya wants tourism to get hard currency. It has to want tourism in a world it did not make, in which it has been assigned a "comparative advantage" in exotic animals and history. It is commercializing that advantage, which is good from the point of view of a world economy, which is itself basically maldistributive and perverse. It can purchase a little happiness for its people—and who, other than a few purist sectarians, is going to reject that?—but only if it subordinates itself to an outrageous international division of labor.

8/26

I walk through the streets to check out a meeting for later today. Some freaks come down Kenyatta Boulevard on motorcycles. America has sent its multinationals to the four corners of the world—and its Beats, its Hippies, its Freaks as well. Once I rounded a bend in the Guatemalan mountains near Chichicastenango, and there was a clump of the alienated American young, searching for their souls (and good marijuana) on the outskirts of Western life. And I was next to a young, obviously far-out, American at the Delhi airport who was in transit to Katmandu, another freak outpost. The locals are furious sometimes. Guatemalan friends told me that the Indians were not at all amused by mixed nude bathing. But eventually American pop culture triumphs. I remember the night Stephanie and I arrived in Warsaw in 1963. I went down to see what was happening in this Communist capital and reported back that the couples were dancing the "twist" in the main dining room of our hotel.

I found the rendezvous point on Tom Mboya street and felt my age and the transitory quality of human life. I had known Mboya briefly on his trips to the United States. I remember him in particular at one civil-rights demonstration in Washington, a handsome, articulate black prince of a trade-union leader. Then he was assassinated (by his own countrymen, not the colonialists, and after the independence for which he fought was achieved). Now I am walking down a street named in his memory in his homeland. I get a Proustian pang, a sense of the unknown interconnections, of the fragility of our moment on earth, but of its weaving too.

Enough French aesthetics. I go now to the U.S. Embassy for some help. That is another ambiguity. I think my government basically, fundamentally wrong in its relations with the Third World despite its fine intentions. Now I will call upon it for aid in finding out how better to expose it. I do so reluctantly, fearing CIA games. But *civis Americanus sum*, and therefore I will confront the ambiguity. I pay taxes; they damn well ought to help me. At a more serious level: I deeply believe that I am working for the best interests of the American people. I am a patriot in my own Leftist way.

I found the USIS after a couple of false starts and was ushered in to see Richard Cushing. He is in his late fifties, I would guess, a former Associated Press newsman who has done USIS tours in Latin America and, for the last five years, in Africa. He was friendly, open, extremely informative. I am sure I could have learned much of what he told me from books—and my ignorance is so great that rudimentary books would have sufficed—but somehow there is an extra dimension when you can ask about something you've just seen.

Kenya—what follows is a summary of what Cushing said, with me responsible for the errors of transcription—is about 12½ million people, with roughly a million concentrated in three cities: Nairobi, 650,000; Mombasa, 300,000; and Kisumu, 200,000. It is overtly capitalist and pro-Western, and has some major corporate investments in place: Del Monte, Firestone, GM is coming in, and there is a fair amount of Japanese capital and British and American banks. The people in the bush are still primitive and poor, though the cash economy has penetrated into most places. There is still strong tribal identification. The Kikuyu are the largest tribe, though split into three political factions; the Luos are next, followed by the Akamba, the tribe that predominates in the Kikuyu-led army.

The people are members of families first, of tribes second, and of the nation last of all. The large, extended family acts as a kind of social-security system, since every employed person supports some of the unemployed relatives. This means, here at least, that the privileges of the working class, if such there are, cannot be simply counterposed to rural poverty. This is a point that I had read about but now begin to understand. The urban workers remain in close contact with their family in the bush and often return home for a period of time. The backbone of the economy is still rural, and the lands are divided up among the sons, which means that viable units are sometimes cut up. Daughters are prized here as valuable, since it is the women who do the farming. The groom's father must, therefore, pay for his son's bride, for he is getting, not simply a daughter-in-law, but a farmhand as well.

Cushing said that four problems stand out in Kenya. First, the poaching of wild animals—of elephants to get their tusks, of cats and zebras for their skins—is not only a blow against natural conservation. It is also a practice that will eventually make Kenya less attractive for tourists, for whom the wildlife is a major reason for coming. Secondly, the chopping-down of trees to make charcoal threatens to turn more and more areas into desert (and Kenya's arable land is already a fairly narrow green belt). One of the reasons for this problem is that charcoal production is commercial, particularly for the (illegal) export market. Charcoal sells for around $1.50 a sack here, but the Arabs, despite their oil wealth, still prefer charcoal cooking and will pay $25 a sack. I had been told about this kind of problem by Lester Brown at the World Watch Foundation in December. At the time, I wondered if it might not be extravagant to identify a new global crisis: after food and industrialization and all the rest, now firewood. But here it is.

Third, population here is going up at around 4 percent a year, which is high even for the Third World. It is the old story. The extended family is the social-security system. Finally, Cushing said, there is a water crisis here, one that could further limit productive land.

After leaving Cushing, a poignant comedy of errors. I had called a business office in the morning and asked for W——, a person who had been recommended to me by a knowledgeable friend in New York. The voice that answered had an African or Indian accent; the man I was trying to reach was Australian. And the person who answered was puzzled, even after I explained that I had heard of him through my New York contact. I decided that W—— might have gone native. So I had made an appointment to meet him in front of a movie theater on Tom Mboya street. I arrived a bit early and stood there for about twenty minutes. The scene was poorer than I had yet encountered in Nairobi. There were some misshapen beggars crawling on stumps of limbs, but it was nothing like the human Calvary of Calcutta. Still, I felt myself in the Third World of hunger, and not in an international bubble with a view, for the first time since I have arrived.

W—— appeared, only he was not the W—— I was looking for. He was an Indian with a fairly unimportant post and could not for the life of him figure out why this Westerner dropped out of the sky and phoned him. I didn't want to say it was a mistake, partly because I was embarrassed for both of us, partly because I did not want to deprive him of what seemed to be an exciting, even mysterious, moment. He introduced me to several of his countrymen in a little shop and then treated me to a cup of thick, sugared Indian tea. Our conversation was disjointed because we were from different worlds and because he couldn't understand what in God's name I wanted. I asked some questions. The cost of living is going up, he said; be careful of con men and thugs, they are all around (a warning I had already heard from the most disparate people). We finally walked to an Indian-owned shop, where he introduced me as a writer—proudly, it seemed to me—to the prosperous-looking proprietor, who jokingly asked if I were going to write a book about the man who had brought me. There was contempt in the joke. After several more confused and embarrassed moments, we parted and I went back to the hotel.

I sat in my comfortable room, sipped a Scotch, and was overwhelmed by a kind of guilty poignance. An accident had brought me into contact with a plain, ordinary man of this place. Neither he nor I really had anything to say to each other, and he will almost certainly live out his life in the crowded, impoverished quarter where I met him, a proud man who has a job where you wear a suit and a tie. I, with my Leftist compassion, will drink Scotch paid for from the wages of that compassion. Yet I will bear up under these contradictions, not least because there is no escaping them. When I wrote *The Other America,* I was not poor, yet I had helped some people see poverty. Still, I sit in my room thinking about a poem by Dylan Thomas, who said that he wrote for the lovers "their arms/ Round the griefs of the ages,/ Who pay no praise or wages/ Nor heed my craft or sullen art." Can one speak on behalf of a people whom you can't talk to? In part, yes. But it is an uncomfortable paradox to live in.

8/27

After a morning of fleeting contacts and missed interviews, a lunch at the City Hall, where the Nairobi Press Club was meeting. Mixed Afro-European group, about forty in number. British banquet etiquette, with formal greetings (Honorable Members, Invited Guests, Ladies and Gentlemen, etc.). The shield on the ceiling was

172 | The Vast Majority

inscribed with the Swahili motto of Kenya: *Harambee*—Let Us All Pull Together. The scheduled speaker, the editor of the biggest newspaper chain in Africa, did not show up, the Chair remarks, "for reasons best known to himself." British-style banquet merriment. We hear Dr. S. R. Sen, a World Bank Director and President of the International Conference of Agricultural Economists (which is meeting at the Kenyatta Conference Center). He is presidential, diplomatic, noncommitted.

I am not an optimist like the Hudson Institute, says Sen; I am not a pessimist like the Club of Rome. I am in between. The world can resolve its problems if it could get a better system of distribution. No one knows, 150 years after he launched his hypothesis, whether Malthus was right or wrong. Sen dwells on the problem of the "niggardliness of nature" and only mentions the world capitalist market euphemistically, noting something about "institutional arrangements." The African journalists try to pin him down. Does the World Bank do enough for the Third World? Yes, it devoted all of its resources to the globe's poor; No, it doesn't have enough resources. He is emphatic on two points. There is no "Green Revolution," only some good research and development which helps some countries. Rice, maize and other foods are left out. Secondly, if the world would spend 10 percent of its armament R&D on food research and development, we could overcome the food problem.

Later I talk to Lee Griggs, the *Time* bureau chief here. Open, friendly, informed. He is not a cheerleader—indeed, his general attitude seems to be that of the cynical journalist, but with a streak of badly concealed sympathy. Per capita GNP has gone down since independence, he says, but that is because of the population growth. However, his basic thesis—implied rather than formally stated—is hopeful. Progress, to be sure, has its seamy aspects. It is, among other things, dominated by the Kikuyu tribe, which counts the President as its most prominent member. The tribe, it seems to me, operates here as a cross between an ancient form of community life and an American Democratic Party machine of the first half of the twentieth century.

Still, things are moving. The small farms are productive, Griggs says, unlike the collectives in Tanzania. To be sure, there is a growing gap between the modern and traditional sectors which is greater than Kenya's only in the Francophone states. And there is a shanty town on the edge of Nairobi; only, it is nothing like the *bidonvilles* in other places in Africa. In the industrial sector, Griggs says, there is thoroughgoing Africanization. Of Esso's 250 employees, for instance, there are only three "expats" (expatriates), and only one of those is American (the others are European). Griggs's own secretary is white, and that is possible only because she is a Kenya citizen.

So, what I get is a report from an experienced observer, who is not a reactionary, which tells me that the capitalist road to modernity is working tolerably well here. Does that mean that Kenya is doing what my theory says is impossible, climbing that ladder to affluence which is dreamed of in the philosophy of Henry Kissinger and Herman Kahn?

I talk to another expert after meeting with Griggs. He complicates, and even counterbalances, Griggs's analysis. He is C. R. Ter Kuile, a tanned, craggy, handsome Dutch agricultural specialist, who works for the FAO.

The real income of the rural poor, he says, is going down—that is, 85 percent of the people are in this situation. I ask if this is merely the result of high oil prices and the recession in the big capitalist powers. No, he replies, it is more structured than that. There is no free market for the farmers. They must sell their crops to government marketing boards at a fixed, compulsory price. The government has left these prices artificially low and thus forced the farmer to subsidize the urban population. But then, I comment, is that a sort of capitalist version of the Soviet system of forcing peasants to pay for modernization? Ter Kuile thinks the analogy right.

Ter Kuile then adds some fundamentals which I should have known, but did not know. Women do most of the farm work; they are about two thirds of the rural population. The men tend the cattle, but that is usually all they do. Otherwise, they engage in trade, work in the city and lead a social life that takes as much time as work itself.

These conversations convince me that reality is more complicated than I imagined it, yet does not diverge too radically from my basic analysis. A kind of "combined and uneven development" seems to be operating here. Just as an underdeveloped country takes over the most modern technology, say a steel mill, rather than recapitulating the evolution from forge to oxygen process, so too it takes over a post-Keynesian, interventionist political approach even if—as in Kenya, Brazil or elsewhere—it follows a "capitalist" road.

8/28

I walk to meet a local journalist, passing through the poorest district I have yet seen in Nairobi. It was almost a relief to be in a slum, crowded with people, a good many of them just hanging around. (They estimate unemployment in the city at 30 percent, which is the level of the Great Depression in the United States.) The shops are run-down and cheap; there are women with babies strapped to their backs and some with them lashed across their chests; tribal people are there with wares to sell. So when I begin to talk to P——, I ask him about a suspicion of mine, which he confirms.

Most of the people who work in Nairobi don't live in town. They live on the outskirts—up to ten miles away—and commute. Some of them have rooms in blocks of City Council housing; many live in huts. One of P——'s friends pays 75 Kenya Shillings (KSh) for one room in a hut with no running water. The minimum wage is 250 KSh a month (roughly $30) and 500 KSh is good pay for workers. Within the city, P—— says, there are three classes: an upper class of executives and top civil servants with 8–10,000 KSh a month; a middle class with 2–3,000 KSh; and the worker with 250–500 KSh.

The rural mass has much less cash income, P—— continues, but they get income in kind from their small plots. We talk of politics. What, I ask, will happen after Kenyatta goes? Is democracy viable here? On the second question, P—— answers, No. He recounts the history of the two-party system in Kenya when Kenyatta, a Kikuyu, was challenged by Odingo, a Luo. This made politics tribal and, according to P——, bad. But then, I said, how can such a system outlive Kenyatta? There are the various Kikuyu factions as well as the hostilities between the Kikuyu and the other tribes. There was even a recent assassination of a Kikuyu leader; and, of course, Tom Mboya, certainly one of the most brilliant and promising of the Kenya leaders—but a Luo—was gunned down some years ago. So what will happen next? No one knows, P—— says. Perhaps civil war; perhaps not. The worst possibility was put in a single word: Beirut.

Walking back from the conversation, I came to Simba street in the posh public spaces around the Conference Center. It triggered a memory. There was a Pete Seeger folk-song album I used to like very much with an African song in it about a lion. (*Simba* is the Swahili word for lion, and after writing this entry I discovered that Seeger's lyric had been based on the Zulu name for the animal. My error did not, however, vitiate the mood it evoked.) That song had been one among many taken from all around the world. It was the refraction of a simple, but decent, internationalism that sometimes had tragic political consequences, as when people romanticized Soviet totalitarianism as the most advanced form of democracy in human history. But what concerns me here is not the intellectual content of that phenomenon, but its aura.

In a brilliant review in *The New York Times* a while ago, Marshall Berman called it the vision of the Popular Front (and note that he, and I in this case, use that term impressionistically, not analytically). In it, one joined Spanish antifascism and the CIO and the black struggles and the New Deal and the Warsaw Ghetto and, for many, the Soviet Union, in a gigantic confraternity of the overwhelming majority of mankind which, if only given its head, if only freed from the plutocrats and fascists and colonialists, would rapidly and instinctively inaugurate a reign of human niceness, of fraternity (they would have said) and sorority (we would add). There were many, many things wrong with that vision, and it was sometimes manipulated to rationalize cruelty rather than promote kindness. And yet, for all of its confusions and evasions and contradictions, if it was a corruption, it was the corruption of something good that always remained in it: of an internationalism that is still the only hope of mankind. I had read and internalized my Orwell; I knew the crimes committed by the GPU in the name of antifascism in Spain; and yet, I never cease to thrill at the songs of the International Brigade.

But walking that street today in Nairobi, I thought with a tired knowledge of how vastly more complicated—and often cruel— reality is than the left-wing myth assumes it to be. Our brothers and sisters here—on whose behalf I picketed in the fifties—could,

176 The Vast Majority

in their free and independent state, turn upon one another in a tribal bloodbath. And I also realized that I am an incurable democrat. Maybe the immediate economic, social and political conditions for multiparty democracy don't exist, as I was told. I don't know. But eventually, they will have to find a nonviolent way to resolve these conflicts, and there is only one I know of and it is democracy.

After that philosophic walk, a chat with a South African (who is completely antiracist). We talk of many things, but one topic sticks in my mind. Tanzania, my friend says (and he is a sociologist who has been living here and working for the UN for some time), has made some conscious choices, like trying to mitigate or even abolish the contrast between city and country. The result, he went on, is that Dar has sort of gone to pot. By Western standards, which is to say the norms of capitalist rationality, that is inefficient. But is the commercial definition of efficiency right and true? Moreover, is B—— right when he says that Tanzania simply doesn't have the human resources to carry out its intentions? Put another way, is the pessimistic prognosis for democratic socialism in the Third World—a prognosis I have made in several books—correct? I find myself hoping that this trip will disprove theses for which I have argued vigorously.

7/29

This was the richest day so far. I rented a car—Avis is located on Kenyatta Boulevard—and, filled with trepidation at sitting in a driver's seat on the right and following British rules of the road, set out for the back country. I drove about eighty miles north, up to the town of Embu.

The farms close to Nairobi were, as I had been told, rich and flourishing. I saw corn and in a few places it was as high as the proverbial elephant's eye. The people walking along the road for the first ten miles or so out of Nairobi wore shoes and looked fairly prosperous. Fairly prosperous? I have the same problem here that I had in India. What is your standard for evaluation? If I see someone with shoes and neat but simple clothing that strikes me as middle-class in this society. But then, I do not really know enough about this place to make any judgments. So the reader of this journal is warned. "Not bad" or "fairly prosperous" means not obviously and abjectly poor.

Fairly quickly, the neat housing disappeared. The landscape became a bit more scraggly, but never downright bad. Huts appeared, some with thatched roofs, others with some kinds of metal on top, some made of mud, I think. Children were everywhere. It gave me a pang when I realized that some of the boys herding cattle or goats—barefoot, ragged children—were about the age of my own son, Teddy (five).

And the women were ubiquitous, too. As I had been told, I saw them working in the fields, cutting wood, carrying heavy loads on their backs, bent double, a bright scarf bobbing just beneath the pack. (The next day at the Cushings' an extraordinary story. A doctor friend of theirs had investigated the results of this heavy carrying. There was a permanent crease in the forehead where the tie holding the water can was bound to the carrier. The women, he discovered, had a permanent headache, though they did not call it such. They regarded it as a normal condition of life, since they begin to carry when they are three or four years old.) The scene was primitive, yet the construction equipment at work on the rutted, boulder-strewn road included big bulldozers and earth-moving apparatus. Tribalism and tractors side by side.

Nothing much happened on the drive, and I didn't stay long in Embu, since I didn't want to get caught at night on an impossible road. But there was an impression: Kenya reminds me of Mexico. The point is not economic. Mexico is much more advanced. It is more a question of mood. The towns here, like the ones I have seen in Mexico, are often dusty clumps along the road, somnolent, with people mainly waiting. For the bus? To gossip? Anglo-Saxon, modern time-clock time has not arrived here for most of the people.

After I got back from my drive up country to the Mount Kenya area—the traditional colonial preserve, I am told—I decided to luxuriate at the fancy rooftop supper club at my hotel. It is called Le Château. At the bar an American businessman who amiably gossiped about African cities as if they were Los Angeles or Chicago. ("Yeah, Lusaka's a nice place, but I really dig the Beach Hotel at Abidjan.") The Kenyan official with whom he chatted was one of those brilliant foreign speakers whose English was just a bit more colloquial and with-it than that of anyone born to the tongue. He and the American were flirting with a Spanish piano player and the Zambian star of the show, Jane Osborne.

In the supper club, there was a table of African central bankers; another table of Japanese businessmen; and an audience that was half black African, including some extremely chic women, and half tourist. Jane Osborne turned out to be a classic night-club chanteuse, except that she sang some of the songs in Swahili (but apologized that, being a Zambian, her accent was not good). I had the conventional sense of the obvious paradox: that one could so easily travel from a boulder-strewn road to a supper club, where an African woman with a "corn row" hairdo and a jangle of bracelets sang to a cosmopolitan group of people. More pertinently, there was an insight into the truly global nature of the capitalist world market, of how it reaches out with its money, its styles, its culture and its mores, to every corner of the planet.

7/30

I talked to the most brilliant and well-informed Kenyan I met here, a journalist, whom I will call R——.

He is not sure that things are going as well as they seem. The dynamic is the result of past accomplishments, but it is not at all certain that it will continue. Investment has been on a hit-or-miss basis. Industrialization is supposed to be based on an import-substitution principle, but the government figures import the very products in which the nation is supposed to become self-sufficient. There has been, he goes on to say, too little attention to agriculture. With the population going up and urbanization taking place, the farms will have to produce more food.

R—— is most enlightening on African capitalism. There are no— or practically no—African capitalists. There are African managers who act as middlemen for the big multinationals that make the basic decisions. But there is no class of African capitalists mobilizing capital for major projects. And people in the government use the system for personal gain on many occasions rather than for innovation. Still, he comments, the average citizen is better off in the years since independence. This is certainly true when you compare Kenya to its neighbors, like Tanzania. Money has motivated people, he remarks, and that works better than the Tanzanian system.

We talk about many things, and our conversation ends as R——

expresses candidly what many sophisticated Third World politicians assume, but dare not say, because of the internal ramifica-
tions in their own country. The poor nations, R—— says sadly,
are simply not going to catch up with the United States. Their
units lack the market scale and the structure to do that. Hong
Kong is not going to surpass America. Justice, he agrees, and the
possible are at loggerheads. A worldwide confrontation will not
solve anything—and what's more, if such a confrontation takes
place, he doesn't want to be around for the apocalypse. I quote
Ortega, telling R—— that I think Ortega's truth is bitter, conservative and, alas, relevant—that the hungry masses sometimes destroy
bakeries in their righteous anger. We end on this note of reluctant
consensus.

After talking to R——, I had lunch with the Cushings. The
really important event came afterward. The Cushings took me
to see the Akamba carvers who do work for them. We drove into
the "native" side of town, past a jammed bus station, which services the outlying country. Then we came to a market place, the
size of two football fields. There was that peculiar scent of open
urban fires, of cooking on city streets. At one end of the market
were some shabby, but permanent, structures. They housed the
cooperative we were visiting. In one of the buildings, the workers
were involved in every stage of making "native" art. Little statues
of cult figures or animals; African canes, et cetera. One group of
men, stripped to the waist, were lathered with wood chips from
planing. Others were actually carving. At the end of the process,
a man was tinting the wood to make it look like ebony. We chatted
with the workers. One was a young boy—I would guess twelve or
thirteen—who had just come to the co-op. The mood, as far as a
stranger could tell, was fairly happy.

In the field outside were shacks made of discarded cardboard,
plaster, stray pieces of wood. Squatters live here without benefit
of water or plumbing. The place was littered with refuse, dotted
with fires, alive with children. It was not filled with a seething
mass, like those squatter colonies I had glimpsed in Bombay, but
I was told that, this being Saturday, many people had gone back
to their villages. Normally, it would be much more crowded. As we
stood in the middle of this extraordinary scene, the Cushings told

me that on two occasions entrepreneurs had bought out the entire stock of the co-op. One was a German, the other a Japanese. Some of the specialty items, they had heard, were doing particularly well in San Francisco.

Suddenly, I was struck by the passage in the *Communist Manifesto* quoted at length in Chapter Four, the one in which Marx and Engels say that "the bourgeoisie gives a cosmopolitan character to the production and consumption of all the countries." I had read, and taught, that passage countless times. But now, standing in the detritus of a poverty-stricken market place in Nairobi, where the workers live in cardboard shacks and make carved napkin rings for the tables of San Francisco, I realized that capital would go to the moon if it thought there was cheap labor there.

DAR ES SALAAM, 8/1

The road into Dar is badly paved, dusty. The Agip Motel, where I am staying, is by American standards spare, even tacky, but it is clean. The bath mat has a hole in it and so does one spread. The lighting is dim, a normal, eye-wrecking tactic of cheap hotels everywhere. Yet it would be criminal to complain. This country is on the UN's list of the poorest nations, and the government deliberately starved a luxury sector that catered to Europeans and Americans. When people in Nairobi told me that Nyerere had let Dar "go to ruins," they meant mainly that the good tailors and cheese stores had closed down.

I wander around, looking at the Russian and Chinese ships side by side in the harbor. There are women in black veils, which they wrap from the head down, all around their bodies. Some people are barefoot; most are wearing simple sandals. Everything is Sunday, dusty, quiet. But then I walk a bit further. Outside a movie, a crowd. Two women stand apart in stylishly cut clothes. There are some young men wearing the high-heeled shoes that are fashionable in Nairobi and among some of the young people back in the States. Another avenue leads me to a new, and luxurious-looking hotel, the Kilimanjaro. I walk in, scouting for British papers or the Paris *Trib*. No luck. But there on the magazine stand is a pile of Soviet English-language publications, including one theoretical organ with articles denouncing the Chinese Communists. Across the lobby, well-dressed people are eating at the "Bruncherie." Back at the Agip, the bar is jammed with Indians. A waiter calls me *Bwana*.

8/2

A lucky series of accidents on my first working day in Dar. Tony Mabbat is the USIS man, and I go to his office to check out some phone numbers. He tells the Ambassador, James Spain, who, it turns out, had heard me speak when he was a "Diplomat in Residence" at Florida State. We have coffee together.

Mabbat and Spain—I purposely muddle their identities so that no comment can be attributed specifically to either of them, but their more or less common point of view can be communicated— are a marvelous example of the problem of the cruel innocence. They are decent, humane, technocratic, liberal, not malevolent.

They are surprisingly sympathetic to Nyerere. They find him personally appealing, and the most they say to me in criticism of his economic and social policy is that perhaps—but only perhaps— he has sacrificed efficiency and productivity to egalitarianism. The country began its independence as a desperately poor place with a scattered peasantry at a primitive technological level. Therefore the rural emphasis is inevitable. There is coercion here, but it usually comes from overzealous secondary officials out to make a name for themselves, and Nyerere, who constantly circulates among the people, tries to correct them.

Tanzania, they say, is dedicated to egalitarian policies, which may retard productivity. There is a drift toward coercion, but it is not the totalitarianism that is sometimes conjured up in the Western press. The Ujama villages, which are 100 percent cooperatives, are not created by force in any case. The formation of villages, but not of Ujama villages, may have involved coercion. But one must differentiate between the villages, which are designed to reduce the dispersion of the population and make it possible to provide social services, and the Ujama villages, which are completely voluntary.

Yes, they admit, international trickle-down doesn't work. Yes, the multinationals are capable of antisocial practices like transfer pricing. I cite some horror stories about the copper companies in Chile. Yes, that is quite believable. But, they then ask me, what are the available options? A global socialist revolution? I agree that this is not exactly likely and that, if it were to take place, its impact on productivity would be uncertain. All right, they reply, we have to get the best out of what is now possible; not some total transformation, but international supervision of the multinationals.

Henry Kissinger's proposal for an international resources bank—in which the bank would protect the Western investor from undue risk (read "expropriation") and the Third World recipient from exploitation and questionable practices—is, they continue, far from perfect. But isn't it a mechanism that might actually facilitate some gains? What do I think of Robert McNamara at the World Bank, they ask. I say that I think he is doing a decent job, that he is sincere, even though I reject the basic capitalist structures and assumptions of the Bank itself.

So, here again is a problem that surfaces throughout my work on this book. Is the moral counterposed to the political and the economic? Does one have to acquiesce in a structure of injustice—the maldistribution of global wealth, and that maldistribution of global productive forces that is its cause—in order to improve the lot of the wretched of the earth just a bit? Are these appealing diplomats, who nevertheless are the representatives of a corporate-dominated administration in Washington, the realists and I an irrelevance? This is not the place to go into my answer. But in the last chapter, when I do, I have to show that what André Gorz has called "structural reforms" are possible—that is, changes which are practicable, yet begin to transform the very mechanisms of planetary inequity.

As I finish my chat with the Ambassador, a welcome surprise. Joan Wicken, the British woman who has been President Nyerere's personal assistant since 1961, and Cran Pratt, a Canadian who used to be a professor here and has just published a book on Tanzanian socialism, are to lunch with him tomorrow and I am invited.

8/3

A day of exhausting fascination. I am almost continuously involved in intense conversations from 12:30, when I went to the Ambassador's office, until 11:30 when a high-ranking diplomat (European, anonymous for reasons of discretion) brought me back to the Agip. I forgot to eat dinner.

The Ambassador's house was an orange-roofed mansion that is, by local standards, sumptuous. It was cool, tastefully appointed, with the Scotch poured on ice that an American could trust—that is, made from boiled, strained water. After the Ambassador and I discovered that we had been at the University of Chicago at the same time, in 1948–49, Joan Wicken and Cran Pratt arrived. She is a British woman, simply dressed, without makeup, with a warm, friendly, appealing face. But she is not, as I first feared, a dour, humorless fanatic. She is self-depreciatory, quick to admit mistakes, with no pretense to omniscience. A Labour Party and Oxford alumna, she came here in 1960 to work on an education foundation modeled on Ruskin College at Oxford (a worker's college). Nyerere was the President of the Foundation, and she soon became his personal assistant. She is, I hear on all sides, one of the most important people here.

Pratt had been on the faculty of the University for some years and, more to the point, is obviously on intimate, personal terms with the country's leadership. He is a Canadian, pleasant, open-faced, a shade more ideological than Joan Wicken, but by no means an ideologue in the pejorative sense of the term. In what follows, I will report impressions that derive mainly from Joan Wicken, but also from Cran Pratt, who agreed on all points under discussion.

Pratt told me that he hoped that the analysis of the Third World in my book, *Socialism,* was wrong. I had argued, sadly, that social-ism was impossible in the poor countries because the technological level was not high enough to allow the abolition of poverty and because the popular movement was not urbanized enough (sophis-ticated in the ways of democratic control) to take charge of the economic and social environment. I told him I hoped I was wrong, too. This theme was to weave in and out of the conversation all afternoon.

We talked of the problem of incentives. Could you, as Che Guevara thought, mobilize the people on the basis of nonmaterial incentives—ideals? We are trying to do it. We might fail, but that will only prove that we have failed, not that the idea is wrong. In this response, and in almost everything we discussed, I did not sense ideological fanaticism but almost its contrary. It seemed to me that these people were improvising their socialism in response to given problems and reality, that they were in no way following a blueprint. At every point, the possibility of error, of change, of new directions, was admitted. If there was a guiding principle, it was an opposition to elites, to bureaucracy, to some people living better than others, to anyone profiteering from the labor of someone else.

What about democracy? In Tanu, the constitutionally "supreme" party, two nominees are picked for every public post and that local decision is ratified in almost every case by the National Executive which does, however, have the right to override it. Then the two candidates, both of whom belong to Tanu, run against each other in a general election. They never speak alone, but always as a pair; they are required to speak in Swahili, so that no one can appeal to tribal prejudices by using a local language. In the process, incumbent legislators and even ministers of the government have been known to lose their seats—and fairly often. The antidemocratic potential of the system, I was told, resides in the right of the NEC to refuse the local preference and give, say, its favored candidate the most incompetent and unpopular person for an opponent.

All this, Cran and Joan told me, takes place within a commitment to egalitarianism. Indeed, they were disturbed that income differentials as large as 9 to 1 were still permitted. This egalitarianism was one of the reasons why the regime had rejected the strategy of the "progressive farmer"—that is, state encouragement for the most efficient, capitalist enterprise in the land, creaming off some of its profits and using that surplus for industrial investment or social services. Had Gunnar Myrdal's three-volume study of South Asia, which advocates a variant of the "progressive farmer" approach, had any influence? Little. The President had read it, but not many other people.

How, I asked, would you define success? If medicine and health and education were increased for the poorest, Joan replied. But then, I went on, do you want Tanzania to become a modern, urbanized society? No. We believe that a socialist system can be built on a much lower economic level than that. We know—this was said later on, when Joan and I were being driven in the Ambassador's car—that we will never catch up with the United States. Still, we don't need your wasteful, destructive standard of living in order to create justice here.

I had read these arguments before. But it is something else to hear them from someone who is engaged in the struggle for socialism in a desperately poor country. I reflected on our conversation. The critique of Third World socialism in my books had been based on the Western-centered assumption (Marx's) that only a society of high productivity and political (democratic) capacity could abolish greed and competition. Now I was being told that there was this other possibility, of socialism at a much lower level of material satisfaction, but one that does meet all of the necessities of existence. I will have to think about that.

I came back to the hotel, tired and exhilarated after some five hours of talk. I managed to calm down over a drink and then went off to the U.S. Information Service auditorium to hear Professor Benjamin Cohen lecture on theories of imperialism.

It was an average American academic performance on the subject, about 80 percent accurate and 100 percent off the real point. The 80 percent was mostly a matter of shooting fish in a barrel: disproving an idiot, vulgar "Marxist-Leninist" theory of imperialism, showing that material interest does not determine absolutely everything, that politics count, and so on. And then there was the point that Western investment since World War II has been primarily in advanced capitalist affluence, not in Third World poverty. I felt reassured. If this was the academic critique of my subject, I could be a little more confident about the truth of my own point of view. I don't want to be snide. Cohen was painstaking, methodical in a good sense of the word, and he rephrased his questioner's sallies so as to make them more effective than they originally were.

But then something happened that had more than a little symbolic significance. All the people who spoke from the floor accepted Cohen's caricature of the theory of imperialism. I had decided to keep quiet when I went to the meeting—no point in having two Americans debate in Dar—but I couldn't seem to stand by while the issue was discussed in such gross fashion. So I got up and said that the theory being dissected was obviously not substantial but that the more difficult problem was to explain why, in spite of the equalization that international trade was supposed to bring, the gap between the center and the periphery was growing. Cohen's answer was, to me at least, reasoned but unsatisfactory. More interesting was that when I finished my two-minute comment there had been a sharp burst of applause from the mainly African audience. (I was later told by the Ambassador that some members of the diplomatic community had complimented him on being extremely clever in having Americans take both sides of the question at the lecture.)

The meeting over, I went out with a high-ranking European diplomat. We picked up a European technocrat working for the government and talked over beer in a comfortable house in the foreign ghetto of Dar.

We discussed many things, some of the comments corroborating things I have already noted. But two insights were new. The press, I was told, is something of an anomaly. The spirit and rhetoric of the *Daily News*, the English-language daily, is dogmatic, hard-lining, "Marxist-Leninist." Nyerere, my hosts said, lets people have their head. He himself does not believe in this militant phrase-mongering, but he allows it. That, however, led to a most crucial question: What happens after Nyerere?

He is a charismatic leader, they say, who utterly dominates this place and has done so since the nineteen fifties. He is personally thoughtful, decent, visionary in the best sense of the word, anti-elitist and antitotalitarian. But what comes after him? Is Tanzanian socialism a construct of this one man so that, when he leaves the scene, a dictator can seize the enormous power now concentrated in his hands, power he uses deftly, sparingly, for the common good? That is basic. And no one even pretends to know the answer. But, then, this is a problem for all of Africa, which is still in its founding-father phase.

8/4

A frustrating morning of phone calls that don't get answered, or do get answered by people who speak only Swahili. I read, write this journal and prowl the streets. Dust everywhere; holes in the road; the people look poor. I walk through a "supermarket" with a pathetically small stock. In bookstores I find works by Left critics of the regime who regard Nyerere as a soft "petty-bourgeois" socialist. A picture book on Trotsky. Cheap novels. Penguins, religious books and tracts. This is not the East Berlin that I visited in 1959 or even the Warsaw that I saw in 1963. Indeed, Joan Wicken had even encouraged me to phone one of the local Leftists, the author of a study attacking the President. (He was one of my telephone failures.)

This afternoon a call from Joan. The President has found a half an hour or so in his schedule. I will see him Friday.

In the early evening, I went to a reception at Tony Mabbat's house. It was a lovely, large place that reminded me of Santa Barbara, California. The Mabbats and their guests of honor were in a receiving line. There were servants circulating with drinks and a cocktail hum of conversation, a scene of upper-class perfection, marred only by the fact that the lights didn't work. By luck, I quickly stumbled upon a young foreign-service officer who had been here as a Peace Corps volunteer ten years ago and who had gone back, out into the bush, to see the changes that had taken place during that decade. Some services, he said, were better: medicine, primary education. Some were worse: buses and mail. Some were about the same: food. He found an internal sense of nationhood, a confused, but appealing, concept of socialism. He was worried by a drift toward authoritarianism, but he did not think that the country had become Stalinist. Like all the official Americans I met here, save one, he was sympathetic to what was going on in Tanzania. Does anyone remember that the "ugly American" was a decent, positive—ultimately tragic—character?

The house cynic spotted me and delivered a lecture. Tanzania, he said, is going the way of Cuba, North Korea and China, no doubt of it. The tone in which this was said was arrogant, contemptuous. I suspect the man was doing his duty in disabusing the dilettante author of his Leftist illusions.

I left the party and had dinner with Joan and Cran. We went over many themes I have already described, but one thing puzzled me. Why the vehemence of the attacks on this country? Why the articles in the Western press equating the Ujama villages with forced collectivization in Russia in the thirties? I had just read a piece by John Bulloch in the *Sunday Telegraph*. It was haughty, patronizing, racist. Nyerere is presented as a figure of fun, "a gentle, amusing and erudite man, whose hobby is translating Shakespeare into Swahili," but also "a man possessed of a vision." "Perhaps it is significant," Bulloch writes, "that President Nyerere still retains an English woman as one of his closest advisors. She is Joan Wicken, a former Transport House official and a graduate of the London School of Economics. That could explain Tanzania." In fact, Joan is a graduate of Oxford, not LSE, but then, many of the other facts in the article are fanciful. More to the point is the Tory drawing-room assumption that the presence of one LSE graduate could explain the fate of a national and social movement of 13 million people during a period of sixteen years.

8/5

This morning I spent about an hour talking to Amir Jamal, the Minister of Finance. He is one of the most intelligent and perceptive individuals I have met on this trip.

I ask him if Tanzania can escape the discipline of the world market, or whether it is permanently fated to "voluntarily" subordinate itself to those structures on the basis of the law of comparative costs. The U.S., he begins, is utterly dominant; the Russians do not play a significant role in international trade, and the Americans should be proud that the demands are all addressed to them. The two possible extremes are autarchy, a total disengagement from the world system in which the United States looms so large, and the open door, which simply gives access to capital to do what it will. What is needed is "selective engagement." Like Tanzania's policy of buying buses from abroad, but not allowing TV to come into the country? Precisely. In some cases, he says, we must protect our own products, even if that imposes a higher cost on us than if we would import. But the practical, determining question there is how big that extra cost is.

There is, he continues, no such thing as a "free market" internationally. It has been "preempted" by the historical and technological weight of the United States and of advanced capitalism generally. It works on the basis of relations between unequals, and therefore following those relations does not lead to good outcomes. And yet, if Tanzania needs a cement plant, it must get the best one it can buy.

What about the rural emphasis in Tanzanian socialism? There is, he says, an intellectual romanticism that holds that the rural is inherently superior to the urban. Yet there is a potential in Tanzania for a more decent rural development than has taken place in the advanced nations. The countryside might thus offer alternatives to city life that are not now dreamed of.

None of this was a radical departure in policy or a startling new insight. What impressed me was the sense of an intelligent man dealing pragmatically with problems on the basis of an analysis that most mainstream economists in the West would think of as "left-wing," but which amounts to a simple common sense—albeit a common sense that requires some penetration to grasp—here on the shores of the Indian Ocean.

That afternoon I chatted with two young clerks from the bank. The contact had been made by one of them who had heard me attack Cohen at the USIS meeting and approached me when I came in to cash a check. They, like everyone else, have a deep commitment to the liberation of South Africa and Rhodesia. This is an obvious nationalist attitude that one would expect. But what impressed me during our hour and a half of conversation on the terrace of the Agip was their familiarity with Western politics, their sophistication about the international economy. Where, I asked, did they learn such things? Certainly not from the local press? No. There were discussions at the University and they could get *Time* and *Newsweek*. They, for example, were quite aware of the complexities of the Socialist-Communist alliance in the *Union de Gauche* in France. In some ways, it was a difficult conversation insofar as it touched on the Third World. We simply agreed, which doesn't make for vigorous exchange.

What struck me at day's end was the nonfanatical, even anti-ideological nature of both of my conversations. It may be that my unscientific sample is excessively reasonable. I have no way of knowing. But it can be said minimally that there is in this country a significant and important stratum that is a million miles removed from Stalinist dogmatism. Again, the ferocity, the lack of balance, the mendaciousness of what I have read in the American press about Tanzania strikes me. American opinion is the real source of fanaticism.

8/6

I go out to Kivukoni College, the party school. The ferry that takes me there is located right next to an open-air market. There are ramshackle structures, built out of random, scrounged materials. The area is packed, but not teeming. Silvery fish and fruit; cooking fires. It is, I learn later on that day, a free market, where nearby farmers bring some of their crops. Bustle, vitality, life; not a sense of unhappiness. The ferry itself was more frame than boat.

A high, narrow bridge, a plaited metal deck. Big trucks rolled on to it, packed without an inch to spare. On the sides, jammed in a little walkway, was a press of local humanity. Moslem women in the black, wraparound dress—but no purdah, no hiding the face— almost all of them very black. Not many Asians. A few soldiers. (The military is not very much in evidence here.) Me. We cross the harbor as dhows sail by, gracefully. On the other side I go down a dusty road, past trees where some birds are hooting. Owls? Do owls hoot in the daylight? Finally, I reach the college, a modern building located in a landscaped setting. Young people, mainly male, wearing military boots and gray fatigues walk by. I meet M——, a faculty member.

Kivukoni, I knew, had been started in the early sixties. The students here, I am now told, are mainly headmasters and head-mistresses from the secondary schools. They first get a three-month training in military ABCs. Then they study Tanzanian socialism, Tanu policies, and various other socialist currents in the world. They are also given a course in elementary bookkeeping, since the Party believes that basic management skills are necessary for anyone who is going to make a contribution to the society. The college has a capacity of 150 students, but it has never had more than 120 at a time. There are 116 now. There are stipends for those who leave family back home; and some women, who must do so, bring their kids with them. The students come from varied educational backgrounds and this sometimes makes teaching difficult.

Is there discussion of various socialist ideas and currents? Yes, but one must realize that we begin from a extremely low level of understanding of what socialism is. Many have some few ideas inherited from the old missionary interpretation of socialism. Most are puzzled by the intricacies of the Sino-Soviet split. Therefore, the various brands of socialism are treated in terms of the concrete experience that gave rise to them. The teacher smiles: I would be quite happy if at the end of the course everyone could give a clear definition of the difference between capitalism and socialism. That, he sighs, is not always accomplished.

Some students come for shorter courses. Law students, for example, take a three-month program. Well, then, I ask, is the point to turn out cadres? No, that would be too ambitious. We are try-ing to see to it that all the leaders of the society in whatever sphere—government, publicly owned enterprise, law, party—have a grounding in the basic principles of national policies. People here discuss Left critics of the regime, but the real problem is to educate them in fundamentals. They don't, however, have any books on the democratic-socialist point of view. As M—— walks me across the field, I promise to send some.

I return to the hotel, the phone rings, and Joan will pick me up in half an hour to take me to see the President.

We meet in Nyerere's private residence, a nice, but not terribly luxurious, white villa on the outskirts of Dar. There are people farming within a minute or two of his house. There is a fence, a few guards, but no great show of force. When I came into the compound, all I could see was one gateman, one soldier. Later on, during the conversation, I could see a couple of soldiers over by a fence. That was all. The house perches right on the edge of the water, and Joan took me to a conference area, an open-air, but roofed, patio. Nyerere came in, dressed in white, exuding an enormous vitality. When I talked to him, the body language, the tension, the energy, was perhaps the most striking visual aspect. There was also an almost teasing sense of humor.

I began by telling him a bit about this book, explaining that I believed that the United States was not moving in a good direction. I asked him what it was that he wanted that went beyond the UNCTAD demands. I added that I thought those demands excessively modest, since they sought only to perfect, not to transform the world market. He answered that I was quite right. UNCTAD is too modest. Even so, he said with a smile, the West did not accept those proposals. Therefore the Third World must continue to be reasonable, to make those moderate demands, although they were not at all the totality of what they wanted. The smaller European countries, he continued, were willing to accept them. The United States and West Germany were not.

But, the President said, the North-South issue is a process, not something that is going to be resolved overnight. In order for that process to go forward, there has to be education, in the Third World countries as well as in the rich nations. Under colonialism, Nyerere commented, the problems were obvious and evident; the evil to be fought was visible and naked and plain to see. At the time independence was achieved, he and Kenyatta and Houphouët-

Boigny and Ben Bella and the others thought that they had accomplished what needed to be accomplished, that no further confrontation was going to be necessary. Then they discovered that they were wrong. And even now, it is necessary to wake up the Third World so that it understands that political independence is, in and of itself, not enough.

In pursuing the struggle, he went on, he does not argue that the Americans are evil, or the Russians, or anyone else. The problem is not evil capitalists, but a system that has a certain logic. It makes no difference whether it is run by saints or sinners, so long as that logic is operating. For example, Nyerere said, the British Labour Party has made a decision to manage capitalism, to accept its limits. It has therefore also accepted fundamental restrictions on what it can do.

In terms of the Third World, he argued, it faces a fundamental struggle with the rich of the globe. It is on the order of the nineteenth-century struggle between the proletariat and the bourgeoisie. It will not be solved by a miracle; it will take a long time. What is needed is something that goes way, way beyond UNCTAD. For now, though, we will take whatever we can get. But what is required is not simply a dialogue between North and South, as people in the West are willing to say, but real confrontation.

What are the means of confrontation? The workers in the nineteenth century, the President replied, organized themselves, went on strike, withheld their labor. He smiled. So for a long time I have been talking about a trade union of the poor of the world. The key in this confrontation is that Africa has resources. The United States has a very high standard of living and it has the resources to maintain that standard of living within its borders. Europe does not. Africa can withhold its resources as the trade-union unionists in the nineteenth century withheld their labor. The Arabs, he said, have pointed the way. They've shown how it can be done in OPEC. They could have done better, but they have pointed the way. The outcome of this struggle will not, in the immediate future, be a socialist world. It will be a welfare world.

When he raised these points with Western politicians, Nyerere said, they gave democracy as their excuse for not doing anything. On a state visit to West Germany earlier in the year, he had posed a question to Helmut Schmidt. The United States has 6 percent of the world's population and 40 percent of its resources. The Soviet Union is emulating the United States, it is trying to catch up with it. The Common Market is emulating both the United States and the Soviet Union, it is trying to outdo both of them. How can there be anything left for us, Nyerere had asked Schmidt, if the United States and the Soviet Union and the Common Market share 120 percent of the available resources of the world?

Schmidt and others in the West to whom he talked said they couldn't respond rationally because their people would not go along with them. He had said to Schmidt, cut the aid to Tanzania if that will help you in the election. If your people are willing to vote and pay for armaments, but they find the trickle of aid to the Third World too much, so be it. But then go on and educate your people so that you don't have to use this democratic excuse.

What, I asked him, would success mean to you? How would you define it? Socialism, Nyerere began, has to combine vision and reality. I am a twentieth-century socialist. Then he paused and amended his statement: I am a twentieth-century Tanzanian socialist. The United States and Western Europe are based on nineteenth-century ideas. They are stuck with their achievements. Now people there are beginning to question those very achievements, wondering if they have not produced a monster. As a socialist, he said, I'm for equality and an end to exploitation. To do that, we have to industrialize. But we don't have to be victims of industrialization, like the people in the West. There are some advantages to our backwardness.

I asked him if this meant that his vision of socialism in Tanzania included much more of a rural component than one now found in the capitalist West? Absolutely. We want to have a civilized rural community where people do more than just farm. We want to create a society in which it is not necessary, in order to have amenities, to go to the cities. We want amenities in the countryside.

But how far, I ask, has this vision penetrated into the consciousness of your countrymen? It's a question of layers of understanding, he replied. In many ways, the vision has not penetrated very deeply. In the rich countries, thus far, only a relatively small group questions the monstrous character of the kind of growth that has taken place there. In Tanzania, the point of view he had been articulating has not reached everyone by any means. He looked to a group of his ministers who had come in and were sitting on the other side of the patio. He pointed to them, laughed, and said, "It has not gone that far."

Europe, the President said, destroyed wildlife and so did the United States. So the first thing the Americans and the Europeans say to us when they come here is, don't destroy the wildlife. At first, we thought they were being sentimental about animals. But now we've come to understand that that's not true. We have something that Europe and the United States don't have. We have clean beaches, clean water, clear air, and that is something we can keep. That, Nyerere continued, is accepted by the broad mass of people. But then he immediately qualified and complicated his own statement. The first thing the people see and know, he went on, is their poverty. They see the United States as the immediate answer. They want ruthless development, they have not grasped the full vision.

At the same time, Nyerere said, the idea that competition, ruthless, cutthroat competition, is wrong has penetrated deeply into Tanzanian society. And the ethic of cooperation has been accepted. On this somewhat ambiguous, yet hopeful, note the conversation ended. The President and his cabinet ministers had to discuss policy for an upcoming Third World meeting in Sri Lanka.

Joan and I came back to the Agip, and we talked a bit about my impression of the overwhelming vitality and humor of the President. Then the question of democracy arose again. Joan told me that when she came here, she was adamant on the need for a multi-party system. Now, she said, she's almost embarrassed for the degree to which she has modified her views. But one has to understand the enormous problem of nation-building in a hostile environment and the fragility of Tanzanian society. I do not know what I think analytically about these propositions. I am somewhat confused, much less certain than when I came here. But one thing I know. These are good people. Perhaps they are mistaken. I am not sure. But they are good. That I know.

8/7

I had tea with the Spains and then went out to the airport. The cab went down the dusty, crumbling streets, past the women in bright dresses, the knots of Moslem women in their black wraparounds. We drove by shanty towns and open-air markets, and there was an "Asian" air to the scene, only it was less oppressive than India, at least for a tourist of poverty. I arrived at the airport and then, after twenty-four hours of travel, reached New York City at four-thirty on a wet dawn.

What had I learned, not so much about Kenya and Tanzania— a couple of weeks of looking and talking is hardly a qualification for profundity—but about a democratic-socialist, Western reaction to them? Obviously, I preferred Tanzania. The corporate, commercial, multinational reality of Kenya put me off. I don't think this is social aestheticism. I am intellectually convinced, on grounds more solid than the glimpses of Africa this trip afforded me, that foreign capital will develop that country perversely. Indeed, I had seen some of the perversion: the contrast between the European center and the market place, where people huddled in cardboard shacks; the inevitable thinness of the development process, which did not, and could not, reach to the people out in the bush; and, for that matter, the pervasive sense of corruption, of venality, of the triumph of the worst of the capitalist vices without a corresponding victory for its virtues. It was obvious that Kenya had made progress. But I had no sense of a new departure, of a Kenyan "spirit" here. Maybe the model is the undeniable, but humiliating, progress that pre-Castro Cuba made as a Yankee plantation and whorehouse. That is too sharp a comparison. But it goes in the right direction.

With Tanzania, I find a real problem. Do I, after having written books and countless articles to the contrary, now think that it is possible to build socialism in a small, desperately poor African nation? No, I do not. I still think that a certain level of technology, of abundance, and a democratic sophistication among the masses, a capacity for self-government, in the economic as well as the political structure, is necessary for socialism. But, a question I have long puzzled over, what do socialists do if fate makes them active in such a country? I am deeply sympathetic to what Nyerere and his brothers and sisters are doing. The supercilious and superficial Western press is often on the side of the worst possibilities in Tanzania by denying and falsifying its best possibilities. Still, my mind may have been changed, not on basic outlook, but on a number of propositions.

First, it is right that the level of abundance necessary for socialism need not—should not, must not—be equated with the wasteful, fraudulent standard of living in the United States. In our rationalized irrationality, we "need" twenty or thirty breakfast foods, all of dubious nutritional value, competing primarily in advertising budgets. Socialism does not need such an "affluence," and Nyerere is quite right on that score. If Tanzania can shield itself from the "demonstration effects" of our criminally conspicuous consumption, it might be able to create cooperative socialist relationships on a material level lower than now exists in America or Europe—but not on the basis of poverty. Poverty is the insidious mother and father of greed.

Secondly, Nyerere may also be right that there are some advantages to his country's backwardness. They can see our rape of the environment. Perhaps they can avoid it.

Third, the democracy question is still critical. It is not that I make a fetish out of Western tradition. It is just that I am convinced that collective structures, including those erected for the best of all purposes, will dominate the people, unless the people can freely—which is to say, ordinarily, uncourageously, without having to go to a meeting every night—dominate them. Without political power in a collectivized society, the masses have no economic or social power. The men and women I met in Tanzania, even if so briefly, are bone of my socialist bone, blood of my blood—but I fear the odds they face.

Chapter Eight **Various Encounters**

I

MEXICO, AUGUST 1972

On this trip I met up with some meaningful clichés. Ordinarily, they would not be worth repeating, particularly since they can be glimpsed by the most casual visitor on the very surface of a society that has one of the deeper, more intricate histories of the Third World. But if my truths are simple enough to find, they are, because of the American innocence, regularly ignored. Tens of thousands of tourists from this country have stumbled over them, yet they have not made any great impression on us. With more than a century of a common border between us, we have robbed Mexico of half of its territory, exploited it, romanticized its pre-Columbian art and civilization and, on the whole, not looked at it.

But then that border experience was rich in a contemptuous familiarity. The first time I crossed over into Mexico, I heard a young American sailor in a Tiajuana street ordering, loudly and without embarrassment, a half a dozen young girls like so much meat at a supermarket. Indeed, that scene and others that I witnessed in Juarez later on could be a seamy, but accurate, symbol for the imperial relationship, one more readily grasped than the complexities of the balance of payments. The invisible hand of the world market converts their "superfluous" population into whores for our pleasure, which is in keeping with the theory of comparative advantage. When I went further into the interior—a trip to Mazatlan on the Pacific Coast in 1962—the reality became less tawdry and more dense, yet it remained as flagrant. From my tourist hotel I looked out in relative comfort on a dusty slum with ragged children and emaciated animals.

But, then, not all Americans were as casual as I or as unseeing as my countrymen. Paradoxically, the ones who sought the deep truths sometimes angered the Mexicans, too. Oscar Lewis, an anthropologist who turned the tape recorder into an instrument of art and drama, transcribed a series of profoundly revealing conversations with Mexican families. But some in that country felt— much like friends I met in India—that the conscientious Yankee was interested only in the degradation of underdevelopment, not in its strengths. When *The Other America* was translated into Spanish, one review played on the title of Lewis's *Children of Sanchez*. The article on my book was entitled "The Children of Smith." The *gringos*, they were saying, have their Third World too.

To avoid any misunderstanding on that count, I should state the obvious. What follows are a few insights and *aperçus*, personalized with the hope that such a technique might get a few of my affluent fellow citizens to open their eyes to a reality that is only next door to us. And the incredible fact of the matter is that these clichés probably will shock and surprise a good many Americans.

I had arrived in Mexico City one evening, rented a car at the airport, and driven along modern roads to an American hotel that maintained that standard of comfortable mediocrity that our innkeepers are bringing to the middle and upper classes of the world. The next morning, I drove through a thriving metropolis with wide, Parislike boulevards and a skyline dotted with construction cranes. The children dressed in dirty tatters and selling gum along the way should have been a signal to me, but they weren't. It wasn't until I got out on the highway to Cuernavaca that the visible, palpable contrasts of this country, of modernity and tradition, industrial wealth and semifeudal poverty, came into focus.

There was a literary reason why my eyes began to see. After I left Mexico City, I began to go past little *pueblos,* somnolent, obviously impoverished, villages clumped along a modern road. And then I began to see *campesinos* walking along the way, wearing the cheap, white cotton pants, the *calzones.* The echoes began. I had first seen those poor rural workers in reproductions of Diego Rivera's revolutionary murals. They were the Zapatistas, the followers of Emiliano Zapata, perhaps the Mexican rebel best known in the United States. Zapata's fame did not derive from any serious American encounter with Mexican history, but from a marvelously romantic film, written by John Steinbeck and starring Marlon Brando, *Viva Zapata!*

I knew a little more about Zapata than I had learned from the murals and the movie, mainly because of an excellent book about him by John Womack. That was why I became puzzled as I drove toward Cuernavaca. Today, that city is one of the most Americanized in Mexico, a place for cheap retirement in a climate of perpetual springtime. Yet it is the capital of the state of Morelos, the home of Zapata and his movement. The revolution that he led began in 1910, and the Zapatistas were, as Carlos Fuentes has argued, a very modern phenomenon: guerrillas as the "natural defense weapon of a settled local culture." It was, then, a precursor of the Chinese and Vietnamese revolutionary movements. Moreover, it was part of a national struggle that eventually saw Mexico stand up to American power. But why, if all this glorious history had taken place, were these poor people walking down the road as if nothing had changed? I had seen a problem in social theory and analysis with my naked eyes.

I will hazard only the outline of a sketch of a possible answer. Some of the factors involved are located in the distant past: in the eighteenth century, a Mexican priest invented the cotton gin before Whitney did, but it was cheaper to exploit fifty peons than to buy a machine that could put them out of work; in the nineteenth century, the British loans not only carried a high interest rate but were sometimes discounted up to 55 percent.* For my purposes, however, begin with Porfirio Diaz, the dictator who dominated Mexico's entry into the twentieth century. Under his rule, the big

* That is, you received only 45 percent of the money on which you paid the interest.

farms, the *latifundia*, expanded at the expense of the peasants, who lost their common land; and the railroads, mines and oil wells were all run either by or for American capital. In 1910, the year the Revolution began, North Americans owned 78 percent of the mines, 72 percent of the foundries, 58 percent of the petroleum, 68 percent of the rubber industry and fifty million dollars' worth of ranches.

From 1910 to 1920, the country was in the throes of revolution and civil war, with the United States intervening consistently on the side of reaction, applauding the assassination of Francisco Madero, a leader committed to democratic rights. Then, from 1920 to 1940, there was a period of reform, climaxing during the presidency of Lazaro Cardenas in the thirties. In 1930 it turned out that, despite a revolution with a radical agrarian wing, 1.5 percent of the proprietors still owned 97 percent of the land. Cardenas pushed forward with land reform and, when the American oil companies openly defied government decrees, was driven to nationalize them. He was met with a boycott by the American corporations, a strike of capital, a refusal to even transport Mexican oil and, of course, the charge of being a Communist.

I remember the latter point quite well. As a very young Catholic in St. Louis, Missouri, during the thirties, I listened breathlessly to a Mexican priest telling how the Reds in his country were persecuting the Church. The ironic point is that Cardenas was a rather pragmatic reformer and certainly no Communist (he gave Leon Trotsky refuge at a time when the Russian secret police were hounding the old Bolshevik leader throughout the entire planet).

Then, from 1940 to 1970, Mexico had more conservative (and sometimes reactionary) leadership. It made tremendous economic strides and was regularly cited as a country at the "takeoff" stage. Under these circumstances, the foreigners got friendly again. Between 1940 and 1961, for instance, direct foreign investment totaled $1.3 billion, but foreign profit-taking amounted to $2.2 billion. As one Mexican scholar put it, the nation was being "decapitalized" by its partners in the United States and the other advanced economies. Still, there was undeniable accomplishment; only, it was distorted. It was not just that the Americans played such a major role. Because Mexico took thirty years of turmoil to get into a position for capitalist development, it did not reach that fabled "takeoff" stage until 1940, and by then the "takeoff" could not possibly repeat the Western experience, with its organic and reciprocal development of technology and work force. The dissonance of modernity and tradition was inevitable.

So it was that agriculture came to be dominated by large units, with 5 percent of the farms accounting for four fifths of the production in the sixties. That was one reason why the *campesinos* walking along the road in Morelos in 1972 looked so poor. So it was that industry crowded into Mexico City, with over half of it located there. So it was that in the early fifties, the richest 20 percent had ten times the income of the lowest 20 percent and, by 1969, sixteen times that income. The result was that, in Fuentes's striking phrase, "the children of Zapata turned themselves into the children of Sanchez," that the agrarian revolutionaries became, not only poor farmers, but poor slum-dwellers as well.

So I arrived in Americanized Cuernavaca, driving past the statue of Zapata, and went to an international labor meeting. There, I confronted another obvious truth: that everyone in Latin America, Left, Right and Center, knows the essential of the history that I have just outlined. To innocent Americans, the notion that their country is imperialist is a Communist myth. To the majority of the world's people with a minimal political consciousness, it is an overwhelming fact of life.

Indeed, America's imperial politics might have kept me from going to Cuernavaca at all. The CIA had used American unions as a front for its operations in Latin America in a number of cases. My friend Norman Thomas, who ran for President as the Socialist Party candidate six times, had been duped by one of those enterprises, a fact that he bitterly resented in the years before his death. Once, in the early sixties, when I was writing about an American union, a knowledgeable friend even pointed out its CIA infiltrator to me. So, normally I would have thought twice about an invitation to go to Mexico for a union conference. In this case, I had no hesitation. The offer had been made at a conference of Labor for Peace, the organization of antiwar unionists, by Jerry Wurf and Vic Gotbaum, the President and New York director of the American Federation of State, County and Municipal Employees. When

Jerry had won the presidency, his first official act was to throw the CIA agent out of the union. So I was delighted to go to Cuernavaca.

In the conference, I presented an analysis somewhat less radical than the one put forward in this book. My critique of the United States was based more on the work of Raoul Prebish, Celso Furtado and the economists of UNCTAD than on the writings of European and Third World Marxists. Even so, I explained how the poor nations of Latin America were transferring wealth to the United States. And I tried to give the Latin unionists—representatives of public employees from around the hemisphere—a sense of why American workers were even more concerned about losing their jobs, and therefore more prone to protectionism, than workers in the more advanced welfare states of Europe. In my country, I said, a man or a woman loses everything—health insurance and vacation pay as well as regular wages—when they become unemployed. It is not like Sweden, where the government can make way for Third World imports because it guarantees every displaced worker a new job. I was, in short, basically critical of the United States, but hardly "anti-American."

Two aspects of the reception I received are particularly relevant. First of all, my theories, which most Americans would probably find strained and far-fetched, struck them as the merest common sense. These people were, for the most part, not intellectuals; they were veterans of the struggle for daily bread. That, however, was the point. My analysis, complex and abstract from the perspective of the American innocence, was reportage as far as they were concerned. Secondly, and perhaps surprisingly, they were not only acutely conscious of what the United States had done to their countries, but enormously heartened that an American would talk about it. Despite all of the outrageous history to which this nation had subjected them, they were ready to respond to that which was good and decent in our heritage.

It was a myth of the Kennedy administration—a myth that, by the way, was a credit to the believer's heart, if not to his or her head—that there was a vast democratic Left in Latin America just waiting for a word of encouragement from Washington. The oligarchs were to be bribed into allowing the masses to have a say, and the latter, given half a chance, would choose democratic social change as against Communist totalitarianism or traditional stagnation. This version of the hemisphere ignored, among other things, the imperial structure that had been put in place. So, I am not suggesting that the United States need only shed its cruel innocence to restore democracy to Latin America. I am saying—a point that I will develop in Chapter Nine—that there is a remarkable potential for forgiveness among some of those whom we have wronged, that there are some possibilities, even if there are no clear-cut solutions.

In Cuernavaca, my dialogue was with unionists. When I got back to Mexico City it was, because of a series of strange circumstances, with the President of the Republic, Luis Echeverria. The accidents which brought us together are not relevant, but the slightly bizarre scene in which the conversation took place might transmit the flavor of the event.

When I went to the National Palace that day, I had no idea that I would talk to the President. I was going to drop off copies of one of my books for Echeverria and an assistant, both of whom I had met in New York earlier in the year. Basically, however, I was being a tourist. My wife, my two sons—one was four years old, the other eighteen months—and my mother-in-law were with me. I wore a rumpled jacket with a missing button. Suddenly, we were in the anteroom to the President's office. Delegations were coming and going, and I once again heard echoes of the movie *Viva Zapata!* When I did get a chance to talk with Echeverria, my sons were chasing around his office, and one of them asked the President how to say "Batman" in Spanish (the answer: "Batman"). It was a strange setting for serious discussion of the Third World.

Echeverria was, at this point, a political surprise. He had been picked for the presidency according to the traditions of the Party of Revolutionary Institutions (PRI) by his predecessor, a conservative man. The nomination was tantamount to election. When Echeverria came to power it was widely assumed, particularly on the Left, that he would continue his country's rightward drift, moving even further away from the turbulent traditions of the years between 1910 and 1940. Moreover, he had been the Minister of the Interior when the police had massacred student demonstrators in 1968; and, the Left thought, that boded ill for their cause. But as soon as he took office—and, as far as shrewd observers were concerned, even during the ritual of the presidential campaign—he became a man of the Mexican Left.

It is important to understand what that means. It is an extension of the point that emerged in the discussion at Cuernavaca, that it is dangerously wrong to equate opposition to American imperialism with Communism or even socialism. That identification was, of course, made by American conservatives during Echeverria's incumbency. It was one of the reasons why foreign investment declined in the seventies. Echeverria raised wages, doubled spending on education and helping the peasants, and raised the prices that the state enterprises charged the private sector. He also denounced the workings of the multinationals, the actions of Mexican corporations in some cases and, while seeking the Secretary Generalship of the UN, became a prominent spokesman for a new international economic order.

And yet, one of the strongest impressions I had from our conversation is that he is *not* a socialist. He was, he made it quite clear to me, in favor of a mixed economy, of reforms, not of fundamental structural change. He did not, he said, agree programmatically with Fidel Castro or Salvador Allende. But, and on this count he was most emphatic, he was in solidarity with Castro and Allende when the United States tried to intervene in the internal lives of their countries. (Later, when America, using indirect financial pressure more than the CIA, helped topple Allende, Echeverria was to give asylum to Allende's widow.) The United States, he noted wryly, had demonstrated the ability to come to terms with Communist China and the Soviet Union (this was the year of Nixon's visits to Peking and Moscow); why could it not act reasonably in its own hemisphere?

He was obviously aware of the flow of funds from South to North and we talked about the trends making for a new maldistribution of global wealth. But again, I was convinced that he found some of my more radical ideas utopian or downright undesirable. And yet, the sense of Third World solidarity that he manifested is extremely important. Among other things, it explodes any simpleminded economic determinism. The underdeveloped countries, as Henry Kissinger clearly understood between October 1973 and September 1975, have their own internal tensions. In particular, poor countries suffered more from the OPEC quadrupling of oil prices than the rich. So Kissinger's strategy was based on a plausible *realpolitik:* set the Fourth World against the Third World, the poorest of the poor against the world's new middle class.

Only, it didn't work, and one of the reasons why was apparent in my chat with Echeverria. Mexico is always cited as part of that new, international middle class (though, as I learned on the road to Cuernavaca, that is much more ambiguous than most proponents of the notion think). To be sure, since it has its own, nationalized oil, it did not need to be concerned about the OPEC policies and could even gain from them. Still, if Echeverria had followed Kissinger's economistic split, he would have sided with the rich powers, not the poor. The point is that the political emotions of the Third World are not the result of mere material calculation. One must take into account the feelings of people who have been patronized and pushed around for centuries. Without sentimentalizing, Third World nations have been quite adept at fighting one another, and the Indians of East Africa could testify bitterly to the fact that nonwhiteness does not necessarily unify people; one must take this political and cultural factor into account with the economic statistics.

After the interview with Echeverria, I went to a dinner party given by Carlos Fuentes. It was interesting politically as well as sociologically.

The people at Fuentes's house were writers and intellectuals, some of them quite prominent in their nation's cultural life. They had been outsiders for years, critics of the conservative drift in Mexico, but without a political base of their own. They had, of course, been outraged when the police, under Echeverria's control, turned on the demonstrators. Octavio Paz, a man of dazzling talent who was among our fellow guests that night, had resigned as Mexican Ambassador to India in protest over the event. In the sixties, Fuentes himself had been a champion of Fidel (so was Lazaro Cardenas, the reforming President of the thirties). Indeed, the first time I met him, in New York, the American government had allowed him only to visit Manhattan. He had secretly violated that restriction and visited Norman Mailer in Brooklyn.

When Echeverria made his turn to the Left, these intellectuals began to move toward him. In a sort of informal agreement it was understood that they could criticize the government within a context of friendship for it. Later on, in 1975 and 1976, this alliance was to break down and Paz was to once again resign in protest—from the editorship of the most distinguished monthly publication in Mexico, *Plural*, a supplement of the newspaper *Excelsior*. Echeverria's friends had taken over *Excelsior* and moved it to the Right. (Fuentes, who by this time was the Mexican ambassador in Paris, stayed on in his post.) These more recent events do not concern me here. What is relevant is the fact that these Mexican intellectuals had embraced Echeverria because they were fearful of a move to the dictatorial Right. They had watched the defeat of democratic hopes in many countries to the south; they had seen young people killed in their own country for demonstrating against the government—ironically, with Echeverria in command.

The point is that these Leftist intellectuals were motivated basically and primarily by a commitment to democratic change. And this was so even though some of them had been strong supporters of Fidel. Indeed, on that count one wonders if their Castroism had not been engendered primarily by America's interventions against Cuba. The other trend that was apparent that evening was social and cultural.

Fuentes's house was substantial and comfortable. Everyone there was deeply immersed in European culture; everyone spoke fluent English. Their politics was based on an identification with Indians and *mestizos*, with the poor people of their country. But they were not poor. They were, for the most part, radicals and yet the drinks and food were served according to the male-dominated Spanish tradition, with men receiving attention first. It would be easy to satirize the situation, to joke about the gulf that separated the people at that dinner party from those on whose behalf they act and think. That would be morally simplistic—is one required to be either a Saint Francis of Assisi or else a bloated plutocrat?—but it would also overlook an immensely important aspect of the Latin part of the Third World.

In Mexico, and throughout much of the hemisphere, there is, in Victor Alba's phrase, the "submerged" nation of the poor, "indifferent to politics, with awareness of the world shrunk to the dimensions of a village." They constitute two thirds of the people; they are not historical actors. Actually, the Revolution and its aftermath has brought more people into active social life in Mexico than in other Latin countries. Yet the basic problem exists throughout all of Latin America. The majority have been "marginalized" by the evils described in this book. They simply do not count. Minorities and elites, like the people whom I met at Carlos's party, were the deciders.

I encountered that fact again later on, when I visited my brother-in-law, a Guatemalan doctor, and stayed at his home in Guatemala City. Berto's family has a long and distinguished history, generally on the Left of Center. Yet it contains people who fought for the Right, and when the CIA helped the latter to overthrow the Arbenz regime in the fifties, one of Berto's relatives went into exile, another was with the victorious forces. And in talking to people in Guatemala City I learned that the politicals of Left, Right and Center all tend to come from the same families and social class. For that matter, in Mexico City in 1972 I had seen university students—a privileged stratum of the society—occupying buildings in the name of the insurrectionary Left.

On this trip, then, I saw some of the things that I had previously only analyzed from afar: the tragic lopsidedness of Mexico's relatively successful economic development that makes of the children of Zapata the children of Sanchez; the well-nigh universal understanding of the imperial role of the United States and a certain solidarity that derives from it; the role of the educated elites, and the marginality of the majority, a reality that America helped create, which makes the democracy we profess so difficult to create in these countries.

II

WASHINGTON, D.C., JUNE 1976

Robert S. McNamara could serve as a symbol of America's cruel innocence. And perhaps I can sharpen the paradox inherent in that phrase if I immediately add that I think McNamara is a man of enormous sincerity, decent values and genuine moral passion. So his participation in our international wrongdoing, like that of the nation itself, is unwitting and even dedicated to effecting results that are nearly the exact opposite of those that are in fact achieved.

I talked to McNamara early on a June evening in his tasteful, spacious office on the twelfth floor of the World Bank building. The building itself is bankerly, echoing, substantial. The room in which we chatted was two stories high, with a giant globe in one corner. McNamara himself was older than the familiar figure of the sixties, the hair not so slicked down as in the photographs of that period, the face more lined. And yet his legendary mannerisms were very much still in evidence. Our discussion was on a "background" basis, which means that I can only summarize, but not quote, him. But the style was as communicative as the substance.

McNamara spoke with an incredible intensity. At first, he reeled off analyses and statistics with such rapidity that I had the distinct feeling that I was hearing a summary of his recent speeches. But then I agreed with him that the question of the Third World posed a basically moral issue, and he seemed charged with a flow of new energy. He impressed me as very much a Protestant in the sociological sense of that term: stern with himself, intent on doing the work of God in the world. He reminded me of another very Protestant genius I have known, Robert M. Hutchins. Hutchins had become president of the University of Chicago at thirty, the *enfant terrible* of the American academy. When I got to know him, he was President of the Fund for the Republic, a civil-liberties foundation. In that McCarthy era, the Right accused him of Communist sympathies, which always struck me as funny (if it were not also sinister), since he was motivated by a combination of aristocratic *noblesse oblige* and missionary zeal. I felt both qualities in McNamara.

But he is a modern missionary—a missionary technocrat. That last quality had, of course, helped him make the most tragic error of his life: the continual miscalculations of the course of the unconscionable war in Vietnam. All of the "kill" statistics and other figures with which McNamara buttressed his arguments omitted only the essential: the political power of a national liberation movement, the political powerlessness of the antinationalist militarists in Saigon, for all of their military hardware. Toward the end of that disaster, McNamara gave a strange speech in Montreal. The poverty of the underdeveloped nations, he said, was the greatest single source of violence, past, present and future, in the post-World War II epoch. "The years that lie ahead," he said, ". . . are pregnant with violence for the nations in the southern half of the globe. This would be true even if no threat of Communist subversion existed—as it clearly does."

That speech, David Halberstam noted in *The Best and the Brightest*, had been one more factor disillusioning Lyndon Johnson and leading him to move McNamara from the Defense Department to the World Bank. It is also a fascinating insight into a man who, playing a leading role in a murderous war in Southeast Asia, was at the same time honestly and passionately moved by the plight of the world's poor. Indeed, I suspect, both commitments derived from the same source, from an internationalism that in one case was served by military terror and in the other by a desire to feed the hungry. McNamara sharpens these dialectical complexities as only a brilliant and powerful man can. He is, I think, an average American writ heroically, and in the case of Vietnam, tragically, large.

My overall impression of our conversation was that McNamara was critical of practically all the actors involved in trying to deal with the problem of Third World poverty. The UNCTAD demands for the stabilization of commodity prices would only aid a few of the biggest exporters among the underdeveloped countries and would not result in any net transfer of income to the globe's poor. The Kissinger proposal for international guarantees to private investors would accomplish some good things, but it was largely irrelevant for a country like India. The current orthodoxy among population experts—that only economic development can provide the social setting in which family limitation becomes possible—is economistic, simplified, negative. (More on this point in a moment.) Foreign-aid patterns had largely been set by Cold War political considerations—hence India's very low per capita assistance—and the rich countries had failed to create real trade opportunities for the Southern powers. But then the internal inequities and conservatism of these Third World nations was another factor inhibiting desperately needed changes. How could one expect land reform to work, when, as in India, it was placed under the direction of landlords?

In short, McNamara was prepared to criticize everyone's sacred cows—the pretensions of the United States and the other advanced capitalist powers, as well as those of the United Nations and of the

Third World itself. He did so, I suspect, precisely because of the sense of moral urgency which motivates him. He talked with a particular passion about what underdevelopment does to children, of how a lack of food may well stunt the brain of a fetus or an infant. This was absolute poverty, he argued, and there should be a worldwide commitment to abolishing it. One can define minimal needs, and those needs should be satisfied for every human being. Indeed, McNamara was optimistic when he spoke in generalities, seeing the possibility of some redistribution of planetary wealth in the next half century. But, then, he seemed to be pessimistic when it got to specifics, noting that India could not expect to raise its per capita income much beyond $260 during the next thirty years.

McNamara was, I thought, most provocative on the issue of population. It has been United Nations orthodoxy since the Bucharest Conference in 1974 that economic development is the only answer to the problem of soaring birth rates. That situation, as Chapter Five defined it, is a direct result of the uneven, nonorganic development of the poor countries. They have, in Carlo Cipolla's phrase, high "agricultural" birth rates and low "industrial" death rates. But, the Bucharest approach argues, this cannot be changed by individualistic "family planning" programs. The reason why people in the underdeveloped economies have so many children is that this is a form of social security, of being sure that there will be someone to take care of you when you are old. However, the sum total of those individual decisions is a national rate of population increase that makes development difficult or even impossible. The Third World, it will be remembered, has had roughly the same growth rate as the developed societies during the postwar period. Only the growing mass of people has pulled the per capita rate down until it only barely keeps pace with the new mouths to feed.

Therefore, this theory concludes, one must break the economic and social circle, and rapid development is the only way to do this. Then there will be enough resources to provide a secure old age for everyone, and the motive for having a large family will be abolished. Thus the poor countries will essentially follow in the footsteps of the rich. Industrialization will give them the low fertility rates typical of industrial economies.

McNamara is not opposed to this line of reasoning. He challenges it, however, when it claims to be the sole and exclusive truth about population. It is correct, he holds, that nineteenth-century industrialization in the West was accompanied by a decline in the birth rate. But does this necessarily mean that the industrialization was the sole, or the prime, cause of that transformation? In fact, a whole series of social determinants changed at the same time. There were industrialization, an enormous increase in education, changes in the status of women, and so on. Who is to define the specific weight of each one of these factors? Who is to say that industrialization was the key to the population trend?

McNamara's skeptical questions have policy implications. He wants to push economic development and industrialization, of course. But he also wants to speed up educational and social changes, and he thinks that they might affect the fertility curves even prior to the coming of the factories. A global shift in the role of women, for instance, might, among many other things, result in a lowered birth rate. There are obvious problems with this line of thought. The place of women in, say, Indian society is clearly related to the parochialism and conservatism of the village life. Is it possible to break into the organic whole of underdevelopment—which is as structured as the organic whole of economic development—and to change only one of its aspects?

It might be possible. That is, economic forces are not the only ones at work in this process. We know, for example, that England and Wales continued with an "agricultural" birth rate after the Industrial Revolution, while France very quickly adjusted and reached an "industrial" level of fertility. Demography, which is not one of the more exact sciences, is not sure as to exactly why this happened. And I think McNamara is right to say that Third World planners should take advantage of every possible indeterminacy. Radios did not exist in the nineteenth century; they do in the twentieth. Which is to say that there are the means for cultural revolution in existence today that just might change some of those economic and social inevitabilities. Clearly, this point of view cannot be counterposed to programs for rapid industrialization. But McNamara is right. It would be tragic if the planners became hypnotized by a unifactor economic determinism in which the only relevant variable for changing population is industrialization.

But if McNamara is as I have described him here, how can I

possibly say that he is a quintessential representative of America's cruel innocence? I have, after all, suggested that he is not only morally committed, but thoughtful and intelligent as well. What then is the fatal flaw?

The building in which our conversation took place provides the beginning of an answer: the World Bank. The Bank is structurally dominated by the principal donors, the so-called Part I countries, who have an influence proportioned to their financial contributions. They have 64.3 percent of the votes and the United States alone has more than 20 percent of them, which constitutes an effective veto power. At times, this can be a most unsubtle and obvious corruption. In 1967, the Bank refused to cooperate with U Thant and the UN in the battle against *apartheid* in South Africa. The grounds were that the Bank could not establish political criteria for its loans.

In the early seventies, with McNamara in control, that position of principled neutrality vanished when the United States organized a worldwide financial blockade against the socialist government of Salvador Allende in Chile. The Chileans suddenly discovered that all of their requests for assistance got lost, delayed, postponed. Rumor has it that by the last year of the Allende regime, 1973, McNamara was working within the Bank to shift that policy, but that he was thwarted by the American votes on the Board. As soon as Allende was overthrown, however, the Bank once again became friendly. Indeed, the group who saw McNamara just before I did was headed by a Chilean cardinal. Even taking this unconscionable incident from a point of view most favorable to McNamara—that he did not personally go along with the vicious policies of the institution he heads—it makes my point. In the sphere of international power politics, sincerity counts for nothing. The World Bank as an institution was, and is, subordinate to the political interests of the United States, and this places a profound limitation on its effectiveness in helping the Third World.

But then there is an even deeper truth, one which is much less obvious and dramatic than the actions taken against Chile. The Bank raises its funds on private money markets and, from the very outset, has had to establish and maintain a reputation for "responsibility"—that is, conservatism, among the rich. Indeed, in 1946 the Bank refused to become a United Nations agency precisely be-

---

cause it feared an adverse reaction on Wall Street if it did. It has, two sympathetic historians have written, "unflinching rectitude on the question of defaults and expropriations," and it has refused to help countries that, like Algeria, Sukarno's Indonesia and Nasser's Egypt, engaged in such practices. There is no question that McNamara, to his credit, changed these attitudes somewhat, for instance that he got the Bank to give up its principled opposition to publicly owned industry. Nevertheless, the Bank tells its borrowers what kind of conduct it expects from them, and sometimes draws up plans, and that its criteria are always sober and orthodox, which is to say *capitalist*.

Leaving McNamara's office, I was somewhat torn as I thought about these things. When I met with Nyerere in Tanzania, I felt a rush of socialist sympathy for him, even though I feared that his audacious project of building socialism in a land of great poverty would be overwhelmed by those conditions not under his control. I did not feel a sense of fraternity with McNamara—he is, after all, a technocrat, not a comrade—and yet, his moral intensity, his commitment, were both impressive and appealing. And perhaps that is why I find him paradigmatic of the nation's cruel innocence. America, like McNamara, is genuinely moved by the suffering of children; its culture shares his Protestant sense of mission. And it too expresses these decent feelings from within a framework of action that is basically conservative. My task would be emotionally easier if those whom I criticize were evil. They are not. But, then, that is why one is permitted to hope.

III

NEW YORK, 1976

The United Nations is a sobering place, particularly if one thinks, as I do, that a genuine world government is an absolute necessity in the twenty-first century. Given that hope, I would like to be able to say that the nucleus of that possibility can be seen, here and now, in the UN. The problem is that, after fifteen years of episodic contact with the institution, I am more impressed by its frail humanity than with its capacity to master the future.

I first began to meet people around the UN in the early sixties, when my wife covered this beat for the *Village Voice*. Perhaps the

most eerily symbolic moment of that period came at the very height
of the Cuban missile crisis. I was waiting for Stephanie in a restaurant where the mood was quite somber, as it was throughout New
York during a week when the outbreak of thermonuclear war was
quite thinkable. She arrived, and I anxiously asked her what
was going on up at the UN. The answer was that the press corps
had opened its new bar on schedule that evening, and reporters
and delegates, none of whom had the least sense that anyone in the
building could control the events taking place, had crowded together in international harmony over drinks.

Then over the years I have moved occasionally on the fringes of
the UN. An original impression was confirmed: that the human mix
among the diplomats was quite uneven. I met brilliant and subtle
people; I also encountered a disturbing percentage of incompetent
politicians who had been dumped in the parliament of the world
because they couldn't fit in in their own countries. The high hopes
of the founding years were, it seemed to me, in something of a
shambles. And yet, I continued to believe in the UN, even if without illusions, because it is the only beginning of a new, global
system that we have.

One of the most competent and penetrating of the UN diplomats
whom I met is the Austrian Ambassador, Peter Jankowitsch. He is
a thoughtful and astute student of world politics; his wife, Odette,
is a specialist in Third World issues. Both are socialists, and that
had been the basis of our original contact. (European social-
democratic governments sometimes appoint conservatives, and
even aristocrats, as ambassadors, and Peter's case is not necessarily
typical.) We had become friends over the years, so I was able to
ask Peter's help when I began to work on this book. He assembled
about ten Third World ambassadors and two or three high-ranking
international civil servants for a *dîner débat* in his apartment.

As we gathered for cocktails, I could have been at any upper-
middle-class party in Manhattan. The only difference was that
several languages were being spoken and even the English was
peppered with bureaucratic phrases: ECOSOC did this or that,
UNCTAD had come up with "integrated" demands, et cetera. The
ambassadors came from Asia, Africa and the Middle East. (Since
our talks were not on the record, I will only identify them with
regional or broad political tags.) They were most emphatically not

of the type that had been sent to New York because they were too incompetent at home. Peter, I realized, had invited some of the best-informed and shrewdest of his colleagues. What follows, then, is a description of Third World opinion as it is stated in semi-private, with most of the official rhetoric removed.

As coffee was served, I began with a brief statement. I was, I said, in complete sympathy with the demands for a new international economic order. The distribution of the world's resources was intolerably unjust and had to be changed. But, I continued, I also felt that the program put forward by UNCTAD at the Nairobi meeting was too moderate. It could be accepted *in toto* by the United States, because it would most certainly not make any significant change in the global maldistribution of wealth. So, I agreed with the Third World generalities, but I had been unable to discover any specific program that would actually have the effect of closing the gap between the rich and the poor. What measures would the assembled ambassadors propose, to implement their declared purposes?

A Middle Easterner spoke and his reply was, with perhaps two exceptions, typical of the responses I heard throughout the evening. The mechanisms for a new order, he said, already exist. They are to be found in the Economic and Social Council (ECOSOC), in GATT (the international tariff organization), in UNCTAD. The real problem, he went on, is that the world, for psychological and economic reasons, will not face up to the issue. For example, Herman Kahn accepts the gap as a permanent feature of global life. If, however, this reluctance to deal with the question were overcome, there would be no real problem in solving it. Currently, he said, inflation is a prime tool of neocolonialism (which meant, I assumed, that the steady increase in the price of manufactured goods was a prime factor in the unfair terms of trade for the Third World). Therefore, "indexing" prices so that the goods of the underdeveloped economies get the same increases as those of the developed would be a major means of dealing with the situation.

Another Middle Easterner spoke in the same vein. He listed the standard Third World package: make the transfer of resources from rich to poor automatic; industrialize the South by transferring technology to it; and integrate all these demands in a single, comprehensive plan. Then he went on to say that he thought these things could be accomplished without great difficulty and that the commodity agreements—for stabilizing, or raising, the prices the Third World gets—were the proper instrumentality of change. He took sharp exception to an article by Geoffrey Barraclough in the *New York Review of Books* which developed an analysis somewhat similar to my own. In the long run, he said, there are global common interests. Just as the capitalists and workers in the West had come to an accommodation, so should the North and the South in the world. The Russians, he commented (and this was something I heard from almost every Third World spokesperson I talked to), were simply not relevant to this process, since they played no great role on the world market.

At this point, a radical African intervened. UNCTAD, she said in agreement with my opening statement, was essentially pro-capitalist and accepted a world-market mechanism that perpetuated, rather than transformed, the problem. An interplay developed. That is all fine and good, said an Asian, and your revolutionary fervor is exemplary. But how do you actually change things if you go completely outside the market mechanism? And in any case, the Communists buy cheap and sell dear; they too take advantage of that capitalist structure. Another African spoke. He was, he said, pessimistic about ever closing the gap. Moreover, he went on, it is a mistake to ask questions about the new international economic order in a setting like this. People will not talk openly about what they really feel. As I understood his drift, he was saying that the private attitudes of at least some of the people present were to the Left of the negotiating positions taken by their governments.

An Asian then commented that one should not talk about systems at all. Each developing country should try to do something for its own people, and the United States should facilitate that effort. But there was no point in talking about systems. A UN expert focused much of the discussion with an analogy. In the advanced countries during the last twenty-five years, he said, the majority of the people have been satisfied. As a result, there is no class struggle in those societies. The poor countries have to follow this pattern. Like the rich economies, they must be prepared to trade off growth and equality—that is, to accept inequality as a mechanism for stimulating growth. On a global scale, as within the Keynesian economies, one can then have a growth whose benefits eventually reach the masses of the Third World.

On their side, he went on, the big powers have to realize that too much inequality in the world is not conducive to peace and stability. (This is the self-interest argument in favor of social justice that Robert McNamara had made with such force in his 1966 speech in Montreal.) And finally, he argued that redistribution is, in fact, taking place, because of the increase in the petroleum price, and he praised the solidarity of the Third World with OPEC. This, despite the fact that some of the nations represented at the dinner had paid much more for OPEC's success than the United States.

There were other interventions, but the ones that I have recorded stated the main themes that came out that evening. I was struck by the utter moderation of what was being proposed. In Daniel Patrick Moynihan's rhetoric as UN Ambassador—and, more importantly, in the consciousness of a majority of Americans—the Third World powers are impatient and explosive radicals who are willing to tear the global structure down if their demands are not met forthwith. And indeed, the manifestos and speeches sometimes convey that notion. Yet, when I pressed them for specifics, they came up with the reasonable proposals that UNCTAD has urged and not much more. And when one in their number voiced the classic left-wing, anti-imperialist position, the statement was rejected in a patronizing way as being fundamentally unserious.

In a famous article in *Commentary,* which played a role in making Daniel Patrick Moynihan UN Ambassador, Moynihan argued that the Third World demonstrated the ideological triumph of British Fabian socialism. That was, I think, a careless overgeneralization, which did not even apply to the country Moynihan had in mind, India, much less to Francophone Africa or Latin America. But now, after this *dîner débat* I had the strange feeling that the ideology that had carried the day was not the Webbs' socialist reformism but the free-trade principles of Adam Smith and David Ricardo. With perhaps two exceptions, these ambassadors and international technocrats believed in the market mechanism. Or, more precisely, they accepted the world market as a given that could not be transcended, and they thought they could achieve their goals within it.

I do not claim to be a political strategist superior to the seasoned diplomats with whom I talked. Perhaps their tactical estimation of the situation, their conviction that there is, in political fact, no alternative to the market mechanism, is right. Julius Nyerere, who has no illusions about the capitalist structure of world trade, had made that tactical point when I spoke to him in Dar. But what I do know is that these people are wrong if they think that commodity agreements or tariff treaties or the whole UNCTAD package will transform the gross inequalities of the world market. It may be that one will live with that inequality for the foreseeable future because there is no political way to abolish it. However, there is no possibility that the mechanisms that were designed to produce that inequality will provide the means for ending it.

It was an enlightening, depressing evening. I had asked, how, specifically, do you move toward a new international economic order. As far as I am concerned, no one among that shrewd, informed and Third World group had answered.

GENEVA, NOVEMBER 1976

I came here for the thirteenth post-World War II Congress of the Socialist International as a member of the delegation from the Democratic Socialist Organizing Committee in the United States. A central topic was the Third World.

Willy Brandt, who was elected Chair of the International at the Congress, roamed the aisles like a friendly Buddha. He had insisted that he would not accept leadership unless everyone agreed to work to break democatic socialism out of the "European ghetto" in which it is largely confined. Yet there were ambiguities inherent in that effort. The members of the International had all rejected dictatorship as a means toward socialism, insisting upon a democratic road. That was a central issue in the split between them and the Communists.

But the movements calling themselves Socialist in the Third World are almost all somewhat authoritarian. At the Congress, Dom Mintoff, the leader of the Maltese Socialists (who have close ties to the Libyans), talked of "undemocratic socialism." That, from the point of view of the International's ideology, is a contradiction in terms. Moreover, one significant section of the Third World movement, the Arab, is dedicated to destroying the homeland of one of the member parties of the International, Israel. And the Israeli delegates at Geneva were more open and hopeful about negotiations, including Israeli withdrawals from some of the captured territory, than in the past.

On the other side, if the Socialist parties of Europe held themselves aloof from the Third World, they would thereby proclaim their irrelevance to the majority of humankind. The solution adopted by the delegates at Geneva—who counted about ten prime ministers among their number—was to plunge into the ambiguities, recognizing that the Third World movements did not meet Socialist criteria, but entering into a dialogue with them to advance the day when they would and seeking to get the West to commit itself to a New Economic Order.

Some delegates, including a Finnish friend of mine, noted that if Europe took its responsibilities to the poor of the globe seriously, then the people's living standard there would grow less rapidly than under the old system. These representatives of the organized workers of Europe looked at that possibility and did not back away from it.

I was heartened on two counts. These Socialist comrades and friends had come to the same conclusion as I, only they represent serious political power. They too were determined to live with the ambiguities, to reach out of the Third World, sometimes despite some of its actions. And they confirmed my theoretical conclusion, that the advanced workers are not necessarily and inevitably counterposed to the poor of the globe.

It is strange that I felt happy being confirmed in what was, after all, a sense of ambiguity. But, since I am convinced that honesty and candor are the preconditions of the first steps away from the four-century system of injustice in which we live, that was indeed the case.

Chapter Nine **The Vast Majority: An Agenda**

The President of the United States should solemnly commit this country to the abolition of absolute poverty throughout the globe. That is the plight of 650 million people who live on incomes of $50 or less. They have been identified by an establishmentarian institution, under effective American control, the World Bank.

Solemn commitments are cheap. As an earnest of our intentions, the President should accept, on principle, the program for a new international economic order proposed by the Seventh Special Session of the United Nations General Assembly in 1975 and amplified by the Nairobi meeting of UNCTAD in 1976. That would mean that we would pledge ourselves to increase and stabilize the prices going to the principal Third World commodities, increase our aid to the UN target of 0.7 percent of GNP, renegotiate the intolerable debt burden from which the earth's poor now collectively suffer, and take steps to facilitate the industrialization of the international South. (These points will be treated in more detail shortly.)

All of these things could be done within the general framework of the existing world social system. That is to say, they are essentially liberal demands that would leave the corporate-dominated

American economy much as it is now. They would require, as will be seen, a much more effective Keynesian full-employment policy in the United States than we have had during the past eight years, but that is an official goal of the Carter administration in any case.

We could, then, take some substantial—even if ultimately inadequate—steps toward a minimum of human decency in the world without too much inconvenience to our own misshapen affluence. I doubt that we will. In the year two thousand, as the third millennium after the author of the Sermon on the Mount begins, I suspect that the poor of this planet will be relatively as bad off as they are now, and quite nearly absolutely so. But as long as there is even the merest chance that this sad opinion is wrong, and since there is a practical, political possibility that the United States could change, we must explore these measures.

In what follows, I will focus on capitalist sins, because the Communist economies play such a minor role in the world market (which is a capitalist world market even when Communists operate within it). Therefore, I should at least note once again that I believe the fat Communists are as outrageously indifferent to the demands of the outcast majority of mankind as fat capitalists. As Che Guevara understood, they charge capitalist prices for their "socialist" goods; and, as I documented earlier, they even accept the major theoretical prop of corporate domination of the planet, the theory of "comparative advantage."

Moreover, I should also warn the reader that the pessimism that will be expressed in this chapter may be overly optimistic.

The future could be grimmer than I have suggested. Instead of stagnating in an institutionalized inferiority, the Third World could retrogress. In what follows I have generally worked on the assumption that during the next twenty-five or so years Western capitalism will stumble, rather than hurtle, toward its end. That distinct possibility, as I wrote in *The Twilight of Capitalism*, would give the system a troubled vitality between now and 2000. However, more apocalyptic alternatives also exist.

For instance, the Trotskyist theoretician, Ernest Mandel, has pointed out that capitalism has gone through a series of "long waves" of expansion in which an innovating ascendant phase of twenty or twenty-five years is followed by an equally long period of much slower growth. The upsurge from the middle of the 1890s to the First World War was succeeded by the stagnation (and collapse) of 1919–39. And the enormous burst of capitalist energy that began in 1940, Mandel hypothesizes, may have ended in the middle sixties. For very different reasons, Lawrence Veit, an international economist for a major American investment house, sees the same possibility. In Europe, he wrote in late 1976, "it is now accepted by many that the future rate of growth will be less than that achieved in the past three decades."

If there is such a chronic capitalist crisis from now until the end of the century, the Third World will suffer from it more than anyone else, just as it paid a very high price for the recession that began in the West in 1973. Markets for its goods will contract; the protectionism of the workers in the advanced countries will probably grow; the affluent will be unwilling to increase foreign aid when there is so much poverty at home; and so on. Thus when Wassily Leontiev's UN Commission charted a scenario for accelerated economic growth in the South, it presumed a high level of activity in the North. That is just one more way of saying that the fate of the world's poor is dependent on the world's rich.

I assume—for the purposes of analysis, but not for prediction—that the future will more resemble Leontiev's version than Mandel's or Veit's. I do so for two reasons. First, it would take a book larger than this one to review the data and come to some kind of tentative estimate of the probabilities in this area. Secondly, and relatedly, this book aims at the simple, if enormous, goal of shattering America's cruel innocence. There is, I think, only so much ideological shock that my hoped-for audience can absorb and, in any case, they can be helped to see through this particular delusion without having to adopt my total world view. So in dealing with positive proposals, I operate on the simplification that things will not be as bad as they well might be.

There is another complicating factor that has already been mentioned. If one assumes that the hostility of the advanced countries to the poor will miraculously end, the Third World leaders, for all their insistence upon a new international economic order, have no precise program for radical change. The more left-wing among them have a rhetoric, not a strategy; the moderates share the ideological assumptions of their capitalist adversaries. So, this chapter, which deals with solutions to the evils I have analyzed, will be most modest in its aims. I do not know "the" answer to these unconscionable problems. I suspect that no one, and no collectivity, does.

Within these severe restrictions, some positive steps can be specified. Wassily Leontiev's *The Future of the World Economy* provides more leads than any other study. However, it should be remembered that Leontiev shows that the present Third World demands in the UN—the so-called International Development Strategy—will not, even if completely successful, alter the present 12-to-1 gap between the rich and the poor. He and his colleagues argue convincingly that a much more accelerated plan could reduce that differential to about 7 to 1 by the year 2000. That, it must be emphasized, is contingent on significant political change in both the North and South, a condition that Leontiev notes, but does not amplify.

Another excellent analysis, the Club of Rome study directed by Jan Tinbergen, recognizes the same limits on hope as Leontiev. Tinbergen and his associates believe that the gap between North and South could be reduced to 3 to 1—the level considered barely tolerable within the advanced economies—in about half a century. But that assumes a 5 percent annual growth in per capita incomes in the Third World, whereas the nonoil poor nations have been averaging only 2.3 percent in recent times and even the United Nations only expects 3.5 percent in an optimistic scenario. Like Leontiev, Tinbergen found that even if the UN targets are met, that will yield only a "marginal improvement in the currently unacceptable situation."

In short, the world is not helpless in the presence of an outrage that scourges a majority of its people, but only the most determined efforts have been an outside chance of success. And that means that the established structures of the global system of injustice will have to be challenged.

In exploring the possibilities for doing that, I will approach the subject in three ways. First, I will describe the historical options within the Third World that would make it possible for it to cooperate with an America bent on a modicum of justice. Secondly, I will examine the Southern program with a particular emphasis upon its moderate quality and therefore the fact that it could be accepted by this country. And finally, I will develop a few of the reasons why the United States could begin to behave, if not justly, then somewhat more decently.

I

The state will play a major role in *any* Third World strategy, even those which are explicitly capitalist. I do not assert this as a cheerful socialist universal. It is, rather, the point of departure for an analysis that must deal with a great deal of complexity.

That complexity eludes the true believers of the American ideology, including the United States government. In 1975, for instance, the conservative polemicist Irving Kristol wrote in the *Wall Street Journal* that the global conflict pits not the rich against the poor, but those who understand that liberal capitalism is the only hope for the backward economies against those who do not. This is, to be sure, an extremist statement of an untruth, since Kristol emphasizes "liberal"—free market, classic—capitalism as the answer for the globe's South. However, in dealing with this essentially frivolous notion, one confronts an attitude that, in somewhat more serious form, underlies all of American policy.

In fact, insofar as countries that are, or claim to be, capitalist exist in the Third World, they are, and must be, highly statified. This, as we have seen, is the case in Brazil; it also holds in Egypt, Mexico and Taiwan. There are some minor exceptions, like Côte d'Ivoire, but they do not change the rule and they are, in any case, totally subordinated to foreign capital. And even in Côte d'Ivoire the elite is administrative, not bourgeois. In Kenya, as Chapter Seven showed, a seemingly free-enterprise agriculture is dominated by the government. Iran, which is sometimes cited as an example of a "white" (or capitalist) revolution, is even less ambiguous than Kenya. The government negotiates foreign deals for its own private businessmen; the state owns strategic industries, like copper and steel, and public investments account for 65 percent of the total.

In India under Indira Gandhi's dictatorial Emergency there was a similar pattern. The regime's ideologists argued that the society had failed to generate a capitalist class, so the state must create one. The model for this approach is found in the top-down industrialization of Japan in the late nineteenth century and in Kemal

Ataturk's revolution in Turkey in the twentieth. In following this line, Mrs. Gandhi used her power to hold down wages, reduce the taxes on the rich and the duties on luxury imports and, in general, to sponsor a conservative revolution from on high. It would be hard to imagine a more "illiberal" capitalism.

These are the facts in the Third World. More to the point of this analysis, they are *necessarily* the facts. Leontiev rightly says:

Accelerated development in developing regions is possible only under the condition that from 30 to 35 percent, and in some cases 40 percent, of their gross product is used for capital investment. A steady increase in the investment ratio to these levels necessitates drastic measures of economic policy in the field of taxation and credit, increasing the role of public investment and the public sector in production and the infrastructure. Measures leading to a more equitable income distribution are needed to increase the effectiveness of such policies. Significant social and institutional changes would have to accompany these policies.

So it is that the inexorabilities of development require pervasive government intervention and extensive nationalization even when a country is bent on a capitalist road to development. This, however, does not mean that socialism is therefore the obvious and historically inevitable path for the Third World.

Socialism, it has been suggested, is the "natural ideology" of a poor society seeking its way out of backwardness. For one thing, the imperial powers were, and are, capitalist, a fact emphasized in almost all the revolutionary national movements. For another, these nations want industrialization, but without the maldistribution of wealth and the urban chaos that accompanies it in the major capitalist economies.

Thus, socialism responds to the love-hate attitude of transitional peoples toward industrialism: it holds out the prospect of rapid progress toward the wonders associated with development, and it presents someone to blame for the painfulness of the process. (In the Third World, the colonialists can be substituted for the frequently non-existent capitalists as the source of the evils of social transformation.)

Would that it were so simple. But, as Julius Nyerere told a Swedish socialist audience in 1969,

Socialism is not poverty. A country cannot claim to be socialist while its citizens live under the conditions which many of our people suffer. Or again: Our people are ignorant. The majority of the adults cannot read and write in their own language; they know nothing of modern techniques of production and are thus unable to take the simple steps which could remedy their own desperate poverty. Not even with our children have we overcome this problem. . . . Mr. Chairman, this ignorance is not socialist.

Socialism, as I argued in Chapter Seven, requires a certain level of productivity and of political development as a precondition. If both those levels need not be defined in present-day Western terms, they are still a basic constraint upon the possibilities open to a poor country. So, my analysis begins to point toward an anomaly: classic capitalism is impossible in the Third World, but so, in most countries, is democratic socialism. Some on the socialist Left have a relatively simple answer. All that has taken place in Africa, they say, is a "mere Africanization of the existing colonial structures." Or, Nyerere's government represents only a "bureaucratic bourgeoisie."

Now, there is some truth in these statements—though not, I think, in the contemptuous dismissal of Nyerere's efforts in Tanzania. Socialism can indeed become an ideology in the classic, and pejorative, Marxist sense of the term: a rationalization and mystification of exploitative economic and social structures. And yet, I am not satisfied with the Left Marxist critique, more for what it omits than for what it says. It tends to imply that there is a rather clear-cut socialist alternative in the Third World if only these movements would fight for it. Yet it rarely specifies in any detail exactly what that alternative is.

I suspect that the Left Marxists are probably thinking of some form of a forced, Spartan march to modernity, usually on a Chinese Communist model (or what passed for that model prior to the death of Mao and the confusing succession crisis it occasioned). Only, that does not solve the problem for, as I have documented in another book, the totalitarian accumulation of capital by a Communist bureaucracy creates a bureaucratic ruling class whose privileges are politically, rather than economically, determined. In the first phase, such a bureaucracy is able to mobilize the society and, by means of extreme coercion, to achieve impressive growth rates. But it increasingly becomes inefficient and conservative, as the Soviet example demonstrates. It too then becomes an obstacle, not simply to human freedom, but to economic development as well. There is, however, another possibility. Surprisingly, the Soviets have something useful to say about it. I say surprisingly, because the official Moscow analyses of social reality are invariably rationalizations of government policy decked out with footnotes from Marx and Lenin. In this case, however, the tactical needs of the state required a rather perceptive account of some Third World phenomena. This is the theory of "noncapitalist development." In effect, this category describes countries that are not Communist but are often hostile to the Western bloc. In a 1972 list it included Egypt, Algeria, Guinea, Tanzania, the People's Republic of the Congo, Syria, Iraq, Somalia, Yemen and Burma. (My guess is that subsequent political events in Egypt—Sadat's turn away from the Russians—have removed it from the role.) In another analysis, India was included under this classification.

According to the Soviet scholars, "noncapitalist development" is characterized by anti-imperialist politics, extensive nationalization, various welfare measures, the regulation of small and medium capitalists and, of course, friendliness to Russia. Clearly, much of this analysis is an attempt to give a Marxist gloss to alliances that Moscow has made in the Third World for big-power purposes. Nevertheless, what I find of value in this theorizing is the recognition of an economic and social reality that, for all the show of pious Leninist orthodoxy, fits none of the classic, Marxist or non-Marxist, categories. So, the Communists are being forced to live with the same ambiguities the Socialist International recognized at its Geneva congress.

The basic, historic alternatives that I have just outlined—state capitalism, Communist totalitarian collectivism, a noncapitalist and non-Communist development that might move toward democratic socialism—will profoundly influence how the poor countries face up to the two critical problems before them: feeding themselves and industrializing.[1]

II

It would, of course, be impossible even to adequately sketch all the factors involved in these massive areas of development strategy within a few pages or, for that matter, in a single book. In any case, all that has gone before should clearly suggest that for food production or manufacture there is no one "model" that can be applied to the enormously diverse societies of Asia, Africa and Latin America. In taking up the issue, then, I have only tried to make a simple statement of a few of the more important inter-relationships that bear upon this vast subject.

To begin with, as almost everyone realizes, there must be an agricultural revolution if hunger is to be eliminated in the South and industrialization made possible. That, Leontiev and his UN Commission believe, is physically possible. By the year 2000, the land under cultivation in the non-Communist Third World could be increased by 30 percent as against 1970, and productivity could grow threefold. To do this, however, would require substantial investment in land improvement, fertilizer, irrigation, research and development and this technological revolution would, in turn, depend "to a large extent on land reform and other social and institutional changes, which are necessary to overcome nontechnological barriers to increased land use and productivity."

Tinbergen's analysis is much less hopeful than Leontiev's about the possibility of expanding the farm area. Most of the good soil is already in production (one third of the land surface), and expansion, Tinbergen argues, will be costly and will face sharply declining returns. Without trying to resolve this serious difference, I will simply focus on the fact that both analyses make social and economic change, rather than technological innovation, the crucial variable.

How, in a very brief compass, does one describe those changes? There are, I think, four options, all of them obviously related to the historic alternatives I have just outlined. There could be forced collectivization, as under Communism; voluntary cooperatives; state capitalist subsidies for an export-oriented, corporate agriculture; a program to create a broad-based efficient system of modest private farm holdings within the framework of a public plan. This last possibility has been advocated for countries like India by Gunnar Myrdal. Indeed, long before the October Revolution Lenin himself considered it somewhat favorably as an "American" alternative to the "Prussian" modernization of the

Russian fields and Teng Hsia-p'ing even apparently thought it might work in China.

Obviously, it is not a matter of indifference as to which agricultural strategy is adopted in the Third World. Two of them—cooperatives, middle-sized private producers working under the plan—are compatible with democracy. Forced collectivization is not, since it requires the forcible suppression of what seems to be an almost irresistible and universal peasant drive for private plots. Moreover, forced collectivization on the Soviet model involves extremely high costs in terms of the immediate, angry destruction of livestock and the persisting hostility of the farm workers. Russian agriculture has yet to recover from Stalin's "revolution from above," though it is too early to say whether China, which took a somewhat less violent path, will face the same institutional inefficiencies. And state subsidies for corporate farming in Brazil have been accompanied, as we have seen, by growing hunger.

So I am disposed toward either the cooperative or the dispersed-ownership model on both democratic and economic grounds. I am, I must quickly and sadly add, not sanguine about the prospects for my preference. The idea of a democratic class of efficient, medium-sized farmers was effectively opposed in India by the entrenched landlord class, which has such great power within the Congress Party. That was one factor in the demise of the most populous democracy on the face of the earth during Indira Gandhi's emergency. And in Tanzania the cooperative road has encountered the many problems recounted in Chapter Seven.

One of the reasons why the Third World will have such difficulty in resolving these problems—problems that, it should be remembered, were solved in the advanced countries by savage attacks upon the peasantry, imports from slave labor, and other violent means—is American policy. Under the Nixon and Ford administrations, the international food policy of the United States became so crassly and voraciously commercial that, to cite one of the most shocking single cases, people in Bangladesh starved because they could not get the cash or the credit to buy 230,000 tons of wheat in this country. Washington refused credit in part because Bangladesh had the temerity to sell $3 million worth of jute gunny sacks to Cuba.

There are similar roadblocks to the industrialization of the poor countries.

If the Third World attempts to industrialize within the framework of the world market it will, if the argument of this book is valid, perpetuate and institutionalize its inferiority even if a happy set of circumstances were to permit some absolute growth. The very notion of profitability—that resources should be allocated to those activities that will produce the highest immediate yield—is a prime instrument of the affluent domination of the wretched. It means that an underdeveloped country will "voluntarily" specialize in those things most useful to the metropolitan powers and thus subvert the very possibility of a balanced internal development. So these nations must, if they are to achieve self-generating growth, protect some of their industries at a cost and reject the antidevelopmental logic of capitalist rationality.

There are two main difficulties with this strategy. One is that the tactic of "import substitution" can, as we have seen, become a mechanism permitting local manufacturers to produce the luxury goods of the wealthy less efficiently than foreigners do and with no great benefits to the society. Or else "infant industries" like Ford and GM will come in to take advantage of the protectionist laws. Secondly, the losses and inefficiencies that could contribute to growth in the long run have to be paid for. There is a limit to the number of such decisions. Still, a policy of "selective engagement" with the world market is crucial. The alternative is continued dependence on—which is to say, subordination to—the profit priorities of an international system guaranteed to keep the poor poor.

It is, I think, wildly optimistic to think that this grim, difficult situation has been changed by the OPEC cartel. The most optimistic militant in Tanzania would not agree with Robert Gilpin of the Brookings Institution that "for the moment at least a perceptible shift is taking place in the global balance of power from the owners of capital to the owners of natural resources." The problem is, as I have already pointed out, that oil is one of the few resources that are appropriate for a cartel strategy (and OPEC is, as I write in early 1977, suffering from severe internal strains and contradictions). Moreover, there are profound ambiguities in the OPEC case itself. Most of those oil profits have been invested in the West—which led one financial analyst to conclude that OPEC is "a funnel, siphoning money from poor people in Bangladesh to rich people in New York, Zurich and Frankfurt."

So it is indeed true, as conservatives love to insist, that the poor countries must reform themselves from within if they are to solve their problems. But it is absurd to think that the agricultural and industrial changes briefly touched upon here are going to take place in a vacuum. Rather, they will occur in an environment that is structurally hostile to the wretched of the earth—an environment that benefits the United States, first and foremost. For our part, we talk idealistically about democracy and the "Free World," while we follow economic policies that contract the already tragically limited possibilities open to the poor of the planet. For that reason I turn now to what is the policy core of this book: not advice for "them," but proposals for us.[2]

Indeed, let me confess what at first must seem a strange fear: that many of the ideas in this chapter will be accepted by the policymakers in Washington. What worries me is that the leaders of American capitalism, who up until now have been incredibly ideological, impractical and emotional in response to very mild proposals from the Third World, will accept the demands for a new international economic order in order to preserve the old international economic order. In 1975, a shrewd and disturbing article by Tom J. Farer appeared in *Foreign Affairs* and urged just such a tactic.

The United States—the industrial West—Farer argued, should co-opt the Third World. It can agree to increased manufactures on the periphery because it is convenient to send some labor-intensive operations there in any case. Smoothing our commodity fluctuations could also be profitable. And since most of the poor nations are ruled by small elites and contain enormous internal disparities in income, it would be possible to corrupt that upper stratum cheaply. It would not even take, Farer says, the modest redistributional concessions which a Roosevelt had to make to the workers in order to maintain the capitalist system during the Great Depression. And finally, if a few key nations were admitted into the rich countries' club—say, Iran, Nigeria, Brazil, Venezuela, Mexico, Indonesia and India—that would damp down the political pressure in the United Nations.

I am concerned because this is a plausible Machiavellian scenario, and a Carter Administration might transcend the rigidities of the Nixon-Kissinger years and adopt it. And yet, I continue to advocate the moderate program even though it could be used for goals which are directly opposed to my own. I do so for a number of reasons. First, there is no immediate possibility of a much more radical program. The existing arrangements of power simply do not permit that. Second, as I have pointed out on a number of occasions in this book, no one has worked out a more radical *program*. There has been much radical rhetoric, but that is something else, and not very relevant to the situation that confronts us.

Third, and most important of all, Farer is too neatly, too confidently, Machiavellian. It is true that the demands that I propose could be used to maintain the ancient structures of inequality in new form. But the achievement of those same demands could also incite and organize people to go beyond them. The welfare state may indeed turn out to have been nothing more than an amelioration of capitalism which is a way-station on the road to a corporate collectivism. But it also might be a popular victory preparing the way for a much more fundamental democratization of economic power. Which of these two alternatives will prevail is an open question that will be settled by political struggle. So is the outcome of the possibilist program outlined here. It could be an instrument of co-optation; it could be a point of departure for basic change. Recognizing—indeed, insisting upon—this ambiguity, I urge these ideas in the name of that latter possibility. For now, let me introduce them by locating them in the hidden history of the reasonableness and patience of the wretched of the earth.

III

There are three basic reasons why the United States could accept the Third World program. All of them outrage the established common sense; each is true. First, the ideology of the demand for a New International Economic Order is impeccably capitalist. Second, the poor countries have been extraordinarily patient and long suffering, and what is surprising is that they have remained so reasonable in the light of a generation of frustration and big-power duplicity. Third, American capitalism could make money from a moderate increase in world social justice.

Since I favor a much more radical program to transform global structures, I should explain that I support these demands as a point of departure, not as a solution. If we can achieve them—and I am not even sure of that—we then have to go beyond them. Far beyond them.

The first Third World summit took place at Bandung in 1955, but it was not until the founding meeting of UNCTAD in 1964 that there was a serious emphasis upon economic policy. At that meeting, Raoul Prebish and the UNCTAD staff worked out a program that rested on assumptions that are still basic to all of the Southern proposals. The core concept is a demand for a more rational capitalist world market. That the major capitalist powers should be vigorously, if discreetly, opposed to taking their own premises seriously should not surprise us, for we are accustomed to the gap between ideology and practice in the business world.

This was the fundamental UNCTAD proposition: "At the root of the foreign-trade difficulties facing the developing countries and other countries highly dependent on a narrow range of commodities are the slow growth of demand for their exports of primary commodities, accounting for 90 percent of their exports, the increasing participation of developed countries in world trade in primary commodities, and the deterioration of the terms of trade of developing countries from 1950 to 1962." More precisely, it was noted that between 1950 and 1962, export prices of primary commodities declined by 7 percent while the export prices of manufactures increased by 27 percent. One of the reasons, UNCTAD said, was that the advanced economies engaged in tariff and excise discrimination against the world's poor.

So it was that the 75 underdeveloped nations at Geneva (the nucleus of what was to become known as the Group of 77, a bloc which now includes more than 100 members) thought that their poverty could be ended if the "trade gap" could be eliminated. This is certainly anything but a radical idea. It assumes that if only the Third World could get a fair deal on the world market, if only that mechanism would cease transferring wealth from the poor to the rich, then its problem could be solved. In fact, even a more equitable world market would institutionalize the fundamental relations of inferiority between North and South. Unequal exchange is only one means of Northern domination among many.

This basic UNCTAD perspective was reaffirmed in the Charter of Algiers in 1967 and again in the Second Session of UNCTAD itself at New Delhi in 1968. At the same time, the New Delhi meeting noted that in the sixties, the poor countries were losing about $2.2 billion a year because of the deteriorating terms of trade. But still, they remained essentially moderate. That reasonableness continued at the Third UNCTAD Session in Chile in 1972 and at the Sixth Special Session of the General Assembly in 1974.

So, the demands for a new international economic order at the Seventh Special Session in 1975 and at the UNCTAD meeting in 1976 came out of more than a decade of long-suffering, frustrated moderation on the part of the world's poor. Most Americans heard the grandiloquent rhetoric. They were ignorant of how patient the hungry had been and how merely incremental their proposals were and are.

There are six main points to the program for a new order. First, the centerpiece: measures to facilitate trade, including the standard proposals for preferences for the poor and a new emphasis on increasing the share of the Third World in industrial production. There were also requests for more concessional aid and private capital, a mitigation of the crushing debt burden of the underdeveloped countries, a transfer of technology from center to periphery and help in building up food production. And there was a proposition that, in effect, endorsed the policy already adopted by the multinational corporations. The major powers, it was said, should "encourage the redeployment of those industries which are less competitive internationally to the developing countries." This was explicitly presented in terms of a profit-making self-interest in the advanced economies, which would take into account the need to move into "more viable lines of production" in the metropolitan countries.

At the Fourth Session of UNCTAD, in Nairobi in 1976, the UNCTAD secretariat had fleshed out some of these proposals. It had called for an "integrated" attack on the problem of the structural disadvantages of the Third World in the terms of trade. Many of the commodities with wide fluctuations in price should be brought under control by a system of buffer stocks. In effect, a world organization would be created, committed to buying a given commodity when the price went down and selling it off when it had increased to a certain point. (The original proposal along these lines came from the shrewdest theorist of twentieth-century capitalism, John Maynard Keynes, right after World War II.) At the same time, prices would be spelled out in real terms, so that inflation in the cost of the industrial products that the poor buy from the rich would be reflected in the return on their own primary products. How serious that last problem is can be grasped from some 1976 figures provided by Julius Nyerere. Between 1970 and 1974, the average annual prices of East Africa's five major export commodities went up by 34 percent and the cost of their industrial imports by 91 percent.

Indeed, shrewd analysts understood that the Seventh Special Session marked the "re-emergence of the moderates" in the Group of 77. Henry Kissinger's intransigence in the period between the OPEC embargo in the fall of 1973 and his somewhat conciliatory speech in September 1975, at the Seventh Special Session, had helped the more militant Third World rhetoricians to gain greater prominence. But the basic, quite reasonable, program was not changed, even though the motivations for it became more shrill. And when Kissinger showed the least disposition to negotiate—as he did in that 1975 address, which was progress only by comparison with the stonewalling that had gone before it—he was given a most sympathetic hearing. His proposals were, as one liberal observer rightly commented, "marginal," yet they were treated as a kind of breakthrough.

So it is that I take the following statement by the Third World Forum, an association of prominent social scientists from Asia, Africa and Latin America, as a fair description of the real content of the proposals of the world's poor: "We wish to make it clear that the Third World is not demanding a massive redistribution of wealth of the rich nations. Nor is it seeking equality of income. It is asking for equality of opportunity." That is, of course, a classic capitalist concept.

There is, then, no *principled* reason why the United States should reject the program of the global South. Yet it did so under the Nixon-Ford administrations and, even if the Carter administration is somewhat better in this area, it will probably oppose the new international economic order in the future. Why does Washington take such an intransigent position against a very moderate, reasonable set of proposals, which provide for just a very little bit of justice for the desperate of the planet?

IV

Recent history supplies part of the answer. During the past several decades, the United States has probably done more to impede the development of the Third World than any other advanced country. This is not because we are particularly malevolent (although it should be noted that the most intransigent Western powers on this issue are usually this country and West Germany), but rather because we are the preeminent capitalist economy. We accomplished this sorry task for the most part quietly, by means of "impersonal" economic mechanisms rigged to our advantage rather than through dramatic displays of viciousness. We invaded only a few places, like Lebanon and Guatemala in the fifties, overthrew only a few governments, like Mossadegh's in Iran and Allende's in Chile, and engaged in only one horrible, full-fledged war against a national revolutionary movement, in Vietnam. The American public, to its credit, often opposed those adventures, and in the case of Vietnam turned Washington's policy around. But the people did not realize, secure in their cruel innocence, that in times of "peace" and "normality" we were carrying out a genteel and proper campaign against the poor, a campaign that is even more effective than the blatant subversions.

Consider just a few cases in point. The United States benefited, of course, from its favorable terms of trade with the Third World during most of the postwar period. But this was not simply a question of world market forces, for this country specifically and consciously discriminated against Southern manufactures even as it proclaimed its support for Southern industrialization. After the Kennedy Round of tariff liberalization in the sixties, the duties on the products of advanced countries were cut in half, but there was practically no reduction for the principal products of the Third World. Moreover, during the last ten years there has been an increase in the nontariff barriers, like quotas, to the exports of the poor. So it is that although the consumers pay more than $200 billion for the commodities from the South and the products derived from them, the underdeveloped nations themselves get only $30 billion out of that sum. The real profits are made in processing, and we have carefully excluded the South from most of that high-payoff activity.

American trade policy has the effect of discouraging development. So does much of our aid effort, which, in any case, has recently become so feeble—0.25 percent of GNP in 1974—that it helped mightily in pulling the advanced world total down to .33 percent—that is, just under half of what the UN recommends. The bare figures, however, overstate our benevolence. American aid has, for the past generation, been directed primarily to those military allies who would be dependable in the struggle against Communism, like Taiwan, South Korea and South Vietnam. In other cases, our charity was used as a lever to facilitate the purposes of multinational corporations. In the sixties, for instance, India was threatened with a cutoff of American funds if it did not meet some American oil company demands in connection with the fertilizer prices they charged in that theoretically independent nation.

More recently, an American Secretary of the Treasury was undiplomatically blunt. "Every sovereign nation," Charles P. Schultz said in 1973, "has, of course, the right to regulate the terms and conditions under which private investment is admitted or to reject it entirely. When such capital is rejected, we find it difficult to understand that official donors should be asked to fill the gap." It did not occur to Mr. Schultz that a poor country might want to determine its own investment policy with concessional funds rather than have it determined for it by a multinational corporation. But then American Secretaries of the Treasury are not appointed to understand that obvious possibility, and grasping it could even disqualify one for the job.

Monetary policy was also used against the have-nots. The United States vigorously opposed linking the new international monetary reserves—Special Drawing Rights, or SDRs—to economic development. So it was that of the $103 billion in international reserves created between 1970 and 1974, the poor got 3 percent, the rich 97 percent. For good measure, Richard Nixon's devaluation of the dollar in 1971 hit hard at those Third World countries that kept their reserves in that supposedly stable currency. They lost, the London *Economist* estimated, $1 billion in purchasing power.

At the same time, that "competitive devaluation" helped to heat up the American economy and ensure Mr. Nixon's re-election.

And finally, the United States carefully kept the Third World out of the international financial institutions under its control. That, for example, allowed Nixon to use the World Bank as a tool against Allende's Chile—and Ford, to use it as a tool for Pinochet's Chile. Why does this country act in this fashion? Is it merely the most hypocritical of the wealthy economies? That is much too simple and misleading a theory. America is both naïvely sincere and Machiavellian when it acts in this way. It is also forcing the wretched of the earth to pay the price for its own domestic inability to achieve anything like full employment.

The naïve sincerity has been noted earlier in this book. The leaders of the United States honestly believe that the spread of multinationals, and of private capital in general, will help the globe's poor to end their destitution. Conversely, Washington is not at all hypocritical when it regards nationalization and expropriation as counterproductive in the struggle for development. The American policy-makers do not, of course, ask why it is that economic wisdom throughout the world and the self-interest of the corporate sector in their own country coincide so providentially. Raising such a question requires that one criticize capitalism as a system, and therefore it does not even occur to most people in this country to ask it.

At the same time, the United States consciously seeks to advance the profit position of its various corporations and industries. In this case, the harm it does to humankind is not good-natured and innocent. For example, the government's response to the UNCTAD proposal for systematic support to Third World commodities was to hold out for a commodity-by-commodity search for agreement. That, as UNCTAD itself explicitly understood, gives maximum room for wheeling and dealing. Washington would face the Third World not as a united collectivity, but country by country, and it could thereby isolate and weaken its adversaries at the negotiating table. With the United States becoming more and more mercantilist in its competition with Japan and the Common Market —putting quotas on various kinds of steel, embargoing soybean imports, and so on—it does not want to sacrifice the least leverage in promoting the interests of various sectors of American industry.

Therefore it came out for more private enterprise (the resource bank) and opposed UNCTAD's integrated approach to commodities.

This is not to suggest that supporting commodities or indexing world market prices is an easy thing to do. It has been pointed out *ad nauseam*—usually by those who want an "objective" argument for rationalizing American policy—that the advanced countries are also major producers of primary commodities and the poor are importers of them. It is true that 60 percent of the world's raw materials come from the rich nations. Indeed, that statistic demonstrates how fraudulent the theory of comparative advantage is: what the rich specialize in is not a question of "natural" advantage but of making money. So it is that Russia and South Africa are net exporters of primary commodities, while India and Pakistan are importers. And there are analogous problems with indexing. These however are technical difficulties. They could be solved if they were taken seriously.

Indeed, in the spring of 1977, the United States, Britain, West Germany and Japan sat down in Geneva for serious talks on a common fund to stabilize commodity prices. As the *Economist* noted, an agreement in this area would help the rich countries as well as the poor, since they too would benefit from the resultant stability. And an across-the-board intervention would be cheaper than a commodity-by-commodity series of agreements, since there are different cycles and money needed to buy sugar could be provided by selling rubber. Predictably, the United States was the most reluctant party to these discussions, but the fact is that serious—established—policymakers are aware that Keynes's scheme would work.

We know, for instance, that the multinationals have developed a computerized system, using satellite communications, which takes account of, and profits from, daily shifts in the world currency market. This was well described by the U.S. Tariff Commission in its conservative report on the multinationals. If the United States was willing to make a principled commitment to the UNCTAD demands, these details—which are complex, major and resolvable—could be dealt with. The critical problem is that the government, in this case as in practically every other case in the postwar period, maximizes the mercantile interests of the

United States. In the process, it makes short-run sense and long-run irrationality.

Indeed, John Cuddy, an UNCTAD economist, has worked out a computerized system for stabilizing ten Third World commodities—only two of them overlap with exports from the North—which could be a major boon to the poor economies. Moreover, this UNCTAD plan envisions that the common fund would make a 6.5 percent return on its invested capital. Since its strategy would be to buy when prices were low and to sell when they are high, it would be all but impossible not to return a profit.

It would be relatively easy for the United States to accept the commodity portion of the Third World package. Indeed, American business might well profit from a system that would smooth out the erratic fluctuations of those prices and make planning much more feasible. The proposal that the South, which now has 7 percent of the world's industrial production, should take over a 25 percent share by the year 2000 is much more problematic, particularly in the United States. The reason is our disgraceful performance in domestic economic management.

"Okun's law"—named after the liberal American economist Arthur Okun—is apropos of this point. Okun has argued that it takes a 4 percent rise in GNP to keep unemployment in the United States from increasing. If one then assumes that the Third World percentage of industrial output rises to 25 percent of the total, then all of those goods must be absorbed on the world market and the workers in the advanced countries who had been employed in making the 18 percent of goods which will now come from the Third World must be put to work at something else. There is, as UNCTAD has pointed out, enormous room for growth in the trade between the underdeveloped countries themselves, which would relieve some of this pressure. And yet, precisely because of the maldistribution of the globe's wealth, the poor are not good customers for the poor. So, the big powers will have to be able to buy the bulk of the new Third World industrial output. To do so would require, given the limitations of Okun's law, that they grow at the rate of 8 percent a year, something they have hardly ever done. Otherwise, they will alleviate poverty in the South by increasing it in the North.

Indeed, it is already clear that the shift of certain industries from center to periphery has adversely affected groups of workers in the United States, for instance, in consumer electronics and apparel. It may be true (I doubt it) that the long-run and over-all effect will be, as the U.S. Tariff Commission argued, to increase American employment. For those who live in the devastating depression created by the short-run trends, that is cold comfort.

This problem explains, I think, one of the main reasons why America is the most reactionary of the big powers in its economic relations with the Third World. Britain, France, Holland, Norway and Sweden were much more sympathetic to UNCTAD than this country. But then during the postwar period, the United States has averaged jobless rates double those found in Europe. Moreover, when an American worker loses his or her job, the effect is much more catastrophic than on the Continent. The welfare state in America is much more limited than any other in the Western world. So, when a worker is laid off, there is no national health to take over where the company medical plan ends; the housing subsidies are less for the poor and the working people; and so on, in almost every area of the nation's life.

Under such circumstances it is politically inevitable that the American unions will fight any transfer of manufacturing jobs overseas *unless* there is full employment. And if the general American economic performance in the next twenty-five years is as lackluster as during the past twenty-five—the Kennedy-Johnson years are only a partial exception to this indictment—there is no hope that the United States will be able to absorb a vast increase in Third World manufacturing output. One cost of the ongoing failure to reach full employment within this country is thus borne by the Third World, which, because of it, finds it much more difficult to win acceptance for its proposals. To be sure, these things are not inevitable. The law which provided guaranteed employment or income to all workers displaced by the Amtrak federalization of part of rail service shows that measures can be designed to cope with the "adjustment" costs of a shift of manufacture to the Third World. But given the failure of the full-employment and national economic-planning movements in the past—and I have participated in both of them—I must confess I am not sanguine.

It would be wrong, however, to look at this issue solely from an American vantage point. The staggering fact is, as the International Labour Office documented in 1976, that the Third World will require *one billion* jobs by the year 2000! That, the ILO study showed, will not only require high growth rates throughout the world but conscious, redistributionist policies designed to see that economic progress actually reaches the most wretched of the wretched of the earth. Specifically, the ILO recommended a "basic employment policy" which would seek to satisfy the "basic needs" —food, medicine, shelter; work; participation in decision making— of all the people of the world by the end of the century. Predictably, the American Government representatives at the ILO meeting (they were appointed by the Ford Administration) were horrified by proposals to interfere with the "market" mechanism, carefully ignoring the fact that the market has been rigged for four hundred years.

The critical fact in all of this is that America and the world could achieve planned full employment if both were willing to make significant changes in the established order of maldistribution. The concerns of American unionists are legitimate; so are those of the people who emphasize the glaring inequalities within a Third World which makes equality among nations its central value. In both cases, the problems can be solved; the difficulties are located, not in fate, but in our politics.[3]

V

There is, however, another area in which positive action is almost certain to come from Washington. The United States is likely to be reasonable about Third World debt. Underlying that probability is a complex reality that suggests how America could change— if it wanted to.

The immediate cause of American sympathy on this issue has to do with money, not compassion. In recent years, as official aid from this country declined, private banks took over a considerable portion of financing the inevitable shortfall in the Southern balance of payments. They did so in part because they could make exorbitant profits by borrowing Eurodollars cheap and lending them dear. So one can look for a statesmanlike attitude from the United States on this count. Funds will be dispatched to the poor countries, possibly with some fanfare, and they will then be returned to the American investors. It would save on postage if the government simply paid off the American banks, but that would be too revealing.

Put in this way, the whole affair is just one more sordid case of affluent manipulation of the poor. There is, however, a deeper trend in all of this. The rich powers are endangered if they are too successful in their exploitation of the Third World. For if they extract various profits and fees and prosper on the basis of unequal exchange, they will turn the poor countries into literal paupers. At that point, they will cease to be a market for commodities, for capital goods, or a desirable site for building an "export platform" behind protectionist walls.

One of the functions of foreign aid was to provide public money, normally raised by tax systems that disproportionately affect the working people, from the advanced world to the underdeveloped societies so that they can buy our goods and services. It was not just the Marxists, like Pierre Jalée, who understood this ingenious system. A 1974 Report of the Foreign Relations Committee was candid about the Marshall Plan: "The infusion of capital goods [to Europe] was to be supplied by the United States, thereby helping to hold up the postwar demand level in the U.S. domestic economy." The same principle was applied when moneys were voted to the poor around the world, and more often than not those disbursements were "tied"—that is, they could be spent only in the American market, even if that meant paying higher prices.

There is a rather important point lurking here: The United States can make money from doing justice throughout the world.

The London *Economist* is one of the most sophisticated, and cynical, periodicals in the West. It has understood the profitability of a modicum of progress for the wretched of the earth for some time. So it was that in 1977 it called for "aid not trade" and advocated a "Marshall Plan for the Third World." The trade deficits of the poor, the *Economist* noted, have been going up and up, particularly since the oil-price explosion engineered by OPEC in 1973. Indeed, 90 percent of the oil producers' surplus, the *Econo-*

mist discovered, is being carried by the counterpart deficits of poor or small countries. (Their portion of the total amounts to $162 billion!)

Under these circumstances, the *Economist* concluded, it is in the self-interest of the rich to send money to the poor—a new Marshall Plan—so as to keep world trade going. This does not mean, note well, that a new international economic order is to be created—that is, that the North is going to finance a structural change in the global economy to benefit the South. It does propose a shrewder and less destructive way of maintaining the status quo, and proves that one of the major Third World demands—the alleviation of the debt burden—could be met by the United States if only it had the intelligence to follow its own main chance.

But doesn't advocating this subject my own argument to an intolerable contradiction? I have said that the misery of the South is systemic and that the basic mechanisms of the world economy will have to be transformed if there is to be any significant progress. And yet, I am now in the position of advocating a sophisticated reform, one which I recognize will shore up the system. How can that be? The answer involves some complications but it is straightforward enough.

The worst thing that could happen to the Third World during the next twenty-five or fifty years would be a catastrophic collapse of Western capitalism. There may be some romantics who think that such an apocalypse would immediately usher in an epoch of planned abundance under the direction of revolutionary Northern regimes, which would forthwith share their wealth with the South. In fact, collapse within the North would, in the future as in the thirties, weaken the Left and open up a road to power toward the Right. The Left, as the fearful events in Germany demonstrate, is weak when there are millions unemployed and open to demagogic appeals directed against the employed and their unions. And conversely, the greatest gains have been made within the advanced capitalist countries under conditions of relatively full employment.

That same rule applies to the Third World. Under conditions of prosperity in the affluent economies, Julius Nyerere's "trade union of the poor" has some leverage. Third World commodities are in demand and in short supply. The threat to withhold them would make an impression then, but not if those commodities were not needed. Leontiev, Tinbergen, and every other serious analyst has therefore made real progress for the hungry partly dependent on the well-being of the affluent. That paradox is not to my liking; but it is real.

More broadly, I have already argued that full employment is a precondition of Northern working-class support for Southern demands to be given the effective right to industrialize. Under those conditions, as Judith Hart, a Labour parliamentarian, told the 1976 Socialist International Congress, a strong Third World insistence on getting the means of that industrialization would benefit the trade unionists in the advanced powers who would produce those capital goods. But in saying this, I am obviously not agreeing with the *Economist*'s purpose, only with its means. They want a Marshall Plan to maintain the old order; I want it because I think it creates the economic and social conditions most conducive to the struggle against that order, domestically and internationally.

That is why I want to point out to Washington that, if it has a shrewd narrow-mindedness, it should spend considerable moneys in helping the Third World out of its debt and toward its goal of industrialization.

So, the key Third World demands—smoothing out the commodity fluctuations, rolling over the debt, getting assistance to industrialize—could be acceptable to the United States, not as it should be, but as it is. Objectively, the interests, not only of American workers, but even of corporations, could coincide in the short run, which is where politics are lived. And that, from my point of view, would hold out the possibility of transforming the long run. However, I must confess that, living in the stagflationist America of the second half of the seventies, I cannot be terribly optimistic.

VI

The United Nations Law of the Sea Conference (LOS) is another argument for a chastened pessimism. It is still in progress as I write, yet all of the evidence suggests that during the past ten years mankind—or, more precisely, the big capitalist powers—has turned its back on one of the greatest, and most painless, opportunities for international justice that has ever existed, or is ever likely to exist.

There are enormous resources under the seas. One estimate figures that 40 percent of the world's petroleum and a literally immeasurable supply of minerals are found there. However, the location of this wealth is of great importance. The Austrian delegation to the UN Conference, the leader of the "landlocked" powers, notes that 87 percent of the hydrocarbons (including petroleum) lie within two hundred miles of the land—that is, within the zone claimed by various countries as their own, national property. Secondly, most of the petroleum in the seas is found adjacent to the petroleum on land—that is, the national exploitation of this resource will benefit primarily the already rich and reinforce the maldistribution of the world's wealth. Still, there are "fabulous quantities" of nickel, copper and other minerals to be found in the deep seabed out beyond the 200-mile limit.

The question is, Who shall own, and profit from, the riches beneath the sea?

The issue was first posed in ironic fashion. Acting in response to a dispute between the federal government and the states, but without any prophetic insight into how important his action would eventually become in terms of energy resources, Harry Truman proclaimed American jurisdiction over the wealth of the "continental shelf" in 1945. Chile, Ecuador and Peru responded in 1952, staking out their claims. This controversy, however, still focused primarily on fishing rights for the Third World, and state's rights in America, not on resources.

By the sixties, a number of the Latin-American powers were insisting on two-hundred-mile, rather than three-mile, limits of national jurisdiction. The African and Asian countries, one UN diplomat remembered, at first thought this idea bizarre. But then a small number of people began to realize that the petroleum and the minerals were, from a dollar point of view at least, more important than the fish. There were international conferences on the subject and in 1967 Arbid Pardo, the Maltese ambassador, defined the concept that was to become central to the subsequent debate. The seas, Pardo said, are "the common heritage of mankind."

Here was an enormous opportunity to solve the problem of poverty in the Third World. There was a tremendous source of new wealth, which was owned by no one. There was a doctrine, going back at least to Hugo Grotius's *Mare Liberum* in 1609, which said, "The sea is common to all, because it is so limitless that it cannot become a possession of anyone. . . ." If these riches could be developed on behalf of the world's poor, it would not be necessary to transfer existing resources from North to South, with all of the political problems that such a move entails. Only this marvelous perspective became the victim of a whole series of national greeds —some of them, let it be said, found in the Third World—and, above all, of the determination of the United States to make the ocean a preserve for multinational corporations.

The solidarity of the South was shattered because there were some countries primarily concerned with fishing rights, and they wanted an "exclusive economic zone" of two hundred miles. That maximized their short-term interest but it had the gigantic side effect of conceding the hydrocarbon wealth, which is normally found just off shore, to the wealthy powers. The landlocked nations had their interest (which was, in general, progressive). They fought for a tax on activities within the exclusive economic zone with the funds to go to an international authority for allocation. But there were further complications. For instance, the big nickel producers —Canada, France (in New Caledonia) and Russia—were disturbed that their land-based mineral would be devalued if it could be mined more cheaply at sea. That pitted the French against the Americans.

However, the most revealing debate had to do with the deep seabed, known as the Area in UN jargon. Here the poor countries once more had a common program, since fishing rights and the distinction between landlocked and coastal powers are not a factor on the high seas. They wanted to internationalize and socialize the Area. An International Seabed Authority would be established with its seat at Jamaica. It would set up an enterprise that would conduct the business of the Authority in the Area, and would be, in effect, an internationally owned corporation. It would be charged with adopting "criteria, rules, regulations and procedures for the equitable sharing among States Parties of financial and other economic benefits derived from activities in the Area, taking into particular consideration the interests and needs of the developing countries. . . ." It was also supposed to protect underdeveloped nations that would lose because of the competition from cheap ocean minerals.

The official American position on all this was one of sophisticated conservatism. During the fall 1976 meeting of the LOS, Henry Kissinger stated Washington's attitude, complete with a Freudian slip.

With respect to the deep seabeds [Kissinger told the Heads of Delegation], we face two realities. One is that developed countries—a few developed countries at this moment—alone possess the technology with which to exploit the seabeds—why don't I use a more happy word?—to mine the seabeds. On the other hand, there is the concept that the deep seabeds represent the common heritage of mankind and, therefore, there is a certain conflict between the realities and the capabilities of certain countries and the theoretical convictions of many other countries.

Kissinger's original choice of word about "exploiting" the deep seabed may not have been "happy" but it was accurate. His next paragraph made that clear. The Third World demand for international socialization is a "theoretical conviction"; the power of America's superior technology is the reality. Kissinger proposed that this country would agree to the establishment of the Seabed Authority and its enterprise; that there would be "revenue sharing" from the proceeds of the mining which would be used to forward economic development *as long as* "all states . . . and their nationals have guaranteed access to seabed mining sites under fair conditions." There must be "adequate incentives and guarantees for those nations whose technological achievement and entrepreneurial boldness are required if the deep seabeds are to benefit all of mankind." So, "the relative economic interests of the countries with important activities in the deep seabeds [must] be protected, even though those countries be in a numerical minority."

In other words, the United States would allow some funds to go for Southern development if its multinationals were given the right to exploit the sea independent of the Authority and if America were to have a weighted vote—taking into account its power, its technological superiority and its capitalist principles—in the Authority itself. This latter fact already operates in the World Bank; Washington dominates it.

Kissinger's attitude was one of sophisticated nationalism, proposing to reproduce the existing international inequities in the middle of the ocean. He was, however, attacked by less-shrewd corporate ideologists as too liberal. The *Wall Street Journal* approvingly quoted S. Fred Singer, a former Interior official, to the effect that "participation [in mining the sea] is open to all individuals or nations who wish to buy stock or otherwise invest in these companies in order to share in any future profits." At this writing, *The Wall Street Journal's* crude position seems to be prevailing over Kissinger's scheme to serve the same corporate ends. The chairman of the House Subcommittee on Oceanography, John H. Breux, wants unilateral American action, and the Ford Administration created regulatory machinery to supervise such a move as early as 1975. Not so incidentally, the efforts to demilitarize the deep sea were also pushed back.

In 1976, this fateful issue became a pawn in American Presidential politics. Under attack from Ronald Reagan on his right, Gerald Ford suddenly reversed American policy and, in April of 1976, came out for the unilateral American control of 25 percent of the world's fish. He then sent his delegate back to the Sea conference with instructions to press for an *international* solution to the question! This development convinced some people that the high hopes in this area were now dead.

And yet, there were possibilities of new alternatives. The "Barba Negra Appeal," a statement signed by Ambassador Pardo, Jan Tinbergen, Maurice Strong (the Canadian who led the UN Environment program) and others, called upon states to share from 1 percent to 20 percent of the mining revenues from the exclusive economic zone with a UN fund which would finance economic development. The percentage each country would pay would vary according to its per capita income. Ironically, it could be that this initiative will fail because of the Third World's nationalistic insistence upon sovereignty in the exclusive economic zone.

The saddest aspect of this history is that it is indeed true, as Elisabeth Mann Borgese has said, that "the effort to build a new international order in the oceans may turn out to be the most important international development of this century." Only, we may now be heading toward the most important failure of this century on the high seas.

VII

Finally, even though a realistic appraisal of positive measures to end the North-South gap leads to pessimistic conclusions, there are still solid grounds for continuing the struggle. The ocean could be a source of enormous wealth for economic development; the United States could accept the entire UNCTAD package on the basis of sophisticated capitalist self-interest. This could be done by a liberal administration and would not, as some on the Left think, require a basic socialist transformation of society as a precondition. In return for a bare minimum of international decency, this country would receive raw materials at stable prices, and even the multinational corporation would find the world an easier place in which to do business. There would be a marked growth in Southern manufactures, and that could contribute enormously to a global prosperity. I conclude that the only realistic hope for some alleviation of the misery of the poor of the world lies along the line of a compromise that is unfair to them, but somewhat less so than the existing, outrageous structures.

And yet, ultimately, I do not accept the realism that is forced upon me in the short run. I think we need international economic planning of the kind Leontiev has produced and along the lines of the FAO's global "balance sheet" on food needs. There should be a world treasury, as Tinbergen says. Indeed, in the long run, which must begin as soon as possible, realism requires moving toward a genuine world government. One of the reasons why the wealth of the planet is so maldistributed is that it has been organized on the basis of nation states. Within a given country, the production of riches tends eventually to spread to every sector, albeit unevenly and only when there is government prodding, as the examples of the American and Italian Souths demonstrate. But internationally, the opposite tendency is at work. Growing development at one pole creates and perpetuates underdevelopment at the other. The only way to overcome this problem is to build a single world. The elimination of frontiers would not simply mean a political liberation;

it is, I suspect, the precondition of world economic liberation as well.

I do not make this point lightly, or even optimistically. It was a work of millennia for the human psyche to proceed from a familial, through a tribal, city and regional loyalty, to the sense of a national identity. It is not at all clear that membership in a world community of billions of people will ever evoke the passionate solidarity that those more focused commitments have achieved. If that is the case, the North-South gap will continue for the foreseeable future, and beyond that. But perhaps it is not the case; perhaps one can hope.[4]

For now, one must be content with very modest first steps. They are there to take, and America could take them. If it wanted to.

Chapter Ten Epilogue

This book, as I have revealed in the journals of my various encounters with the Third World, has been a personal and emotional as well as an intellectual experience. Its completion leaves me profoundly ambivalent. In the spirit of the "phenomenology" which prompted me to report on my feelings in India, East Africa and Mexico, I want now to briefly face up to the tensions within me. I do so because I think those tensions refract contradictions in reality.

First of all, I was surprised to find out how much I agreed with the neo-Marxist theory that America is an imperialist power.

For some years, as I recounted in Chapter Five, I have argued against the neo-Leninist theories of American imperialism, primarily because I found them simplistic and overgeneralized. I still do. But what I now realize is that there is an imperial reality which, even if Lenin's analysis of more than a half century ago does not apply to it, is still quite substantial. My error was a sophisticated variant of the one I saw in Dar: I too accepted the neo-Leninist position as the only one. Now, I see the problem in much broader terms, as defined in a tradition deriving from the Marx of the

Grundrisse and from Rosa Luxemburg and as containing utterly new developments as well.

America is at the center of a complex, structured and interdependent system, historically and presently suffused with capitalist values and priorities, which massively reproduces the injustices of a world partitioned among the fat and the starving. In the not-so-long run, there is no practical political possibility of making a progressive change in this basic injustice. Fundamental mechanisms must be transformed to do that. There must be, as the last chapter concluded, not merely a world political government, but a world government that would allocate the goods and resources of the earth on something like a fair basis. What we need is a commonwealth of humanity.

In the here and how, that is the sheerest utopianism, in the worst sense of that abused word. Yet even as I sort out the tacky compromises that have to be made to get a crust of bread for the hungry, I insist that this is the only hope.

And yet, if I am persuaded by the intellectual power of the Marxist analysis—always understanding that I am talking of that minority of serious Marxists and not of the totalitarian ideologues who have usurped his name—I am painfully aware of how meager their practical proposals are. The problem is that our account of the imperial system is designed to account for trends that operate in decades, or even centuries. It is, however, a most defective instrument in trying to deal with political proposals for the desperately pressing immediate future. So it is that Christian Palloix, a brilliant French Marxist, wrote a two-volume study of the world capitalist economy. At the end of Volume 2, he candidly admitted that his theory is "purely negative," that strategies, even radical strategies, for dealing with the reality he had so complexly defined have not yet been formulated. He then proceeded to give eight pages of ideas on how to cope with a system that has taken two volumes to define, not to mention four hundred years to build.

Palloix had the courage to admit his limitations. His colleagues are not always so candid. They sometimes write in the arrogant spirit of a Marxist integralism that pretends to have all the answers. But they, like Palloix, like me, are much better at explaining the historic, economic and political agencies that determine what is wrong in the past and present than at coming up with roads to a future that is both humane and possible.

In some ways, I wish that the Leninist fantasies were true, that one could "smash" the bourgeois state apparatus and begin the liberation of mankind. But they are only fantasies. And the Third World is a much more complicated and intricate place than is dreamed of in our—or its—philosophies. Therefore, even as one adopts a grand historical perspective and understands the imperial nature of American power, one must be chastened, humbled, prepared to search for the miserable, inadequate increment of change that will help us to transform the structure.

There is a broader political problem in all of this. It was once thought on the Left that there would come a day, a "final conflict," in which history would leap from necessity into freedom. Reality turned out to be much more ambiguous. Capitalism will die, but it could be followed by bureaucratic collectivism, by a new form of class society, which might well exploit the globe's poor as well as the metropolitan workers. Or it could be succeeded by socialism— that is, by a libertarian, democratic and humane communitarianism. That issue will not be settled in the lifetime of the youngest of my readers. In the battles within the advanced economy as well as in relation to the Third World one must prepare for a long struggle whose end is not clearly defined. There is no one "answer" for Africa, Asia and Latin America.

So I find myself—and more importantly, I think the world finds itself—torn by tactical and strategic dilemmas when confronted by a moral problem that is utterly straightforward: Shall the wretched of the earth be fed, clothed and housed? Or, more precisely, will the world be reorganized—re-created—so that they can feed, clothe and house themselves?

It is certain that America will not be able to answer that question, or even to pose it, so long as it remains cruelly innocent. It is because our history has exempted us of any sense of wrongdoing that we can be so complacent. For this reason, this attempt to develop a historical and even emotional understanding of our complicity in a monstrous injustice is a political act. If Americans could become conscious of our place in the system of international inequity, that could be the beginning of change. We are a decent and charitable people. We want to do right. But in this overwhelming area of human life, with the fate of the vast majority of human-kind at stake, we do not even suspect what the right is.[1]

We sincerely and unwittingly participate in that system that makes children leprous in Bombay, furrows the foreheads of women in Kenya and turns Indians in Guatemala into drunkards. Indeed, even within the United States, our affluence is misshapen, and cities rot and workers are unemployed, in part because corporations range to the end of the earth to find cheaper labor. Our editorial-ists are always telling the wretched of the planet that they must change themselves if their agony is to come to an end. That is a comfortable, paternal truth. It ignores a more difficult problem: that we the people of America are, in our cruel innocence, at the very center of the system; that we, the most decisive power in the world, must change from within too. The shocking, incredible fact is that we could, if we wanted to. If we do not, that will not signify a tragedy. It will be a crime against billions of men, women and children, including hundreds of millions of the halt, the blind and the maimed.

Notes

Chapter I

1. Hunger: "World Food: A Perspective," by Thomas Poleman, in *Food: Politics, Economics, Nutrition Research,* Philip Abelson, ed.; "Myths of the Food Crisis," by Nick Eberstadt. Third World statistics: UN 1974 Report on the World Social Situation; interview with Robert McNamara, June 1976; *Reshaping International Order,* Jan Tinbergen, ed., pp. 38, 66, 6. Per capita income: UNCTAD, *New Directions and New Structures for Trade and Development,* p. 4; *World Social Situation,* pp. 38, 101, 107, 51. New middle class: "The Response to the Third World," by C. Fred Bergsten, p. 10. Shift: "Three Models for the Future," by Robert Gilpin, in Bergsten and Krause, eds., *World Politics and International Economics,* p. 53. American public opinion: "Public Opinion: The Beginning of Ideology," by William Schneider. Moynihan: "U.S. Mission to the UN," Press Release, October 5, 1975.
2. Heilbroner: *The Human Prospect,* p. 42. Ribicoff: Quoted, "Atoms for Brazil," by Norman Gall. Brookings on proliferation: "Nuclear Proliferation," by Phillip J. Farley, in Owen and Schultze, eds., *Setting National Priorties. Tucker: The Inequity of Nations,* pp. 91, 93, 94. Overseas profits: "The Political Economy of Global Corporations and National Stabilization Policy," by Ronald Muller, in *The Multinational Corporation and Social Change,* David Apter and Louis

257

Goodman, eds. John Rawls: *A Theory of Justice*. Lester Thurow: *On Generating Inequality*. Kahn: *The Next 200 Years*.
3. Rostow: *The Stages of Economic Growth*, p. 4. Marx on India: Shlomo Avineri, ed., *Karl Marx on Colonialism*, pp. 132–139. "Take-off figures: Simon Kuznets, *Economic Growth of Nations*, Table 2, p. 24; Wassily Leontiev, *The Future of the World Economy*, Table 1, p. 75. Caste system. Ali A. Mazru, in Bhagwati, ed., *Economics and World Order*, p. 298.
4. No insurmountable barriers: Leontiev, *op. cit. supra*, p. 46. *New York Times:* editorial, October 18, 1976.

Chapter II

1. Samuelson: Samuelson, ed., *International Economic Relations*, p. 9. Ricardo: *Principles of Political Economy and Taxation*, pp. 71, 151–52. Russians on comparative exchange: V. Solodnikov and V. Bogoslovsky, *Non-Capitalist Development*, p. 199. Gunnar Myrdal: *The Political Element in the Development of Economic Theory; An International Economy; Economic Theory and Underdeveloped Regions*, p. 123. Heckscher-Ohlin-Samuelson: Bhagwati, ed., *International Trade*, *passim*. Myint: *Economic Theory and Underdeveloped Countries*, pp. 124–25. Hicks: *A Theory of Economic History*, p. 161. Tucker: *The Inequity of Nations*, p. 15. Myrdal: *Economic Theory and Underdeveloped Regions*, p. 141. Balogh: *Fact and Fancy in International Economic Relations*, p. 1.
2. International Finance Corporation origin: Mason and Asher, *The World Bank Since Bretton Woods*, p. 347. *Economist:* "Rich Man, Poor Man." Nationalization: Brzezinski, "America in a Hostile World." Macrea: *Survey*, S-15. World manufacturing: UN, *Survey of Economic Conditions in Africa*, Tables 5 and 6, pp. 88–89; *World Economic Survey*, Pt. I, pp. 17–19. American overseas investment: "International Economics and International Politics" by Bergsten, Keohane and Nye, in Bergsten and Krause, eds., *World Politics and International Economics*, p. 23, n. 30; UN, *Multinational Corporations in World Development*, Table XII, p. 148. Profits: *Ibid.*, Table XXXVII, p. 187; "Three Models for the Future," by Robert Gilpin, in Bergsten and Krause, eds., p. 53. Vernon: *Sovereignty at Bay*, *passim*. Amin: *L'Accumulation à l'échelle mondiale*, pp. 107ff. United Nations Industrial Development Organization: *Industrial Development Survey*, p. 192. Ranis: Apter and Goodman, eds., *The Multinational Corporation and Social Change*, p. 112.
3. Vernon: in Apter and Goodman, eds., p. 41. Industrial hostages: *The Economics of Imperialism*, by Barret-Brown, p. 326. Multinational retreat: "Yankees Go Home," by Daniel Yergin, *New Republic*, September 4, 1976; David Vogel, University of California

Business School (Berkeley), communication with author. Myint: *Economic Theory and Underdeveloped Countries*, p. 96. Brookings economists: "The Multinational Firms and International Regulation," in Bergsten and Krause, eds., p. 176. Multinational testimony: Walter Goldstein in Apter and Goodman, eds., p. 155. GM spokesperson: UN, *Summary of Hearings* . . . , p. 75. Oligopoly: Vernon, *Sovereignty at Bay*, p. 12. Agnelli: UN, *Summary of Hearings*, p. 147. US Tariff Commission: p. 159. DuPont Vice-Chair: UN, *Summary of Hearings*, p. 121. Transfer pricing: Vernon, *op. cit.*, pp. 53–54. Edith Penrose: UN, *Summary of Hearings*, p. 336.

Chapter IV

1. The "Gap": "The Haves and Have Nots Around the Year 2000," by P. N. Rosenstein Rodan in Bhagwati, ed., *Economics and World Order*, pp. 20–32; Wassily Leontiev, *The Future of the World Economy*, Introduction and Summary; Address to the Board of Governors, International Bank for Reconstruction and Development, Robert S. McNamara, pp. 3–4. Terms of trade: UN, *World Economic Survey*, 1974, Pt. I, pp. 4, 8. Manufactures: UNIDO, *Industrial Development Survey*, p. 3. Population: *World Economic Survey*, 1974, Table 3, p. 47. OECD: *Development Cooperation*, p. 11. Manufacturing percentage: *Industrial Development Survey*, p. 11.
2. African population: "Perspectives on Future Economic Prospects and Problems in Africa," in Bhagwati, ed., *Economics and World Order*, p. 274. Academic critique: Cohen, *The Question of Imperialism*, p. 35. Luxemburg: *Gesammelte Werke*, IV, pp. 49ff. Sixteenth-century Europe: Butterfield, *The Origins of Modern Science*, p. 89. Zero concept: Joan Robinson, *Freedom and Necessity*, p. 61. European level: Wallerstein, *The Modern World-System*, p. 53. Gershenkron: *Economic Backwardness in Historical Perspective*, p. 20. Eastern rigidities: Wallerstein, p. 85; Rodinson, *Islam and Capitalism*, pp. 61ff; Marx, *Grundrisse*, pp. 375ff; Karl Wittfogel, *Oriental Despotism*, passim. City: Kuznets, *Modern Economic Growth*, p. 5.
3. Marx on world market: *MEW* XXV, pp. 345–46. Wallerstein: pp. 98–99. Montesquieu, *De l'Esprit des lois*, I, p. 265. Lattimore: quoted, Wallerstein, p. 91. Williams: *Capitalism and Slavery*, p. 63. Marx on climate: *MEW* XXIII, pp. 536–37; *MEW* IV, p. 456. American colonies: Lichtheim, *Imperialism*, Chapter IV. Hamilton: quoted, Hacker, *Alexander Hamilton and the American Tradition*, p. 182. "Kith and kin": Barret-Brown, *The Economics of Imperialism*, pp. 139, 261. Necessary conditions: Barret-Brown, p. 74. Joan Robinson: *Freedom and Necessity*, p. 60. Weber: *General Economic*

History, p. 300. Cipolla: *Economic History of World Population,* pp. 55–56. British 1%: Kuznets, *Modern Economic Growth,* p. 464.
4. Smith: *Wealth of Nations,* pp. 360, 354. Ricardo: *Principles,* pp. 151ff. Marx on Ireland: *MEW* XXXII, pp. 668–69. Capital international: *Grundrisse,* pp. 311–13, 319; Barret-Brown, p. 134. Hymer: "Multinationale Konzerne and das Geset der ungleichen Entwicklung," in Senghass, ed., *Imperialismus und Strukturelle-gewalt,* p. 204, n. 4. *Manifesto: MEW* IV, p. 466. Marx's error: Avineri, ed., *Karl Marx on Colonialism,* p. 136. Luxemburg: *Werke,* V, p. 349; Lenin, *Collected Works,* Vol. XXII, p. 243; Hilferding, *Das Finanzkapital,* p. 441. Marx on division of labor: *MEW* XXIII, p. 475. "Fit of absence of mind": quoted, Langer, *The Diplomacy of Imperialism,* p. 69. Marx on imperialism not paying: *MEW* XII, p. 284. Anti-imperialism: Barret-Brown, p. 107; Langer, p. 70. Chamberlain: Langer, p. 77. Luxemburg, IV, p. 82. British exports: Barret-Brown, Table 3, pp. 104–5; John Knapp, "Economics or Political Economy," p. 38. Upper classes: Barret-Brown, p. 128. Racism: Kiernan, *Lords of Human Kind, passim.*
5. Bukharin: *Imperialism and the World Economy,* p. 164. Welfare state expansionism: Knapp, p. 42; Robinson, p. 91; G. Myrdal, *The Challenge of World Poverty,* p. 297. Emmanuel: "The Socialist Project in a Disintegrated Capitalist World," p. 71; *L'Échange inégal,* p. 209. Meany advisor: Nat Goldfinger, "What Labor Wants on Trade," p. 1. Texas Instruments: Benjamin Sharman, p. 220. European Workers: Walter Goldstein, in Apter and Goodman, eds., p. 158. The Federationists: "A Realistic Approach to World Trade" by Elizabeth Jager; "The Danger from Raw Materials Cartels" by Stanley Ruttenberg. Textiles: "Textiles Threaten . . . ," *Business Week,* January 31, 1977.
6. Robinson-Gallagher: *Imperialism,* William Roger Louis, ed. Arendt: *The Origins of Totalitarianism,* p. 126. Kissinger: "The Law of the Sea," p. 2.

Chapter V

1. Amin: *L'Accumulation à l'échelle mondiale,* pp. 28–29. Food corporations: Martin McLaughlin, "The World Food Situation and the U.S. Role," in Hansen, ed.; "The Grain Drain," by Joel Solkoff, *New Republic,* December 18, 1976; "The Grain Drain," *Economist* (London), January 22, 1977. Hong Kong: Emmanuel, "Current Myths of Development," p. 63. Ultramodern sectors: Amin, *op. cit.,* p. 75. World Bank: cited, Radice, ed., *International Firms and Modern Imperialism,* p. 91.
2. Hicks: *A Theory of Economic History,* pp. 164–65. Dualism: Alberto Martinelli, "Dualismus und Abhangigkeit" in Senghass, ed.,

Imperialismus und Strukturellegewalt. Myint: *Economic Theory and Underdeveloped Countries,* p. 72. Guatemala: Walter Sullivan Report on the Pacific Science Congress, *New York Times,* August 26, 1975. Amin summary: *op. cit.,* pp. 323–34.

3. Vernon: *Sovereignty at Bay,* pp. 195, 307 n. 3; Barret-Brown, p. 143; Karl Deutsch in Rosen and Kurth, eds., *Testing Economic Theories of Imperialism,* p. 30. Frank on metropolitan intervention: *Capitalism and Underdevelopment in Latin America,* p. 287. Furtado: "Externe Abhangigkeit und ökonomische Theorie," in Senghass, ed., pp. 316ff.

4. Terms of trade: Senghass, ed., p. 249; Cohen, p. 169. On Lenin: Jalee, pp. 158ff. Mandel: I, pp. 108, 112–14, 138, n. 23; Barret-Brown, pp. 245–48 and Table 26. U.S. Latin investment: Lichtheim, 153 n. 14. Fees: UNCTAD, 1976, p. 7. Third World debt: *Ibid.,* p. 10. Leontiev: Table 60, p. 244. Valdes: quoted, Frank.

5. Marx on unequal exchange: *MEW* XXV, p. 248. Mandel: Vol. II, Chapter XI. Wages: Barret-Brown, Table 24, p. 232. Emmanuel on difference: *L'Échange inégal,* p. 288. Real wages in Greece: *Ibid.,* p. 101. Myint: p. 115. Amin on exports: *Accumulation à l'échelle mondiale,* p. 75. Guest workers: Klee, ed., *passim.*

6. *Wall Street Journal,* September 15, 1975. *New York Times* on Brazil: January 25, 1976; July 6, 1976. Brazil wages: Heller, p. 61. Kendell: August 24, 1976. Finance Minister: quoted, "The Rise of Brazil," by Norman Gall. Incomes: OECD, *Development Cooperation,* p. 62. Riots: *New York Times,* December 5, 14, 1974. Food: "Food First!" by Lappe and Collins, p. 7. Geisel announcement: "Brazil," *Business Week,* December 6, 1976.

Chapter VI

1. OECD: *Development and Cooperation,* p. 24. Leontiev: p. 15. Cipolla: p. 86. Agricultural revolution: Hill, Pt. I, Chapter 3; Pt. II, Chapter 3. Mauritius: Cipolla, p. 102. Net exporter: UN, *World Food Conference,* p. 33; Eckholm, p. 179. Sahel: Lappe, p. 2. Wheat exports: UNIDO, *Industrial Development Survey,* p. 215. Washington agricultural subsidies: "The Great Food Fumble," by Fred Sanderson, in Abelson, ed., *Food: Politics, Economics, Nutrition Research,* p. 3; *The Twilight of Capitalism,* p. 226. High prices for poor: "Different Issues Underlying Food Programs" by Henry Walters, in Abelson, ed., *op. cit.,* p. 25. Cartel conditions: "Trade in Raw Materials: The Benefits of Capitalist Alliances," by Stephen D. Krasner, in Rosen and Kurth, eds., p. 193; "The U.S. in the World Economy," by Edward R. Fried and Phillip Trezise in Owen and Schultze, eds., p. 171. Williams: *The Root of the Modern American Empire.* 1974 Secretary of the Treasury: "Less Food, More Politics,"

Leslie Gelb and Anthony Lake, p. 179. "Free Trade": "The World Food Situation and the U.S. Role," by Martin McLaughlin, in Hansen, ed., p. 82. Grain-meat ration: "World Food: A Prospect," by Thomas T. Poleman, in Abelson, ed., p. 11; Cipolla, p. 40; UNIDO, p. 209; "Myths of the Food Crisis," by Nick Eberstadt.
2. UN, World Food Conference: *Report*, p. 33. Hungry countries: "Myths of the Food Crisis." Sanderson: Abelson, ed., pp. 1, 23. Ehrlich and Harriman: *How to Be a Survivor*, pp. 43ff, 53, 86. Indian birth control: *Soft State*, by Bernard Nossiter, Chapter 3. Lester Brown: quoted, Nossiter, *op. cit.*, p. 21. Myrdal on Green Revolution: *The Challenge of World Poverty*, pp. 125ff. Walters: "Different Issues Underlying Food Problems," in Abelson, ed., p. 27. Schumacher: *Small Is Beautiful, passim.* Energy in food production: "Energy Use in the U.S. Food System," by John S. and Carol E. Steinhart, *Bread for the World*, pp. 20ff., 38.

Chapter IX

1. Mandel: *Le Troisième Âge*, Vol. I, Chapter IV. Veit: "Troubled World Economy," p. 273. Tinbergen: *Reshaping the International Order*, pp. 94ff. Irving Kristol: *Wall Street Journal*, July 17, 1975. Côte d'Ivoire: Samir Amin, *Neo-Colonialism in West Africa*, p. 64; "Le Côte d'Ivoire est le plus prospère des états d'Afrique noire francophone," by Pierre Biarnes, *Le Monde hebdomadaire*, 20–26 Août, 1970. Iran: David Housego, *A Survey of Iran*. India: Anon., *Ein Jahr nach dem Ausnahmezustand*, p. 24. Indian taxes: Intercontinental Press, September 27, 1976, p. 1352. Leontiev on government: Leontiev, pp. 49–50. Socialism: Preface, *Socialism in the Third World*, Desfoses and Levesque, eds., p. v. Nyerere: *Freedom and Development*, p. 127. Africanization: "Frelimo and the Mozambique Revolution," in Arrighi and Saul, eds., p. 379. "Bureaucratic Bourgeoisie": Shivji. Russian analysis: Solodnikov and Bogoslovsky, pp. 97, 102.
2. Leontiev on agriculture: Leontiev, pp. 12–21. Tinbergen: *op. cit.*, p. 89. Private farm holdings: Myrdal, *Challenge of World Poverty*, p. 111; Lenin, *Collected Works*, Vol. XV, pp. 43ff; Teng: "Economic Growth in China and the Cultural Revolution," by Dwight Perkins. Bangladesh case: "The Economics of Starvation," by Emma Rothschild. Gilpin: in Owen and Schultze, eds., p. 53. Oil profits: "Key Currencies," by Richard F. Janssen, in *Wall Street Journal*, December 13, 1976.
3. Tom J. Farer, *passim*. UNCTAD: *Trade and Development*, pp. 8, 120, 66ff. Second Session: Vol. I, pp. 431ff. *History of Group 77*: Jankowitsch and Sauvant, *passim*. Seventh Special Session: UN, *Resolutions Adopted by the General Assembly During Its Seventh*

Special Session, p. 7. Keynes: UN, *A New UN Structure*, p. 72. Nyerere: Address, May 4, 1976, p. 11. Moderates: "The Crisis of Interdependence: Where Do We Go from Here?" in Hansen, ed., pp. 60–61, 62. Tariffs: Tinbergen, p. 89. Processing: *Ibid.*, p. 34. Aid levels: Introduction, Hansen, ed., p. 24. Schultz: *New York Times*, September 23, 1976. Special Drawing Rights: "The Response to the Third World," by C. Fred Bergsten, pp. 4–6. Devaluation: *The Economist* (London), February 17, 1973. Common Fund: *The Economist* (London), March 11, 1977, p. 85. Commodity Importers and Exporters: "The New Economic Order," by Nathaniel Leff; "How Best to Help the Third World Industrialize," by Frances Cairncross; "Industrieländer und Rohstoffländer," by Alfred Lauterbach. U.S. Tariff Commission: pp. 141–42. "UNCTAD Commodity," *Business Week*, May 19, 1977, p. 80ff. Okun's Law: Baraclough, p. 33. *Employment Growth and Basic Needs*, International Labour Office, *passim;* Joseph Holland, memorandum 5, Center of Concern (November, 1976).

4. Debt: *The Economist* (London), December 25, 1976, "Locked in With the Poor"; Emma Rothschild, *New York Review of Books*, June 24, 1976. Committee on Foreign Relations: p. 12. Jalee: pp. 164ff. *The Economist:* "Aid Not Trade," January 29, 1977. Sea Resources: Kissinger, "The Law of the Sea," p. 2. Petroleum: "An Economic View of Marine Problems," by Bertrand de Jouvenal in Borgese and Krieger, eds., pp. 22–23, 30. Truman: Alva Myrdal, *The Game of Disarmament*, p. 96; Borgese and Krieger, pp. x, 331. Grotius: Department of State, *A Constitution for the Sea*, p. 3. Sea Authority: UN, *Third Conference on the Law of the Sea*, Vol. V, pp. 129ff. Kissinger: Press Release, U.S. Mission to the UN, September 1, 1976; *Ibid.*, August 13, 1976; "The Law of the Sea." Breux: Letter, *New York Times*, October 1, 1976. U.S. policy: "How to Make Peace on the Seabed," by Jack N. Barkenbus, p. 212. Demilitarize: Alva Myrdal, pp. 96ff. John J. Logue: "Carter's Ocean Opportunity." Borgese: *New York Times*, Op Ed, October 1, 1976.

Chapter X

1. Palloix: *L'Économie mondiale capitaliste*, Vol. II, pp. 228ff.

Bibliography

Abelson, Philip H., ed., *Food: Politics, Economics, Nutrition Research.*
New York: American Association for the Advancement of Science,
1975.

Alba, Victor, *The Mexicans.* New York: Pegasus, 1967.

Amin, Samir, *L'Accumulation à l'échelle mondiale.* Paris: Anthropos,
1971.

———, *Neo-Colonialism in West Africa.* New York: Monthly Review
Press, 1973.

Anon., "Indien—Ein Jahr nach dem Ausnahmezustand," *Die Zukunft*
(Wien), June 11, 1976.

Apter, David, and Goldman, Louis, eds., *The Multinational Corporation
and Social Change.* New York: Praeger, 1976.

Arendt, Hannah, *The Origins of Totalitarianism;* 2nd ed. Cleveland:
Meridian, 1958.

Arrighi, Giovanni, and Saul, I. S., eds. *Essays on the Political Economy
of Africa.* New York: Monthly Review Press, 1973.

Avineri, Shlomo, ed., *Karl Marx on Colonialism and Modernization.*
New York: Doubleday Anchor, 1969.

Balogh, Thomas, *Fact and Fancy in International Economic Relations.*
New York: Pergamon Press, 1973.

Baraclogh, Geoffrey, "The Haves and Have Nots," *New York Review of Books,* May 13, 1976.

Barkenbus, Jack N., "Peace on the Seabed," *Foreign Policy,* Winter, 1976–77.

Barnet, Richard, and Müller, Ronald, *Global Reach.* New York: Simon and Schuster, 1975.

Barret-Brown, Michael, *The Economics of Imperialism.* Baltimore: Penguin, 1974.

Bergsten, C. Fred, "The Response to the Third World," *Foreign Policy,* Winter, 1974–75.

———, and Krause, Lawrence, *World Politics and International Economics.* Washington: Brookings Institution, 1975.

Bhagwati, Jagdish, *Economics and World Order.* New York: Free Press, 1972.

———, *The Economics of Underdeveloped Countries.* New York: McGraw-Hill, 1966.

———, ed., *International Trade.* Baltimore: Penguin, 1969.

Borgese, Elizabeth Mann, and Krieger, David, eds., *The Tides of Change.* New York: Mason Charter, 1975.

Brzezinski, Zbigniew, "America in a Hostile World," *Foreign Policy,* Summer, 1976.

Bukharin, Nikolai, *Imperialism and the World Economy.* London: Martin Lawrence, n.d. [original Russian, 1915].

Butterfield, Herbert, *The Origins of Modern Science.* New York: Free Press, 1965.

Cairncross, Frances, "How Best to Help the Third World Industrialize," *Manchester Guardian Weekly,* September 20, 1975.

Cipolla, Carlo, *The Economic History of World Population;* 6th ed. Baltimore: Penguin, 1974.

Cohen, Benjamin, *The Question of Imperialism. New York:* Basic Books, 1973.

Desfoses, Helen, and Levesque, Jacques, eds., *Socialism in the Third World.* New York: Praeger, 1975.

Eberstadt, Nick, "Myths of the Food Crisis," *New York Review of Books,* February 19, 1976.

Eckholm, Erik, *Losing Ground.* New York: Norton, 1976.

Ehrlich, Paul, and Harriman, Richard, *How to Be a Survivor.* New York: Ballantine, 1971.

Emmanuel, A., "Current Myths of Development," *New Left Review* (London), May–June, 1974.

———, *L'Échange inégal.* Paris: Maspero, 1969.

———, "The Socialist Project in a Disintegrated Capitalist World," *Socialist Thought and Practice* (Belgrade), September 1976.

Farer, Tom J., "The United States and the Third World: A Basis for Accommodation." *Foreign Affairs,* October 1975.

Federationist, "Labor's Stake in the World Economy," January 1977.

Frank, André Gunder, *Capitalism and Underdevelopment in Latin America.* New York: Monthly Review Press, 1965.

Fuentes, Carlos, *Tiempo Mexicano.* Mexico City: Joaquín Moritz, 1972.

Gall, Norman, "Atoms for Brazil," *Foreign Policy,* Summer, 1976.

———, "The Rise of Brazil," *Commentary,* January 1977.

Gelb, Leslie, and Lake, Anthony, "Less Food, More Politics," *Foreign Policy,* Winter, 1974–75.

Gershenkron, Alexander, *Economic Backwardness in Historical Perspective.* Cambridge: Belknap, 1966.

Goldfinger, Nat, "What Labor Wants on Trade," *New York Times,* March 4, 1973.

Grant, James, "Development: The End of Trickle Down," *Foreign Policy,* Fall, 1973.

Hacker, Louis, *Alexander Hamilton and the American Tradition.* New York: McGraw-Hill, 1964 [1957].

Hansen, Robert G., ed., *The United States and World Development.* New York: Praeger, 1976.

Heilbroner, Robert, *The Human Prospect.* New York: Norton, 1974.

Heller, Walter W., *The Economy: Old Myths and New Realities.* New York: Norton, 1976.

Hicks, John A., *A Theory of Economic History.* Oxford: Oxford University Press, 1969.

Hill, Christopher, *Reformation to Industrial Revolution.* Baltimore: Penguin, 1967.

Housego, David, "A Survey of Iran," *The Economist* (London), August 28, 1976.

International Labour Office, *Employment Growth and Basic Needs.* Geneva: ILO, 1976.

Jalee, Pierre, *L'Impérialisme en 1970.* Paris: Maspero, 1969.

Jankowitsch, Odette, and Sauvant, Karl P., *The Evolution of the Non-Aligned Movement into a Pressure Group for the Establishment of the New International Economic Order* (ms.).

Kahn, Herman, *et al., The Next 200 Years.* New York: Morrow, 1976.

Kiernan, V.G., *The Lords of Human Kind.* New York: Little, Brown, 1969.

Kindleberger, Charles E., ed., *The International Corporation.* Cambridge: MIT Press, 1970.

Kissinger, Henry, "The Law of the Sea." Washington: State Department, April 8, 1976.

Klee, Ernest, ed., *Gastarbeiter, Analyseen und Berichte.* Frankfurt-am-Main: Suhrkamp, 1972.

Knapp, John, "Economics or Political Economy," *Lloyd's Bank Review* (London), January, 1973.

Kuznets, Simon, *Economic Growth of Nations.* Cambridge: Belknap, 1971.

———, *Modern Economic Growth.* New Haven: Yale University Press, 1966.

Langer, William, *The Diplomacy of Imperialism;* 2nd ed. New York: Knopf, 1968.

Lappe, Frances Moore, and Collins, Joseph, "Food First!" New York: Institute for Food and Development Policy, 1976.

Lauterbach, Alfred, "Industrieländer und Rohstoffländer," *Die Zukunft* (Wien), February 20, 1976.

Leff, Nathaniel, "The New Economic Order," *Foreign Policy,* Fall, 1976.

Lenin, V. I., *Collected Works.* Moscow: Foreign Language Publishing House, 1973.

Leontiev, Wassily, *et al., The Future of the World Economy.* New York: United Nations, 1976.

Lichtheim, George, *Imperialism.* New York: Praeger, 1971.

Logue, John J., "Carter's Ocean Opportunity." *Commonweal,* April 29, 1977.

Lopez Gallo, Manuel, *Economía y Política en la Historia de Mexico.* Mexico City: El Caballito, 1972.

Louis, Wm. Roger, ed., *Imperialism.* New York: Franklin Watts, 1976.

Luxemburg, Rosa, *Gesammelte Werke;* 5 vols. Berlin: Dietz Verlag, 1974.

Macrea, Norman, "Survey," *The Economist* (London), October 31, 1975.

Mandel, Ernest, *Le Troisième Âge du capitalisme;* 3 vols. Paris, 1976.

Marx, Karl, *Grundrisse der Kritik der politischen Ökonomie.* Berlin: Dietz Verlag, 1953.

———, and Engels, Friedrich, *Werke.* Berlin: Dietz Verlag, 1960.

Mason, Edward S., and Asher, Robert E., *The World Bank Since Bretton Woods.* Washington: Brookings Institution, 1973.

McNamara, Robert S., Address to the Board of Governors, October 4, 1976. Washington: I.B.R.D., 1976.

Montesquieu, *De l'Esprit des lois;* 2 vols. Paris: Garnier Frères, 1973.

Moore, Barrington, *Social Origins of Dictatorship and Democracy.* Boston: Beacon, 1966.

Moynihan, Daniel Patrick, Speech, October 5, 1975. New York: United States Mission to the United Nations, 1975.

Myint, Hyla, *Economic Theory and Underdeveloped Countries.* Oxford: Oxford University Press, 1971.

Myrdal, Alva, *The Game of Disarmament.* New York: Pantheon, 1977.

Myrdal, Gunnar, *The Challenge of World Poverty.* New York: Pantheon, 1970.

————, *Economic Theory and Underdeveloped Regions.* London: Duckworth, 1957.

————, *An International Economy.* London: Routledge and Kegan Paul, 1956.

————, *The Political Element in the Development of Economic Theory.* London: Routledge and Kegan Paul, 1957.

Nossiter, Bernard, *Soft State.* New York: Harpers, 1970.

Nyerere, Julius K., *Freedom and Development.* Oxford: Oxford University Press, 1974.

Organization for Economic Cooperation and Development, *Development Cooperation.* Paris: OECD, 1974.

Owen, Henry, and Schultze, Charles, eds., *Setting National Priorities.* Washington: Brookings Institution, 1976.

Palloix, Christian, *L'Économie mondiale capitaliste et les firmes multinationales;* 2 vols. Paris: Maspero, 1975.

Perkins, Dwight, "Economic Growth in China and the Cultural Revolution," *China Quarterly,* January–March, 1967.

Radice, Hugo, ed., *International Firms and Modern Imperialism.* Baltimore: Penguin Books, 1975.

Rawls, John, *A Theory of Justice.* Cambridge: Belknap, 1971.

Ricardo, David, *Principles of Political Economy,* R. M. Hartwell, ed. Baltimore: Pelican, 1971.

"Rich Man, Poor Man," *The Economist* (London), May 1, 1976.

Robinson, Joan, *Freedom and Necessity.* New York: Pantheon, 1970.

Rodinson, Maxime, *Islam and Capitalism.* New York: Pantheon, 1973.

Rosen, Steve, and Kurth, James, eds., *Testing Theories of Economic Imperialism.* Lexington, Mass.: D. C. Heath, 1974.

Rostow, Walt W., *The Stages of Economic Growth.* Cambridge: Cambridge University Press, 1960.

Rothschild, Emma, "The Economics of Starvation," *New York Times,* January 10, 11, 1977.

Samuelson, Paul, ed., *International Economic Relations, Proceedings of the Third Congress of the International Economic Association.* London: IEA, 1969.

Schneider, William, "Public Opinion: The Beginning of Ideology," *Foreign Policy*, Winter, 1974–75.

Schumacher, E. F., *Small Is Beautiful*. New York: Harper Torchbooks, 1973.

Senghass, Dieter, ed., *Imperialismus und strukturelle Gewalt*. Frankfurt-am-Main: Suhrkamp, 1972.

Sharman, Benjamin A., "Labor's International Role." *Foreign Policy*, Spring 1977.

Shivji, Issa G., *Class Struggles in Tanzania*. Dar es Salaam: Tanzania Publishing House, 1973.

Smith, Adam, *The Wealth of Nations*. New York: Modern Library, 1937.

Solodnikov, V., and Bogoslovsky, V., *Non-Capitalist Development*. Moscow: Progress, 1975.

Thurow, Lester, *On Generating Inequality*. New York: Basic Books, 1976.

Tinbergen, Jan, Coordinator, *Reshaping the International Order: A Report to the Club of Rome*. New York: Dutton, 1976.

Tucker, Robert W., *The Inequity of Nations*. New York: Basic Books, 1977.

Ulynovsky, *Socialism and the New Independent Nations*. Moscow: Progress, 1970.

United Nations, *Multinational Corporations in World Development*. New York: United Nations, 1973.

————, *A New UN Structure for Global Economic Cooperation*. New York: United Nations, 1975.

————, *1974 Report on the World Social Situation*. New York: United Nations, 1975.

————, *Resolutions Adopted by the General Assembly During Its 7th Special Session*. New York: United Nations, 1976.

————, *Summary of Hearings Before the Group of Eminent Persons to Study the Impact of Multinational Corporations*. New York: United Nations, 1974.

————, *Survey of Economic Conditions in Africa, 1973*, Pt. I. New York: United Nations, 1974.

————, *Third Conference on the Law of the Sea*, Vol. V. New York: United Nations, 1976.

————, *World Economic Survey, 1974*, Pt. I. New York: United Nations, 1974.

————, *World Food Conference Report*. New York: United Nations, 1975.

United Nations Conference on Trade and Development, *Final Act and Report*. New York: United Nations, 1964.

———, *New Directions for Trade and Development*. *Nairobi:* UNCTAD, 1976.

———, *Second Session*. New York: United Nations, 1968.

———, *Third Session*. New York: United Nations, 1972.

United Nations Industrial Development Organization, *Industrial Development Survey*. New York: UNIDO, 1974.

United States Department of State, *A Constitution for the Sea*. Washington: U.S. Department of State, August 1976.

United States Tariff Commission, *Implications for World Trade and Investment and for U.S. Trade and Labor of Multinational Corporations*. Washington: Senate Finance Committee, 1973.

Veit, Lawrence, "Troubled World Economy," *Foreign Affairs*, January 1977.

Vernon, Raymond, *Sovereignty at Bay*. New York: Basic Books, 1971.

Wallerstein, Immanuel, *The Modern World-System*. New York: Academic Press, 1974.

Weber, Max, *General Economic History*. Glencoe, Illinois: The Free Press, 1950.

Williams, Eric, *Capitalism and Slavery*. New York: Putnam, 1966.

Williams, William Appleman, *The Roots of Modern American Empire*. New York: Random House, 1969.

Wittfogel, Karl, *Oriental Despotism*. New Haven: Yale University Press, 1957.

Womack, John, *Zapata and the Mexican Revolution*. New York: Vintage, 1968.

Index

Adelman, Bob, 71
Advanced powers, *see* Capitalist powers
AFL-CIO, 122, 123
Africa, 119, 120, 133, 146, 161, 162, 178, 246; colonization of, 107–12, 114; decolonialization of, 166; nationalization in, 42–43; national populations, 107; per capita income, 16; resources of, 192; *see also* East Africa, North Africa
Agnelli, Giovanni, 51
Agriculture, 105; in Brazil, 149–50; and food supply, 161–64; in India, 209; vs. industrialization, 134–35, 163; in Kenya, 172–73, 176–77, 178; in Mexico, 201; and population, 154–55; in Tanzania, 184; in Third World, 228–29; in U.S., 157–59, 163; *see also* Wheat
Akamba (Kenya), 169

Alba, Victor, 206
Algeria, 166, 213
Algiers, Charter of, 234
Allende, Salvador, 204, 212, 236, 238
Alliance for Progress, 19
Amazon River (Brazil), 150
America, *see* United States
American Association for the Advancement of Science, 161
American Federation of State, County and Municipal Employees, 201
American Indians, 113, 114
Amin, Idi, 15
Amin, Samir, 26, 46, 130, 132, 136–137, 143*n*., 144–45
Apartheid, 28, 212
Arab countries, 108, 192, 170, 218–219
Arbenz regime (Guatemala), 207
Arendt, Hannah, 127

About the Author

For more than twenty-five years, Michael Harrington has been an activist in social movements. He is currently the National Chairman of the Democratic Socialist Organizing Committee, the main successor organization to the Socialist party of Eugene Debs and Norman Thomas. He is a Professor of Political Science at Queens College of the City University of New York, and the author of several books, including *The Other America,* a classic work on poverty in the United States, *The Twilight of Capitalism, The Accidental Century,* and *Fragments of the Century.* He lives in New York with his wife and children.